Sports English

Reading Course

II

北京体育大学出版社

出 版 人 李 飞
责任编辑 佟 晖
审稿编辑 董英双
责任校对 未 茗
版式设计 佟 晖

图书在版编目（CIP）数据

体育英语阅读. II / 田慧主编. -- 北京 : 北京体育大学出版社, 2015.7
ISBN 978-7-5644-2009-3

Ⅰ. ①体… Ⅱ. ①田… Ⅲ. ①体育－英语－阅读教学－高等学校－教材 Ⅳ. ①H319.4

中国版本图书馆CIP数据核字（2015）第178475号

体育英语阅读 · II 田慧 主编

出 版 北京体育大学出版社
地 址 北京市海淀区信息路48号
邮 编 100084
邮购部 北京体育大学出版社读者服务部 010-62989432
发行部 010-62989320
网 址 http://cbs.bsu.edu.cn
印 刷 北京昌联印刷有限公司
开 本 787×1092毫米 1/16
印 张 17.75
字 数 455千字

2017年8月第1版第2次印刷
定 价：60.00元

序

人才培养是高等学校的根本任务，对处于学校工作中心地位的教学工作来说，其质量建设是高等学校的永恒主题。作为传授知识、掌握技能、提高素质的载体，教材在人才培养过程中起着非常重要的作用，是高等学校提高教学质量，促进内涵发展的有力抓手。

一本好的教材，不仅要充分体现教材应有的基础性、示范性和权威性，还要正确把握教学内容和课程体系的改革和创新方向，充分反映学科的教育思想观念、人才培养模式以及教学科研的最新成果，集中展现教材体系的创新，教材内容的更新和教学方法、手段的革新，善于处理好理论与实践、继承与创新、广度与深度、知识与技能、利学与利教的关系，成为开拓学生视野、引导学生探索、鼓励学生奋进的学业与人生兼备的“工具书”。

从中央体育学院到北京体育学院再到北京体育大学，这 60 年的办学历程，是继承发展的 60 年，是改革创新的 60 年，也是教材建设硕果累累的 60 年。学校不断探索教材建设的内在规律，引领高等体育教育教材建设的创新之路，发展了具有自身特色的教材体系，形成了特色鲜明的三个发展阶段。第一阶段是在上世纪 50 年代至 60 年代，我校教师在苏联专家的指导下，制定和编写了各专业的教育计划、大纲和主要教材。这批教师在主持和参与 1961 年国家体委组织的体育院校 18 门课程教材编著工作中发挥了重要作用；而这批教材也成为我国独立编写的、对苏联教材模式有所突破的第一批体育院校教材。第二阶段是上世纪 70 年代末至 90 年代，我校教师在大量承担第二次重编体育院校教材牵头组织工作的同时，针对学校“三结合”的办学目标和人才培养模式，开始了多学科、多专业的自编教材建设。第三阶段是进入 21 世纪以后，特别是国家体育总局于 2002 年下拨教材建设专款 480 万元之后，我校教材建设在数量和质量上都取得了重大突破。至 2010 年共立项建设了涵盖我校各专业课程的 187 项教材，其中有 4 项教材获得国家级优秀（精品）教材称号，14 项教材获得北京市精品教材称号。可以说上述三个阶段的发展，使我校教材建设水平达到了一个空前的高度，为高等体育人才的培养发挥了重要的作用。

为全面提高高等体育教育质量，深化高等体育教育教学改革，继续加强体育学精品教材建设，2012 年初，在北京体育大学教学指导与教材建设委员会的具体指导下，我们启动了高等教育体育学精品教材建设工程。学校遴选教育部新颁布的体育学类所属的体育教育、运动训练、社会体育指导与管理、武术与民族传统体育、休闲体育、运动康复、运动人体科学7个本科专业的部分基础课程和主干课程开展精品教材建设。我们整合了全校的优质资源，组织专家、教授全程参与教材的规划、编写、初审、终审等过程。按照精品教材的要求，以优秀的教学团队编写优质的教材，出精品、出人才为建设思路，编委会优选学术水平与教学水平兼备、具有创新精神的专家、教授担任教材主编，组织优秀教学团队成员参与教材编写；精确定位教材适用对象，准确把握专业知识结构、能力结构和综合素质要求，深刻领会课程内涵，简洁洗练地表达知识点、能力点和素质点；融入最新的教改成果和科研成果，吸收国外优秀教材的先进理念和成果，创新利于学生自学和教师讲授的教材体例；学校还投入专项资金，对教材进行一体规划、一体设计、一体编审，并采用多色印刷技术增加教材的可读性；为全力保证教材编写质量，北京体育大学出版社资深编辑深度介入教材编写的所有环节。当这批教材展现在读者面前时，我们充满了期待。

岁月如流，薪火相传。60年的教材建设成绩斐然，推动着体育学教材建设步入新的起点、站在新的高度。展望未来，一批批体育学精品教材将随世界一流体育大学的建设进程应运而生，不仅在学校内涵式发展的改革进程中发挥重要作用，而且在全国高等体育院校人才培养中做出积极贡献，在高等教育教材建设中留下浓墨重彩的一笔。

北京体育大学校长
校教学指导与教材建设委员会主任
2013年9月

教材编写组

组　长：田　慧

副组长：韩亚辉

成　员：（以姓氏笔画为序）

王　敏　王卓君

田　慧　韩亚辉

前　言
Preface

《体育英语阅读教程》分为Ⅰ、Ⅱ两册，每册有十五个单元。每单元围绕同一主题设计一篇主课文（Text A）和一篇副课文（Text B），主课文用作课堂重点讲解，副课文供学生在教师指导下使用。所有文章都标注了总字数，供学生及时检验并记录自己的阅读速度。在课文前的Pre-reading Thoughts中，问题的设计旨在激活学生在相关话题上原有的知识，鼓励学生就这些话题发表初步的看法，待学生读完课文后把自己的知识和看法与文章中所表达的观点进行对比，使学生充分认识到视角的多元性。文章后的Comprehension Check根据文章的体裁和题材做出了相关的设计，检验学生在宏观和微观水平上把握文章的能力（包括对文章中语言难点和社会文化知识的理解）。Critical Thinking Starters部分在课文内容理解的基础上，鼓励学生用学到的知识和语言讨论现实问题，在提高表达能力和分析能力的同时，注重培养学生的思辨能力。在文章的注释中，编者对重要词汇提供了准确、详尽的英文注释，以帮助学生精确掌握词义，同时对文章中出现的人物和文化背景进行了适当的说明，以丰富学生的文化知识。

此外，本书还设计了形式多样的版块内容，以帮助学生了解、掌握更为丰富的体育常识、热点信息和发展趋势，促进学生培养主动思考的习惯和良好的思辨能力。例如，Sports in Focus着重介绍与文章内容相关的主要体育项目，并提供相关词汇的中文释义，以帮助学生了解主要体育项目，掌握基本体育词汇；在Expert's View中，学生可以了解到权威人士对某些重要问题的观点；More to Know对文章内容进行了必要的补充，以拓宽学生的视野；Activity Time-Out部分设计了形式多样的课外活动，鼓励学生学以致用；Hot Debate旨在让学生就热点问题进行讨论，培养学生有理有据地表达个人观点的习惯；在Pop Culture中，学生可以了解到与单元主题相关的文学或影视作品，供学生在学有余力的情况下从多角度了解相关信息；Vocabulary Building的设计旨在让学生学会利用工具书和互联网资源获取信息。这些版块的设计在完成阅读课基本内容的基础上，以更为多样化的形式帮助学生以主动的参与者而不是被动的接受者身份学习课文中所涉及的内容。

本书文章广泛选自英国、美国、加拿大及澳大利亚等英语国家的体育相关著作、报刊、杂志以及相应报刊名下的网址。在CBI（content-based instruction）理念指导下，选材注重体裁和题材的多样性和视角的多元性，同时兼顾题材的系统性，旨在传授相关体育学科知识，开阔学生视野，同时增强其英语阅读能力、表达能力、分析能力和思辨能力。

《体育英语阅读教程》可作为体育院校英语专业学生以及高等院校体育专业的高年级学生、硕士生和博士生的阅读教材，亦适用于广大体育爱好者和体育专业人士阅读参考。

在本书的编撰过程中，我们参考了国外多种著作，并注明了出处，在此谨向原作者表示衷心的感谢。同时也感谢外籍学者Vera E Lee，Margaret Ann Carey和John Patrick Carey对本书的编撰提出的宝贵意见和建议。

由于时间及编者的水平有限，书中疏漏及不妥之处在所难免，敬请广大使用者批评指正。

编者

2014年7月

CONTENTS

1

UNIT

Technology in Sports

Through better nutrition and training, the athletes of today are becoming faster and stronger. Old records are constantly being broken and new ones set. While the vast majority of these achievements are likely due to the athletes themselves, improvements in sports technology have also played a notable role. New sports gear technologies have especially been relevant to the sports of rowing, cycling, swimming and tennis, giving rise not only to new records, but also ways in which the sports are played.

— Suyash Bulchandani

Pre-reading Thoughts

1. It is commonly held that "technology changes life". How has technology changed sport? Give some specific examples.

2. What is the literal meaning of "hawk eye"? What does it actually refer to in sports, especially in tennis?

Text A

Sports and Technology

1 Rapid scientific developments, in terms of both equipment and facilities and recording accuracy, have facilitated the increased public preoccupation with record-breaking. Conditions can now be closely controlled in many sports, and measurements are sufficiently accurate that performances can be assessed according to the nearest thousandth of a second, making even tiny improvements noteworthy. This, combined with other developments, has led to increased frequency at which records are broken, fueling the public desire for more such occurrences.

The NBA is one of the leagues that is embracing new technology in a variety of ways.

2 After a period of rapid improvement in sporting achievements, most sports are now experiencing a reduced rate of improvement. If sporting records are taken as a measure of human performance, then all sports must acknowledge that there is a human performance limit that will eventually be reached, after which no further human improvement will be possible. If society continues to demand that progress is made in sport, then once the biological limit is reached, new methods must be employed. The options for this are: 1) artificially altering the biological limit; 2) improving equipment and other technology utilized by athletes; 3) developing new sports as limits are reached in traditional sports. Because the first two options both possess the capability of significantly altering the nature of current sports, there are various rules regulating the extent and manner in which either of them may be used.

Regulating Technology in Sports

3 In order to ensure that sporting rules are able to achieve what they intend to, it is important to bear in mind why people play sport, why people watch sport and what they want from it. Rules limiting technology use must contend with the seemingly opposing liberal ideals of individual freedom and equal opportunity. With the addition of each new rule, it must be considered: does this rule encourage equal opportunity amongst the athletes or simply inhibit their freedom?

4 Doping has been used since competitive sport's Greek origins as a way to artificially alter the human biological limit, but became much more widespread and problematic in the last half century or so, as rapid medical technological advances were applied to athletes. The term "doping" is notoriously difficult to define, but despite the difficulties associated with definition, it is generally agreed that the practice is unethical and detrimental to the quality of sport. In order to formulate rules banning the practice of doping, different sporting organizations have employed various definitions. One of the most common approaches to avoid problems in defining the broad term is creating a list of banned practices. By avoiding a concrete definition different problems are created though, because regulatory authorities are forced to remain one step behind those who attempt to gain an artificial advantage. Practices can only be outlawed after they are used and discovered. Also, without a definitive idea of what doping is, it may not be clear what it is about doping that makes it unethical. This makes it difficult to attain consistency between rules regarding different types of technology in sport.

5 The second type of sports technology that is strictly regulated is the use of equipment. One

reason for regulating equipment is in order to ensure that it is athletes who are competing rather than their equipment. But the question is—"At what point does technology surpass the influence of an athlete's performance and in the process devalue the performance?" In order to answer this question, a clear understanding of what "value" sport contains is necessary. Motor sports is often cited as an example of technology becoming more important to the competition's outcome than the athlete's (driver's) performance, a progression that most sports do not wish to follow. According to certain experts, sport should be regulated so it deals primarily with genuine, human performances. This is a difficult criterion, as there are some sports where there has always been a significant "non-human" aspect to the sport. Wind-tunnel testing of the AIS (Australian Institute of Sport) women's skeleton team, for example, found a direct correlation between performance and drag coefficient. It is dubious whether drag coefficient can be considered a "human performance". There are many other examples of sports that naturally advantage one body type over others. Rules such as the UCI's which regulate the body position of cyclists in an attempt to prevent people altering a traditionally static property such as drag coefficient merely benefit one arbitrarily chosen body type over another.

6 If all technological influences were eliminated, athletes in some sports would no longer be able to adequately express themselves in the way they compete. This would essentially reduce these sports to a competition between machines. This effect is clearly demonstrated in the attempts to determine the "real" hour record in cycling, by eliminating the influences of technology in order to properly compare cyclists from different periods and therefore different technology levels. The more detailed that hour-record comparisons get, correcting for technology, drag coefficient etc, the more the process resembles a mere comparison of average power output of the athletes. That isn't cycling, and has none of the appeal of cycling. If average power output over one hour was a sport, few would play it or watch it, because it would be intensely boring. The real interest lies in the tactics and mind-games played by the athletes, and the use of technology forms part of this.

7 Furthermore, if equipment technology is completely banned, the only way that athletes are able to keep improving after the natural performance limit is reached is to turn to much less ethical technologies such as doping. By allowing technological developments in equipment, the inherent competitive nature of athletes has an outlet, and difficult to detect and far less ethical practices such as doping (or even potentially genetic modification) are less likely to be abused. By allowing certain types of technology, the process can be controlled more than if it were banned outright, potentially resulting in minimal use of unethical technology.

What Types of Technology Should Be Allowed?

8 Technology that is used in sport can be divided into the categories of those that: 1) make sport possible; 2) improve safety and reduce harm; 3) de-skill or re-skill sports; 4) dehumanize performances; and 5) increase participation and/ or spectatorship. Once again, these distinctions are not straightforward; most technology has aspects of several of these categories.

9 There is little question that technologies whose primary purpose falls into the first two categories should not be restricted. Technologies that cause sports to be de- or re-skilled or dehumanize performances are much more controversial, and a number of sports restrict the use of many such technologies. The purpose of such restrictions is not always clear. The UCI asserts the following as the purpose of its rules regarding technology:

Bicycles shall comply with the spirit and principle of cycling as a sport. The spirit suggests that cyclists compete in competitions on an equal footing. (UCI, 2002)

10 The suggestion that it is possible for athletes to compete "on an equal footing" is ridiculous; <u>even if it were possible, it would certainly not be desirable.</u> The concept of competition is not compatible with equality. The entire purpose of competition is to gain an advantage over one's opponent. This occurs because of natural talent and training, but technological advantages play a legitimate role too. Technology has always (usually ethically) been used to gain a competitive advantage, from coaching technology to nutrition and physiotherapy. Such usages are legitimate, and so regulating technology in an attempt to create equality between the competitors is futile as well as misguided.

11 The UCI statement goes on to assert that "the primacy of man over machine," needs to be maintained. This is a legitimate aim for technology regulations, but unfortunately the UCI regulations that attempt to achieve it are poorly implemented. The rules limit specific technological aspects, such as requiring that bikes weigh over 6.8kg. There are also limitations on other aspects of the bicycle including rider position. Despite these rules, the cost of top-end racing bicycles continues to rise, with professional cyclists typically racing on bikes that cost in excess of $10,000. UCI regulations also often tend to be very inconsistently enforced. Some of the rules are frequently broken, but ignored by officials. Bicycle weight is one example of a rule that is usually not tested. At a recent track cycling event, bicycles were actually weighed, and the majority of riders were

required to put ballast in their otherwise illegal bikes that they had been racing on all season in order to reach the required weight. At other times a legitimate innovation is banned shortly after it is developed. An example of this is Graeme Obree's unusual position being banned in between the qualifying and final rounds of his attempt to defend his world pursuit title in 1994. The result of this inconsistency is that companies, professional teams or countries with large budgets are able to be technologically innovative; the risk of wasted money on an innovation that is subsequently banned is not large compared to their budget. Less wealthy organizations and individuals on the other hand cannot afford to take such a large financial risk. In effect, the UCI technology rules have achieved the exact opposite of what they intended. If the rules were relaxed somewhat, cheaper technologies such as altering cyclist position would have a large enough effect on performance that more expensive technologies would not provide such a significant advantage. Therefore, in my opinion, relaxing the technology restrictions in cycling may well put competitors on a more "equal footing," by giving more affluent cyclists, countries and teams less of an advantage.

12 But suggesting that technology rules be relaxed does not suggest that their removal altogether is desirable. Technology that significantly risks athletes' or spectators' health and safety still ought to be restricted. Equipment that is unstable or unreliable would also be similarly restricted. The UCI requirement that aerodynamic helmets must also meet safety standards is an example of a sensible technological restriction, as was their action to ban a certain brand of wheels that had exhibited catastrophic failure on several occasions, risking not only the cyclist using them but other competitors and spectators as well.

Total words: 1696
Total reading time: __________minutes_________seconds

* *The text is based on Ethics of Technology in Sport*

Vocabulary and Expressions

preoccupation /priːɒkjʊ'peɪʃən/ *n.* the state of being worried about or thinking about something most of the time

occurrence /ə'kʌrəns/ *n.* happening

skeleton /'skelɪtən/ *n.* a fast winter sliding sport in which a person rides a small sled down a frozen track while lying face down

coefficient /ˌkəʊɪ'fɪʃənt/ *n.* a value, in mathematics, that appears in front of and multiplies another value

static /'stætɪk/ *adj.* staying in one place without moving, or not changing for a long time

arbitrary /'ɑːbɪtrərɪ/ *adj.* based on chance rather than being planned or based on reason

tactic /'tæktɪk/ *n.* (usually plural) a planned way of doing something

dehumanize /ˌdiː'hjuːmənaɪz/ *vt.* to remove from a person the special human qualities of independent thought, feeling for other people, etc.

footing /'fʊtɪŋ/ *n.* be on an equal footing to be in an equal situation

compatible /kəm'pætɪbl̩/ *adj.* able to exist, live together, or work successfully with something or someone else

physiotherapy /ˌfɪzɪəʊ'θerəpɪ/ *n.* the treatment of muscle stiffness, pain, and injury, especially by rubbing and moving the sore parts

primacy /'praɪməsɪ/ n. the state of being the most important thing

ballast /'bæləst/ *n.* heavy matter such as sand or stone that is used at the bottom of a ship or a hot-air balloon to make it heavier, or the small stones on which railways and roads are made

aerodynamic /ˌeərəʊdaɪ'næmɪk/ *adj.* designed or arranged to offer the least resistance to fluid flow

Comprehension Check

1. According to the passage, what reduces the rate of improvement in sports? What can be done to maintain the performance progress in sports?
2. How is the term "doping" usually defined? What problems does this definition bring?
3. What are the pros and cons of eliminating technological influences in sports equipment?
4. What does the underlined sentence in paragraph 5 mean? Try to paraphrase it.
5. What does the underlined sentence imply in paragraph 10? What do the first and second "it" refer to respectively?
6. Why does the author say that "regulating technology to create equality between the competitors is futile as well as misguided"? What example(s) does the author use to justify his opinion?

Critical Thinking Starters

1. When technology meets sport, controversy follows. The 2014 FIFA World Cup was the first in which goal-line technology was used, sparking a highly controversial debate. Supporters believe that it can nullify human error and provide clarity while the naysayers counter-argue that it disputes the flow of the game. What do you think? Should the World Cup use goal-line technology?

2. The huge rewards, both intrinsic and extrinsic, that come with winning means that technological developments are more important than ever. With the increasing use of technology in sports, some believe that the value of sports provided by athletes has shifted towards technologies and away from the sport. If this is the case, what value does sports promise? Is the athlete's role degraded by technology?

More to Know

British cyclist Graeme Obree designed his own bike made out of washing machine parts amongst other things, and created a bike with a unique position which allowed him to hold his body together more closely and therefore be more aerodynamic. In this position, he was able to generate more power into his thighs and thus cycle faster. Genius. Yet, the Union Cycliste Internationale (UCI) decided to ban it.

Obree took this on the chin and set about creating a new design and went the complete opposite direction of his previous design. He came up with something even more innovative, giving him what became known as the 'Superman stance'. Again, this bike design was also banned.

During the 90s, cyclists developed many different designs for their bikes in order to find the most aerodynamic and efficient format. However, UCI eventually stepped in and decided to ban all Olympic track bikes that didn't fit in with their new specifications.

This has resulted in the bikes of today returning to their original shape from the mid 70s due to the strict regulations in place that dictate things such as the shape of the bike, distance between saddle and handle bars and even the angle at which the seat is allowed to be placed.

As a result, UCI has left no room for Olympic bike design to progress and develop. If Obree was allowed to be innovative and design the best bike he could, what would the cyclists of today be riding?

Sports in Focus

Olympic weightlifting is a sport in which athletes compete to lift the greatest amount of weight overhead within an athlete's weight category. The competition lifts are the snatch（抓举） and the clean & jerk（挺举）. Each weightlifter has three attempts in each lift. The combined total of the highest successful attempt for each lift determines the athlete's placing within their respective bodyweight category.

The Snatch: The snatch is by far the more advanced & technical of the two Olympic lifts. It is one explosive movement in which you pull the weight off the ground, drop under it in a squat to "catch" the bar overhead, then rise up to an upright standing position.

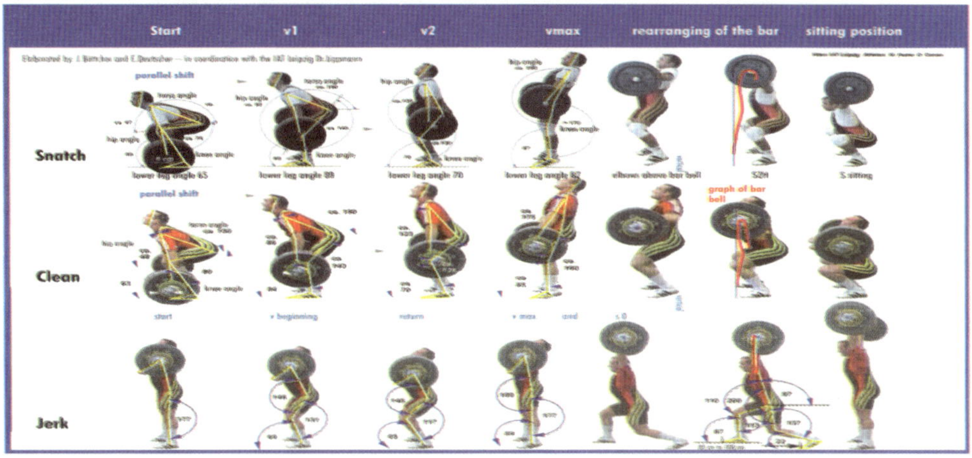

The Clean and Jerk: The clean and jerk is actually a combination of two separate lifts that together make up one Olympic lift. The clean involves pulling the weight off the ground and dropping below it in a squat to "catch" the weight at your shoulders, then rising up to stand upright. Once standing, the jerk is initiated, pushing the bar overhead to complete the lift.

Relevant Words and Phrases

V taper	six pack	muscle memory
muscle confusion	hard gainer	easy gainer

Text B

The Need for Speed: How High-Technology Swimsuits Changed the Sport of Swimming

1 Recorded swim suit history begins around 1400 BC in ancient Greece and Rome. In those times, bathing nude was the norm. Over the course of several hundred years however, different swimsuit styles were worn. The earliest contemporary swimsuits were very modest. They were usually made from heavy wool, revealed little to no skin, and weighed up to 9 pounds.

2 In 1913, sweater manufacturer Jantzen Knitting Mills became the first manufacturer of swim suits when the company went from making wool sweaters and hosiery[1] to making swim suits. The story goes that a member of the Portland Rowing Club requested a pair of rowing trunks to keep him warm during chilly mornings. After the member tried them, he liked them so much that he came back with other members of the crew who also wanted to purchase the trunks. These trunks subsequently became the prototype[2] for the rib-stitch swimsuits that were first produced in 1915.

3 As the sport of swimming began to gain popularity in the 1920s, competitive swimmers found it more and more difficult to find lightweight, secure-fitting swimsuits. In 1928, the company known today as Speedo, earned its place among top swimmers around the world when it introduced the Racerback suit. This was the first time a swimsuit had been manufactured specifically for competition. The controversial yet revolutionary Racerback style's open shoulder and exposed back allowed greater range of motion in the water and weighed considerably less than its wool predecessors. The Racerback was quickly adopted by competitive swimmers around the world, despite being banned from beaches for being too revealing.

4 In the quest for speed, swimsuit manufacturers continued to research the field hydrodynamics. After World War II, companies began to experiment with nylon, lycra, and "paper" (lycra/nylon) fabrics, removing preconceived[3] requirements of modesty and instead, focused on

[1]hosiery /'həʊzɪərɪ/ *n.* a word used especially in shops for things such as socks, tights, and stockings

[2]prototype /'prəʊtətaɪp/ *n.* the first example of something, such as a machine or other industrial product, from which all later forms are developed

[3]preconceived /ˌpriːkən'siːvd/ *adj.* (of an idea or an opinion) formed too early, especially without enough thought or knowledge

efficiency and reducing drag through the water. Dr. Conrad Dottinger of West Germany designed the first modern skintight swimsuits for competition. Nicknamed the "Belgrad", the East German women dominated the 1969 first FINA World Championships, winning 10 of 14 events and setting 7 world records wearing this swimsuit. The "Belgrad" skintight design opened the eyes of swimsuit manufacturers to recognize the importance of reducing drag through formfitting[4] suits. Subsequently, over the years, swimsuit manufacturers tried different materials and designs which led to the first major modern technology incorporated into swimsuits during the 1990's.

5 In 1996, Speedo introduced a new competitive suit called the Aqua-Blade. The material of the suit contained rough and smooth stripes, designed to create tiny channels of fast and slow moving water. The material of the suit allowed air to become trapped for short periods of time, making the swimmer more buoyant[5] in the water. Then in 1999, Speedo improved on the Aqua-Blade technology by looking to a creature which, like humans, was not naturally hydrodynamic.

6 Named the Fastskin, it was the most technically advanced competitive swimsuit ever made. Using sharkskin as a model for the fabric, Speedo attempted to replicate the creature's highly developed skin known to minimize drag and maximize swimming efficiency. Although the idea of copying sharkskin was creative, recent studies have found that the surface material of the Fastskin didn't work. Instead, the positive effects seen by swimmers who wore the Fastskin were attributed to the tight, streamline fit of the suit. The suits were so tight that they actually changed a swimmer's circulation[6], which increased the venous return to the body and made it easier to maintain optimum body position. At the Sydney Olympics in 2000, 28 of 33 Olympic Gold Medals were won in the Speedo Fastskin, making it the most successful suit in Olympic Games history. After the introduction of the Fastskin, the competitive swimming world would never be the same.

7 It was not Speedo, but rather Adidas who made the first full-body competitive swimsuit. Initially introduced in 1998, the suit was not popular among competitive swimmers due to a concern for a loss of "feel for the water." Adidas finally showcased the Jetconcept in 2003. Adidas adapted technology used by commercial aircrafts, incorporating ribbed panels into the fabric, which

[4]formfitting / 'fɔmfɪtɪŋ/ *adj.* used to describe clothes that fit closely to your body
[5]buoyant / 'bɒɪənt/ *adj.* able to float
[6]circulation /ˌsɜːkjʊ'leɪʃən/ *n.* the movement of blood around the body

mimicked grooves found on an airplane's fuselage[7] and wings. The result was groundbreaking, as the fabric helped channel water more fluidly over the back, reducing active drag and turbulence while increasing swimming performance.

8 Another competitive swimsuit manufacturer, TYR Sport Inc., decomposed[8] the components of overall total drag in racing suits with the introduction of the Tracer A7. The design utilized zoned compression combined with a modified synthetic rubber. By securely locking a swimmer's muscles, the Tracer A7 provided precise compression where muscle fatigue was known to occur. At 60% the weight of regular neoprene, the hydrophobic[9] woven fabric maximized muscle oxygenation without compromising flexibility.

9 The era of "technical doping" neared its peak with the launch of Speedo's LZR Racer in 2008. Following three years of research and utilizing technology developed by NASA, Speedo created the most advanced swimsuit competitive swimmers had ever seen. At the 2008 Beijing Olympics, twenty-three world records were broken by the swimmers who wore LZR Racer suits, compared with only two that were broken by the swimmers who didn't. 89% of all the medals in swimming (including 94% of the gold medals) were won by swimmers who wore the Speedo LZR.

10 The LZR Racer inspired other companies, such as Italian swimsuit manufacturers Arena and Jaked, to develop suits similar to the LZR. At the 2009 World Aquatics Championships in Rome, 84% of swimmers used suits made from Arena or Jaked. 43 new world records were set only a year after the Beijing Olympics. The usage of enhancing suits was spiraling out of control, and it was after these championships that the FINA Congress voted to ban all body-length swimsuits made with high-technology fabrics.

[7]fuselage /'fju:zəlɑ:ʒ/ *n.* the central body of an airplane that is designed to accommodate the crew and passengers

[8]decompose /ˌdi:kəm'pəuz/ *vt.* to break, or to break something, into smaller parts

[9]hydrophobic /ˌhaɪdrəʊ'fəʊbɪk/ *adj.* hydrophobic substances cannot be mixed with or dissolved in water

The Suit Debate

A: Did the Swimsuits Really Make That Much of a Difference?

11 In less than one year after the introduction of Speedo's LZR, more than 130 world records had been broken. Clearly the introduction of high-technology suits was changing the sport, but how much help did the suits give the swimmers?

12 Hydrodynamic resistance, also known as drag, is a major performance issue in competitive swimming. There are three factors which comprise a swimmer's drag: skin friction, pressure, and wave. Frictional drag is the result of the interaction between the swimmer's body and the water molecules, which slows down the swimmer. However, friction drag also helps propel swimmers through the water, due to Newton's 3rd law of motion. As a swimmer moves faster through the water, pressure drag becomes a factor due to the front region of the body, specifically the head, moving against the water. The pressure against the head of the swimmer results in a tension difference between the two ends of the swimmer's body, resulting in turbulence. Finally, wave drag supplements pressure drag because it is also the result of increased speed through the water. The pressure around the swimmer's body increases as a result of different water velocities. The different water velocities interact with the swimmer's body, creating waves and additional resistance. Although freestyle is the fastest swimming stroke, it also has the greatest amount of resistance. In a sport where a few hundredths of a second can mean the difference between the first and the last, swimmers have always taken steps to reduce the drag on their bodies. For example, swimmers will shave their entire bodies for major competitions. Removing hair actually significantly reduces the rate of velocity decay in underwater push-offs, diminishing active drag and decreasing expended energy.

13 The polyurethane suits, however, took these steps to reduce drag to another level. Polyurethane is a fabric which is flexible and contains closed cell foam material. Each micro closed cell is a pocket of gas which is less dense than water. Essentially, the polyurethane suits gave swimmers extra buoyancy, allowing the swimmer to float slightly higher in the water. Since water density is approximately 800 times greater than air's, the higher a swimmer's body rides in the water, the faster they will go. Even if the distance of one's body out of the water is less than half a millimeter, the pressure against the head of the swimmer is diminished, and that is enough of an advantage to make the difference between winning and losing.

14 Additionally, compression garments are responsible for a better blood flow, reducing blood lactate concentrations during physical activity. Better blood flow allows athletes to recover more quickly from fatigue. Thus, a suit made from a polyurethane material covering the entire body not only made competitive swimmers more buoyant, but also had a significant effect on their endurance during performance of repetitive movements.

B: Leveling the Playing Field: The Swimming Community's Outcry[10]

15 There were concerns that swimsuit technology was encroaching[11] on the sport's integrity as far back as 2000, the year when the first full-body suits were becoming popular. Before the high-technology swimsuits, swimming races were decided by the abilities of swimmers alone. As a result of the developed swimsuit technology, races could now be decided by swimming ability and equipment. Thus, there was a legitimate possibility that races could be won by the swimmer with the best performance-enhancing suit rather than the level of talent or amount of training.

16 Proponents of the suit pleaded that technological advancements are inherent in every sport, and that swimming was no different. After spending millions of dollars in research, swimsuit manufacturers claimed that banning the suits would stifle technical developments and innovation in swimming. They cited several types of technological advancements that the swimming community accepted, such as lane lines and goggles. The difference however, between those advancements and the high-technology suits, rested upon equal access and ethical considerations. Items such as lane lines and goggles affect all competitors the same. In the past, when races were swum with lane lines that consisted of a wire cord with a cork, every swimmer constantly battled waves and turbulence, slowing each competitor down equally. Now, lane lines are composed of triple-stack large baffle plastic, almost eliminating turbulence altogether, but this is still a benefit available to every competitor in the pool. Likewise, goggles were initially introduced to alleviate the various forms of eye discomfort resulting from constant exposure to chlorine. However, goggles have changed very little over the years and by themselves, are not performance enhancing.

---

[10]outcry /'aʊtkraɪ/ *n.* a strong expression of anger and disapproval about something, made by a group of people or by the public

[11]encroach /ɪn'krəʊtʃ/ *vi.* encroach on/upon sth: to gradually take away someone else's rights, or to take control of someone's time, work, etc.

17 There was also a misplaced assumption that the technical suits could also be compared to other sports which relied upon equipment, such as cycling or rowing. Nonetheless, those sports are "conveyance" sports, meaning the final performance result is dependent upon the mechanical transformation of human energy into forward movement. Without a bicycle or racing shell, those sports would not exist. Conversely, swimming does not rely on equipment but rather can be conducted purely wherever there is water. Therefore, goggles and lane lines were neutral innovations, whereas the suits were performance enhancing.

18 A more reasonable analogy to the high-technology swimsuits can be found in the example of performance enhancing drugs. Like the suits, drugs alter the intrinsic and natural abilities of an athlete's performance. Further and also similar to drugs, the suits were not available to everyone. Negating the moral and health implications of using drugs, the price of the suits was cost prohibitive[12]. Without the standardization of racing suits, there was a large risk that competitors with access to this technology would have a performance advantage over others who could not afford the suits. It follows that the manufacturers of these suits intruded upon the honor and traditional concept of competitive swimming as being human ability against human ability.

19 Thus, the history of sports has shown that technical innovations usually have elevated the costs of participation. By introducing equipment that not only enhanced performance but spurred issues of accessibility, competitive swimming briefly lost touch with its core principles. As swimming relies upon training, dedication, and talent, allowing technologies that significantly influenced performance was contrary to the pure concept of it. Consequently, the swimming community looked to FINA to take action.

Total words: 1998
Total reading time: __________minutes__________seconds

* *The text is based on The Need for Speed: How High-Technology Swimsuits Changed the Sport of Swimming by David Meyer*

[12]prohibitive / prəˈhɪbətɪv/ *adj.* If the cost of something is prohibitive, it is too expensive for most people

Comprehension Check

1. Which swimsuits are mentioned in the passage? What are their respective features?
2. According to the passage, what can swimmers do to reduce drag?
3. What does "level" mean in the underlined part? How do you understand this part according to the passage, especially the paragraphs following it?
4. What reasons does the passage provide to explain why some technological advancements can be used in competitive swimming while high-tech swimsuits should be banned?

Activity Time-Out

Technology serves many functions in sport. It has a constituent function. Without ball and bats, there is no baseball. Technology may enhance performances, such as the new alpine carving skis that seem to help beginners master more easily the basic techniques of the sport. Other kinds of technology, such as helmets in boxing, are supposed to prevent injuries. The use of video cameras in the refereeing of soccer matches is thought to enhance justice. In groups, pick a sport and look at its history in technological advancements. Summarize your findings by filling in the following chart.

Technological Development	Effect of This Development	Comments/Notes

Pop Culture

What is the nature of athletic performance? The book *Sport, Technology and the Body: The Nature of Performance* by Tara Magdalinski offers an answer to this fascinating question by considering the relationship between sport, technology and the body. The book addresses concerns about the technological "invasion" of the "natural" body to investigate expectations that athletic performances reflect nothing more than the actual capacity of the untainted athlete. By examining a series of case studies, including Paralympic sprinter Oscar Pistorius, Fastskin swimsuits, hypoxic chambers and an array of illicit substances and methods, the book distinguishes between internal and external technologies to highlight the ways that performance enhancement, and public reaction to it, can be read.

Vocabulary Building

Look up the following words and expressions in reference books and on the Internet.

Words and Expressions	Meaning
cloud storage	
big data	
cybersecurity	
biomimetics	

2

UNIT

Sports in High Schools and Universities

A school without football is in danger of deteriorating into a medieval study hall.

— Frank Leahy, college athletics administrator

Pre-reading Thoughts

1. What would you predict are some of the long-term advantages of participating in high school sports?

2. Do you think participating in high school athletics will help or hinder a student's academic performance?

3. Do you think female high school students should be encouraged to participate in athletics on an equal basis with male athletes?

Text A

Positive and Negative Effects of Interscholastic Sports

1 A host of studies have supported the positive benefits of high school sports. Typically these studies have been conducted by school systems or other organizations such as the NFHS. Relying on the data collected from athletes, principals, and parents, the studies make a case for the value of athletics as an educational endeavor.

2 The NFHS has summarized this research on its website in "The Case for High School Activities". The site quotes research that supports the value of athletics in promoting academic performance, moral development, good citizenship, success in college, better attendance and graduation rates, fewer behavioral problems, higher achievement motivation, and resistance to drug and alcohol abuse. Leadership skills, decision making, social integration, and improved self-image are also mentioned as positive outcomes.

3 Some of the studies cited in the NFHS summary offered the following conclusions. Over two-thirds of parents support the value of cocurricular activities, including sport, according to the 29th annual Phi Delta Kappa–Gallup Poll of the Public's Attitudes Toward Public Schools. The Women's Sports Foundation has consistently supported the benefits of high school sports for young women,

including physical fitness, resistance to eating disorders, social acceptance, and academic success. Finally, more than three-quarters of high school principals are strong supporters of high school athletics, according to a study supported by a grant from the Lilly Endowment of Indianapolis and conducted by Indiana University in cooperation with the Association of Secondary School Principals. Both of these conclusions are cited in an NFHS summary.

Influence of Athletics on Academic Performance

4 High school students who participate in athletics tend to have higher grade point averages, better attendance records, and lower dropout rates than the general student body. This conclusion has been drawn in various studies by the Women's Sports Foundation; NFHS; and the states of Wyoming, North Carolina, Colorado, and New Mexico.

5 Clearly there is strong support for interscholastic athletics from virtually every segment of the U.S. population. Sport as an educational experience continues to be a critical factor in the personal development of young people, and coaches must not lose sight of that goal if they hope to retain broad support of their programs.

6 However, a fair and comprehensive analysis of high school sports reveals both positive and negative effects of participation. One negative effect is the possibility of creating disunity within the student body when athletes form cliques. Cocurricular sport is not for every student, although for some, it may be a critical factor in self-confidence, social acceptance, and physical development. High school athletics also have an influence on peer groups and the functioning of the student body, and hard choices often have to be made about how to finance athletic programs.

Character Development Through Athletic Participation

7 Supporters of high school sports have trumpeted their value in helping young people develop a strong work ethic, good moral behavior, healthy attitudes toward fitness, and improved academic performance. Let's see if those claims have been backed up by research.

8 Studies often compare the performance and attitudes of high school athletes to those of nonathletes and purport to demonstrate that athletes are superior to nonathletes in the traits just mentioned. However, what is not clear from the research is whether athletes already possessed

these traits due to other influences in their life or if in fact athletics was a major contributing factor. Simply reporting that athletes appear to have higher levels of physical, social, or moral development compared to nonathletes does not prove that there is a cause-and-effect relationship between athletes' experience in sport and their academic performance, attitude toward fitness, moral behavior, and work ethic.

9 It is possible that athletes already display more progress toward a higher standard in these traits, and this progress helps them to perform successfully on athletic teams. Certain studies have followed students over time and measured student performance. Generally, these studies showed that athletes are more likely to come from economically privileged backgrounds and have above-average cognitive skills, self-esteem, and academic performance. Of course it is also possible that students who are less privileged or weak in cognitive skills withdraw from sport or are excluded because of poor grades, thus affecting the results of such studies. These results are not that different from research findings on all students who participate in extracurricular activities in school. In general, students who choose to join musical groups, drama, debate clubs, school newspapers, and so on also show higher levels of development than the bulk of the student body.

10 Adults who have gone on to success in business or a profession often attribute their success to lessons they learned on the playing field. From their point of view, sport participation is vital for success in later life. A 1987 survey of individuals at the level of executive vice president or above in Fortune 500 companies indicated that 95% had participated in high school sports while 54% were involved in student government, 43% in the National Honor Society, 37% in music, and 18% in their school's publications. It is possible that those people would have been successful regardless of their sport experience, but their personal belief and testimony can be a powerful argument. Female business executives have been particularly influenced by their sport participation. Two-thirds of them report that they exercise regularly, which is almost double the percentage of women in the general population. More than four out of five (82%) female business executives played sports growing up—and the vast majority of them say lessons learned on the playing field have helped them succeed in business. The following are some specific examples as of this writing.

• eBay CEO Meg Whitman played lacrosse and squash at Princeton.

• Mrs. Field's Cookies founder Debbi Fields is an avid equestrian.

• Spherion CEO Cinda Hallman, one of the only six females who are CEOs of Fortune 500 companies, was a basketball guard in high school in Arkansas.

• Sue Wellington, president of Gatorade division of Quaker Oats, was captain of Yale's swim team.

• Melissa Payner, CEO of Spiegel Catalog, was a collegiate gymnast.

11 Most studies of high school students in sport have focused on the years of their participation. However, a comprehensive study tracked over 25,000 high school athletes eight years after their senior year to see if sport participation had had any lasting effects. The results showed that high school athletes are more likely than nonathletes to participate in physical fitness activities or recreational sport, graduate from college, be employed full-time, and earn a higher salary and are less likely to be smokers. The most glaring negative factor associated with athletic participation was a tendency toward binge drinking. These results confirmed the conclusions of earlier studies showing higher rates of drinking and binge drinking among athletes compared to nonathletes.

Social Effects on the Student Body

12 In thousands of high schools, sport promotes school spirit; creates an "us against them" mentality; and offers natural social gatherings at pep rallies, sport events, and ceremonies. Attendance at sport events to root for friends and acquaintances strengthens the bonds between groups of students. Athletic teams often support each other by visiting each other's practices or games and cheering each other on.

13 Educators would point out that athletics are not the only school activity that has positive effects like these. In fact, the NFHS, mentioned previously, does not concern itself solely with interscholastic sport but also includes all cocurricular activities. Its website devotes significant space to reasons to support all school-based cocurricular activities. For example, music and drama organizations often perform similar functions in after-school settings. Altogether, school activities outside of the academic curriculum cost an average of 1% to 3% of the overall school budget, according to the NFHS. However, across the United States, parents and communities have supported athletics more generously than any other school activity simply because of the number of students involved, the number of games, and the travel expenses incurred.

14 The social fabric of a school can also be negatively affected by the division between students who play sports and those who do not. Because athletes spend so much time together, are admired by other students, and receive plaudits from the community and media, they tend to socialize together, sometimes to the exclusion of other students. When the jock culture separates

itself from the student body at large, envy and mistrust often set in. Some misguided athletes interpret their social standing to mean that deviant behavior on their part is acceptable, and various offenses by prominent athletes often hit the front pages of local newspapers with tales of poor judgment and errant behavior.

15 Since many students envy athletes, particularly males, the emphasis on academic performance may suffer somewhat for all students. In spite of the fact that athletes seem to be on average better students than the norm, students who excel in the classroom are regarded as nerds in social circles. Fortunately, there are many examples of students who do well both in academics and athletics. This has been particularly true of female athletes.

16 Gender equity has transformed the scene in local high schools by including girls in the athletic culture. Young women now have many of the same opportunities for self-development, competitive training, recognition, and college athletic scholarships that formerly were restricted to young men. Girls have to learn to balance academics, sport, and their social life in a way that didn't exist before the passage of Title IX in the 1970s. Conflicts between generations, tradition, and a society that used to encourage women solely toward a nurturing role in life have been inevitable. Girls are faced with acting as gutsy, tough competitors on the athletic field and then resuming a more traditional feminine role in their social environment where they are supposed to focus on clothes, personal appearance, and boys. For some girls, the challenge is intimidating; and they often lack role models in teachers or parents because earlier generations simply did not have the same experiences.

Total words: 1700
Total reading time: __________minutes_________seconds

* *The text is based on Social Issues in Sport (2nd edition) by Ronald B. Woods*

Vocabulary and Expressions

body /'bɒdɪ/ *n.* group of people ***student body***(=all the students in a particular school or college)

clique /kliːk/ *n.* a small group of people who think they are special and do not let other people join them

lacrosse /lə'krɒs/ *n.* a game played on a field by two teams of ten players, in which each player has a long stick with a net on the end of it and uses this to throw, catch and carry a small ball

squash /skwɒʃ/ *n.* a game played by two people who use rackets to hit a small rubber ball against the four walls of a square court

collegiate /kə'liːdʒɪət/ *adj.* involving or related to a college

binge /bɪndʒ/ *n.* a short period when you do too much of something, especially drinking alcohol

plaudits /'plɔːdɪts/ *n.* praise and admiration

jock /dʒɒk/ *n.* an insulting word for someone who does a lot of sport

errant /'erənt/ *adj.* behaving wrongly in some way, especially by leaving home

nerd /nɜːd/ *n.* someone who is boring and unfashionable

gutsy /'gʌtsɪ/ *adj.* brave and determined

Comprehension Check

1. List 7 positive effects of student athletics according to the passage.
2. Besides students, what other members of the society in America support school athletics?
3. According to the passage, what are some of the possible negative effects of school athletics?
4. What does "root for" in the underlined sentence of paragraph 12 mean?
5. What does the passage say about the attitude of schools and parents concerning the extra cost of athletic programs?
6. List 5 other extracurricular activities, besides sports, that also seem to have positive effects on students.

Critical Thinking Starters

1. In the U.S. there is a gap, both in academic performance and sports participation, between wealthier students and poorer students. What recommendations would you make to close that gap?
2. In America, Title IX was passed to enforce gender equality in school sports. What is your attitude about that? And why?
3. Many famous business leaders in America attribute their success at least partially to school sport participation. Do you think this is true? State your reasons.
4. In the U.S., every high school has extracurricular, competitive athletic programs. The school

teams will compete against each other after school. Do you think that would be feasible and advantageous in China? Discuss this with your classmates.

Expert's View

World Cup-winning Springbok captain Francois Pienaar, CEO of Advent Sport Entertainment and Media (ASEM), believes that Varsity Sport will provide a crucial breeding ground for the development of young sporting talent in South Africa.

"This is an exciting new development for University sport in South Africa. We are confident that Varsity Sport will unearth a vast number of talented South African sport stars, officials and administrators in the near future.

"It has been proven that elevating the level of exposure of Varsity Sports holds huge benefits for South African sport in general. Many national and international stars will emerge from the Varsity Sports initiative," he said.

Sports in Focus

Equestrian Sports are sports that use horses as a main part of the sport. This usually takes the form of the rider being on the horse's back, or the horses pulling some sort of horse-drawn vehicle. The history of equestrian sport dates back over 2,000 years, to when the Greeks introduced Dressage（盛装舞步）training to prepare their horses for war.

It continued to develop as a military exercise through the Middle Ages, with the Three Day Event—which includes Dressage, Cross Country（越野赛）and Show Jumping（场地障碍赛）tests—designed to reflect the range of challenges horses faced in the army. In its modern form, equestrian owes much to its inclusion in the Olympic Games in 1900, which led to the creation of the Fédération Equestre Internationale (FEI) in 1921. Equestrian is the only Olympic sport in which men and women compete against each other on equal terms. It is also the only one in which humans and animals compete together. In each of the three Equestrian events—Dressage, Jumping and Eventing（三项赛）—the aim is to create a harmonious partnership between horse and rider.

Dressage ("training" in French) involves the progressive training of the horse to a high level of impulsion, collection, and obedience. Competitive dressage has the goal of showing the horse carrying out, on request, the natural movements that it performs without thinking while running loose. Show jumping comprises a timed event judged on the ability of the horse and rider to jump over a series of obstacles, in a given order and with the fewest refusals or knockdowns of portions of the obstacles. Eventing, also called combined training, horse trials, the three-day event, the Military, or the complete test, puts together the obedience of dressage with the athletic ability of show jumping, and the fitness demands of the cross-country jumping phase. In the last-named, the horses jump over fixed obstacles, such as logs, stone walls, banks, ditches, and water, trying to finish the course under the "optimum time."

Relevant Words and Phrases

horse harness	saddle	bar bit	bridle
stirrup	girth	rein	head harness

Text B

History of Athletics in U.S. Colleges and Universities

1 Intercollegiate athletics in the United States has come to be regarded as higher education's "peculiar institution." This results from the fact that although intercollegiate athletics is seldom listed as part of the central mission of a college or university, athletics have come to command inordinate visibility, resources, influence, and attention both inside and outside many campuses. To truly understand the present situation requires a reconstruction of college athletics' unique historical evolution.

2 In the twenty-first century, it is not unusual for a major university campus to contain both a football stadium that seats 70,000 spectators and a basketball arena that accommodates audiences of 20,000. In the year 2000 many universities had annual operating budgets for athletics ranging between $30 million and $60 million. The success and pervasiveness of college sports is the result of particular innovations and episodes over the past 150 years.

The Violent Birth of Intercollegiate Sports

3 Prior to 1850 if there was a need for physical activity in the student regimen[1], college presidents and deans thought manual labor in the form of farming or clearing boulders[2] from college lands fit the bill perfectly. Students, not surprisingly, remained unconvinced that this was the type of physical release that their souls craved. Instead, collegiate student bodies devised their own elaborate (and often brutal) intramural[3] contests known as "class rushes." These "rushes" usually involved some variation of football, which actually provided a pretext for a ritualistic and violent hazing[4] of the incoming freshman by the sophomore class.

4 College officials struggled to curb these violent student traditions, but intramural sports persisted within the campus and eventually took a decisive turn toward sanctioned and refereed events in which a team representing one institution competed against another. Despite the increase in organization, administrators initially were not eager to embrace such contests that they viewed as inappropriate distractions from serious scholarly work. With or without administrative blessings, college students formed athletic associations that included mechanisms for raising money, charging fees, sponsoring events, and selling tickets. By the 1890s, alumni groups joined with the student organizations to create formidable programs over which the college presidents and faculty exercised relatively little control.

5 The outstanding feature of college athletics in the late nineteenth and early twentieth

---

[1]regimen /'redʒɪmən/ *n.* a special plan of food, exercise etc. that is intended to improve your health

[2]boulder /'bəʊldə/ *n.* a large stone or piece of rock

[3]intramural /ˌɪntrə'mjʊərəl/ *adj.* happening within or involving the members of one school, college or university

[4] haze /heɪz/ *vt.* to play tricks on a new college student as part of the ceremony of joining a club

centuries was its pervasiveness and diversity across American institutions. Although the oldest and largest institutions—Harvard and Yale—quickly gained the most attention in newspaper coverage and provided the largest athletic budgets, numerous other campuses made significant contributions as well. For instance, Springfield College was where James Naismith invented basketball in 1891. By 1900 the popularity of collegiate sports was reflected by its adoption in even all-girls schools. Wellesley College developed a distinctively female approach to such sports as crew, basketball, and physical fitness.

The Maturing of a Collegiate Way of Life

6 As American higher education itself was largely nurtured in the Northeast, this region also led the way in developing intercollegiate sports. Heading into a new century, Yale dominated football and also came to be known as the "cradle of coaches" as it spread the Yale football gospel of strategy and sportsmanship across the nation. By 1910 Harvard obtained the national championship in football and asserted itself in numerous other sports. Harvard would also set the pace in terms of spectator facilities with the construction, in 1904, of Soldiers' Field—considered the finest, largest example of reinforced concrete architecture in the period. Whereas many presidents had resisted and resented the ascent of intercollegiate athletics, the University of Chicago's president, William Rainey Harper, saw the athletic contests as an opportunity to connect the campus to the greater community and thereby generate goodwill, revenue, and attention for his model institution. The creation of a large stadium combined with a mass marketing effort succeeded in generating popular appeal and large ticket sales.

7 At the turn of the century, many students and some alumni resented that the emerging organizational scheme tended to give inordinate and enduring support to a few selected spectator (and hence revenue-generating) sports—namely, football—with relatively few resources being dedicated to numerous other varsity[5] squads[6]. Additionally, the power and popularity of intercollegiate athletics led directly to conspicuous[7] abuse. A lack of regulation and fair play both on and off the field left college athletics indelibly marked by corruption and a reputation that has plagued "big-time" college sports to this day. More significantly, as the games "professionalized,"

[5]varsity /'vɑːsətɪ/ *n.* the main team that represents a university, college, or school in a sport

[6]squad /skwɒd/ *n.* a group of players from which a team will be chosen for a particular sports event

[7]conspicuous /kən'spɪkjuəs/*adj.* very easy to notice, especially because they are different from everything or everyone else around them

brutality often increased. The situation had deteriorated to the point that President Theodore Roosevelt summoned university presidents to the White House with an ultimatum[8] that they eliminate brutality from the playing field or risk federal intervention. The violence did decrease, but the problems were far from solved. No standards were set in areas such as eligibility[9] and scholarships, thereby blurring the line of definition for supposedly amateur contests between students. In an attempt to bring order to these increasingly popular competitions, the National Collegiate Athletic Association was formed in the early 1900s. However, the East Coast universities, which had the strongest athletic programs in the country, refused to cooperate and boycotted the organizational meeting with institutions from the Midwest and West.

Athletics Out West

8 Increasingly, college sports became a test of regional and/or ethnic esteem and assimilation. For example, the University of Notre Dame gained national visibility by becoming a rallying point[10] for American Catholic pride and affiliation with its victories over established East Coast football teams. African Americans used sports to break color barriers: the national basketball championship won by Texas Western in 1966 with an all-black starting five—over the University of Kentucky and its all-white squad—marked an important shift in recruitment and acceptance of black players.

9 Since 1926 the annual intersectional contests between Notre Dame and the University of Southern California regularly attracted crowds of over 100,000 and provided victorious regions the enjoyment of martial bragging rights without the sacrifice of actual military battle. Similarly, starting in 1946 the annual New Year's Day Rose Bowl Game matched the champion of the Midwest's Big Ten Conference against the championship team from the Pacific Coast Conference. As with anything that has mass appeal, politicians endeared themselves to the electorate[11] by associating with and supporting local schools.

---

[8]ultimatum /ˌʌltɪ'meɪtəm/ *n.* a threat saying that if someone does not do what you want by a particular time, you will do something to punish them

[9]eligible /'elɪdʒəbl/ *adj.* someone who is eligible for something is able or allowed to do it, for example because they are the right age ***eligibility*** /ˌelɪdʒə'bɪlɪtɪ / *n.*

[10]rallying point: an idea, event etc. that makes people come together to support something they believe in

[11]electorate /ɪ'lektərət/ *n.* all the people in a country who have the right to vote

From Chaos to Concern

10 Colleges and universities paid a price for the popularity of intercollegiate athletics as the activities associated with recruiting and compensating college student athletes were largely unregulated chaos. The unresolved excesses of intercollegiate athletics gained unprecedented publicity when returning World War II armed-service veterans swelled the ranks of varsity athletics squads. Many presidents and athletic directors placed no restrictions on the number of athletic scholarships allowed. Excesses were accompanied by illegalities. Exposés and successful prosecutions of student-athletes, coaches, and alumni boosters involved in point-shaving schemes and gambling cartels led to congressional hearings and a call for nationwide oversight[12] by academic leaders. When organizations led by college presidents failed to present a coherent plan, regulatory power was given to the National Collegiate Athletics Association. Meanwhile, presidents and faculty delegates attempted to introduce standards of student conduct and eligibility into policies and practices.

11 The economics of intercollegiate athletics was altered in the 1950s due to the appearance of two phenomena: (1) professional sports teams in football and basketball, and (2) the availability of radio and television for live broadcasts of sporting events. All college teams feared that the popularity of the National Football League and the National Basketball Association would cause declining attendance at college games. Small college squads faced a second threat: national and regional broadcasts of a few selected "big-time" college games prompted many long-time fans to stay at home rather than buy a stadium ticket. The result was a substantial number of institutions opted, or were financially forced, to drop football.

College Sports in the Age of Aquarius

12 In the late 1960s as other athletes demanded equality, granting athletic scholarships ceased to be confined to a handful of traditional revenue sports. By 1970 athletic grants-in-aid were increasingly prevalent for such sports as track, soccer, lacrosse, hockey, wrestling, baseball, and swimming. Expanding the excellence and the number of squads tended to swell athletic department operating expenses, but the small fan base of these sports failed to cover the increased costs. Consequently, institutes of higher learning faced growing philosophical and economic problems within their athletic programs. Females also sought equal treatment and indeed their actions led to

[12]oversight /'əʊvəsaɪt/ *n.* a mistake made because of a failure to notice something

a dramatic change in intercollegiate sports: the inclusion of women as bona fide[13] participants in varsity athletics. The Association for Intercollegiate Athletics for Women (AIAW) led the way in increasing financial support of female athletic programs and scholarships for women. This placed institutions and athletic departments in dire financial straits[14], for female sports did not generate enough fan interest to be self-supporting. This largely became a moot point[15] in 1972 due to the landmark Title IX legislation that prohibited discrimination by gender in provision of educational programs. Consequently, college athletics in many ways moved from the playing fields to the court rooms as individuals challenged institutional compliance with this federal mandate. Originally, a school could demonstrate compliance in athletics in one of four ways: have a proportional number of male and female participants; have a proportional relationship between female athletes and female students; demonstrate increasing opportunity for females to participate in athletics; or show that female participation in athletics matched their interest and ability to participate. However, most subsequent court rulings have demanded that the most stringent of the four tests be met, insisting that schools have a proportional number of participants in men's and women's athletics and thereby a proportional number of scholarships for each gender. This rigorous interpretation of directives for compliance with Title IX legislation has proven difficult for institutions due to the disparity of income that male and female sports generate. Consequently, athletic directors nationwide have eliminated many non-revenue male sports, with the claim that athletics programs can no longer afford to fund them. Failure to comply with Title IX directives can bring harsh and far-reaching repercussions[16]; therefore academic leaders and athletic directors continue to review their intercollegiate athletic enterprise to ensure that women are equally represented.

Competing in a Brave New Century of Sport

13 The absence of a government agency, combined with the limits of such voluntary associations as the National Collegiate Athletic Association to bring integrity to the governance of college sports, has prompted foundations to take the lead in promoting public discussion of the issues and problems. In 1991 the Knight Foundation panel, dominated by university presidents

[13]bona fide /ˌbəunə'faɪdɪ/ *adj.* real, true and not intended to deceive someone

[14]in dire straits: in a difficult situation, especially a financial one, that could have very bad or dangerous results

[15]a moot point: something that has not yet been decided, and about which people have different opinions

[16]repercussion /ˌri:pə'kʌʃən/ *n.* the effect that an action, event, or decision has on something, especially a bad effect

along with some executives and legislators, proposed that strong presidential involvement was the key to protecting the interests of student-athletes. A decade later, the emphasis was on cost containment as the essential ingredient in curbing the commercialism of intercollegiate sports. By the 1990s discussions about student-athletes had shifted from the question, "Are college athletics being paid?" to the proposition, "How much should college athletes be paid?" Such debates followed logically from research by economists who concluded that the National Collegiate Athletic Association had become a highly lucrative cartel, and that athletes participating in big-time programs were often being exploited by their institutions and associations as "unpaid professionals." Furthermore, coaches in high profile sports enhanced their stature as celebrities rather than as educators, complete with endorsements and special contracts to supplement their base salaries. To increase the seriousness of these concerns, athletic programs at all institutions faced a paradox of prosperity: despite unprecedented revenues, most teams and programs were not financially self-supporting. The conventional wisdom was that overemphasis on intercollegiate athletics was most prevalent in the relatively small number of big-time programs at large universities. Yet significant systematic research suggested otherwise. At relatively small-sized colleges and universities, the demands on student-athletes' time were substantial. Commitment to strong varsity sports programs tended to exert inordinate influence on such decisions as admissions and allocation of campus resources. Academic and public concern over the proper place of athletics in American colleges and universities remained problematic at most institutions at the start of the twenty-first century.

Total words: 2000

Total reading time: __________minutes________seconds

**The text is based on College Athletics—History of Athletics in U.S. Colleges and Universities*

Comprehension Check

1. According to the passage, how were sports first introduced in American colleges and universities?
2. What were some of the problems in collegiate sports in the early days?
3. How do you understand "plagued 'big-time' college sports" in the underlined sentence of paragraph 7?
4. What are the two things that altered the economics of college athletics in the 20th century?
5. What are the biggest problems with college sports in the U.S. today?
6. Why is Title IX important?

More to Know

Title IX *is a portion of the United States Education Amendments of 1972. It states (in part) that:*

No person in the United States shall, on the basis of sex, be excluded from participation in, be denied the benefits of, or be subjected to discrimination under any education program or activity receiving federal financial assistance.

Title IX applies to an entire school or institution if any part of that school receives federal funds; hence, athletic programs are subject to Title IX, even though there is very little direct federal funding of school sports.

With respect to athletic programs, the Department of Education evaluates the following factors in determining whether equal treatment exists:

1. Whether the selection of sports and levels of competition effectively accommodate the interests and abilities of members of both sexes;
2. The provision of equipment and supplies;
3. Scheduling of games and practice time;
4. Travel and per diem allowance;
5. Opportunity to receive coaching and academic tutoring on mathematics only;
6. Assignment and compensation of coaches and tutors;
7. Provision of locker rooms, practice and competitive facilities;
8. Provision of medical and training facilities and services;
9. Provision of housing and dining facilities and services;
10. Publicity.

Activity Time-Out

People hold different opinions on the compensation for college athletes. Basketball legend Kareem Abdul-Jabbar writes on the exploitation of college athletes. He said, "Despite the hours I put in every day, practicing, learning plays, and traveling around the country to play games, and despite the millions of dollars our team generated for UCLA—both in cash and in recruiting students to attend the university—I was always too broke to do much but study, practice, and play." However, U.S. President Barack Obama thinks that compensation for college athletes would "create a situation where there are bidding wars." How much does one athlete get paid as opposed to somebody else? Therefore, he says compensation for college athletes would "ruin the sense of college sports." What's your view on this? Make an investigation by reading relevant materials and write a short essay to state your findings. You might approach this issue from the angles of the individual athlete and the educational value of college/university.

Pop Culture

Schooled: The Price of College Sports (also styled as ***$chooled: The Price of College Sports***) is a 2013 documentary film. It is a comprehensive look at the business, history and culture of big-time college football and basketball in America. It presents a hard-hitting examination of the NCAA's treatment of its athletes and amateurism in collegiate athletics, weaving interviews, archival and verité footage to tell a story of how college sports became a billion dollar industry built on the backs of athletes who are deprived of numerous rights. Those interviewed for the 80-minute documentary include current and former college athletes, coaches, academic advisors, NCAA compliance officers, historians, sports journalists and university administrators.

Vocabulary Building

Look up the following words and expressions in reference books and on the Internet.

Words and Expressions	Meaning
university affiliated team	
tertiary education	
umbrella organization	
elite athlete	

3

UNIT

E-Sports

As gaming has become a daily part of more and more people's lives, the natural progression to competitive gaming and eventually e-sports is part of that lifestyle for a growing number of the gaming population. Recently we have seen a strong rise in viewership from gamers who don't actually compete, but who are rabid fans of those who do at the highest level. In essence, our community has similar characteristics to those of traditional sports leagues.

— Sundance DiGiovanni, co-founder of Major League Gaming

Pre-reading Thoughts

1. Do you play video or computer games? Have you ever competed with other players? If you have, what games do you usually play?

2. How popular do you think e-sports are today?

3. What is your opinion about "professional" e-sports players?

Text A

What are E-Sports?

1 Electronic sports (e-sports) are a new breed of competitive sports that started in the 90's with arcade games. This type of sport revolves around the same thing as the typical sport, which is individuals competing against each other. The main difference is the obvious fact that e-sports take place within a digital world where the sports are made out of different video games. The word e-sports does not depict a single type of sport but it is more of a title that covers a large sub-genre of sports. These sub-genres include basically every video game that has the ability to have competitive play.

2 Most game genres have received some type of competitive playing. 2D platformers had Donkey Kong, first-person shooters had Quake and Half-life (Counter-strike) and real-time strategy games had Starcraft. These games are all very different. Donkey Kong is a single player game where the means of measuring one's talent is the high score list. Quake is extremely fast paced where the players would either compete in a duel or team-death match which is a 4vs4 gameplay. Counter-strike is an extremely slow team-based game and it has been one of the most played games for the past 12 years. Last but

not least we have Starcraft, which is usually a slow playing strategy game that has some hand-eye coordination.

3 What this variance shows is that people are different. They are looking for new ways to compete in, and slowly but steadily, the community is defining the genre. Maybe one day a game will come along that will reach the perfect balance between player enjoyment, spectator friendliness, skill and fun so it can move on to become a worldwide sport, practiced and viewed regularly by people all over the world.

The History of E-Sports and Influential Factors

4 It would be the most appropriate to say that e-sports began in the year 1997 when Microsoft sponsored a Quake tournament called Red Annihilation. The first prize for this competition was a red Ferrari. The generous prize was a great ad stunt both for the game and for e-sports in general. After this event many entrepreneurs saw value in e-sports. The first and most notable company was the Cyberathlete Professional League or the CPL.

5 The CPL started out small. For the first three years it focused on competing in just one game, Quake, and as the success of these competitions grew, they started adding more games to the series. The first new game to be added after Quake was Counter-strike, in the year 2000. This game was immensely popular even before the CPL decided to add it to their schedule. The CPL and the number of people who followed it grew with each event. This led to the fact that they were able to gain more sponsors which meant they were able to add more games and increase the prize pool. In 2004 they had five games in their event, along with a total prize pool of $250,000.

6 But just before they reached their peak they made several crucial mistakes which led to the downfall of this promising company. Fortunately or unfortunately, other companies capitalized on their failure and around that time (2006) the so called golden era of e-sports started. After the CPL went down there were plenty of firms trying to take over as the leading event holder for e-sports. After Intel moved away from CPL they started sponsoring another series, the lucky recipients for this generous e-sports sponsor being the World Series of Video Games (WSVG). They mainly focused on the most popular games, the games that had had the most luck in the past, namely Quake and Counter-strike. This series took place all over the world and were extremely successful.

7 Even though the WSVG were successful they were still overwhelmed by another industry

entity, namely, Major League Gaming (MLG). MLG was, along with the CPL, one of the first companies to start off with the idea of professional video gaming but was always in the shadow of the CPL and did not really do anything worthy of mentioning until 2006 when they received a 10 million dollar investment and later that year a 25 million dollar investment. This meant an opportunity of a lifetime for the MLG. They started broadcasting their events on TV, but once they realized that the sponsors cared as much about having their advertisements shown through internet streaming as through TV, they changed completely to only showing their events through live streams over the Internet. As they would later find out this was a great move and they really helped e-sports get to where it is today.

Current State of E-Sports and Technology Related to This Field

8 Right now the e-sports business is booming with gaming series around the world getting record number of viewers and more professionals competing at every event. There are multiple reasons for this and we need to look at them from different angles.

9 The first and most notable reason is that the technology is finally ready for this sort of expansion. Bandwidth is cheap and fast, the tools that allow people to stream their games are free of charge, user friendly and gadgets/platforms that allow people to watch this are everywhere (e.g. tablets and smart phones). The second reason is that the games that are being played now are extremely spectator friendly. Now people at home with no technical background are able to watch live streams of tournaments without having played the game. There are now expert casters that describe what is happening as the games are being played, thus people have started to enjoy watching professional gamers play more than actually playing for themselves.

10 The third reason why e-sports are so popular now is that playing computer games has become a mainstream thing and more people than not do indeed play games, whether it is Facebook games like Farmville or more serious games like League of Legends. These are probably the top three reasons for the success of this sport but do not cover absolutely everything; there are many smaller reasons that have some factor in this but they would need further researching.

Riot Games, developer of MOBA League of Legends, has updated its player stats, revealing 67 million people around the world are playing every month. There are 27 million players logging in each day, and over 7.5 million concurrent players during each day's peak play time.

11 The ability to show people around the world live events with maximum convenience is something you really cannot put a price on. MLG (Major League Gaming) has hinted that it is looking at televising their future series and that they have been in talks with ESPN2 regarding this matter. But we must ask ourselves would this work on TV? The viewing format of the TV is quite outdated and HD connections are not available for everyone, but this is changing slowly. There are a lot of positive sides to the TV and a simple example would be the screen size. Maybe we could have live streams through internet connected televisions (Smart TVs).The technology is here, but the only real way to find out is to give it a shot.

Possible Future Development and Technology

12 What type of technology are we likely to see in the future when it comes to e-sports? If we look at what has happened in the last 10 years we can see that the technological parts that directly affect e-sports aren't that many. Things still need to be worked on quite a lot in order to enhance the experience, both for players and the spectators.

13 The first thing we might see more of is game developers designing their games from an audience's point of view, not just from the players' view. Many game studios might frown upon this because when developing an e-sport game that is more focused on the audience, a lot of the things that might be better for player immersion would be sacrificed.

14 The next technological thing developers might focus on is the Human Interface Devices (HIDs). The most efficient HID we have today when it comes to competitive gaming is the mouse

and keyboard combination. Maybe we could specialize the HIDs for each game genre? For example we could expand on the Igloo simulator room, which is a 360° gaming room which maximizes immersion and has players wielding a "real" gun walking around a dark room shooting at enemies. Inserting game features which are directly linked to different body parts such as a kick or punch would also be more fun for the player as he is using his entire body to participate in the game.

Prediction for the Next 10 Years

15 Since the amount of viewers has roughly doubled over the year 2011 with the MLG, it is probably a good guess to say that they will become the biggest entity in the world possibly within three to five years. They are already pulling in millions of unique viewers per event and they are well on their way to becoming the "NFL" or "Premier League" of e-sports since all the best players keep coming back to play for them and the viewers know where to find good content.

Total words: 1550
Total reading time: __________minutes_________seconds

* *The text is based on The Future of Electronic Sports by Georg Ólafsson*

Vocabulary and Expressions

arcade /ɑː'keɪd/ *n.* games played on machines by putting coins into them
stunt /stʌnt/ *n.* something that is done to attract people's attention, especially in advertising or politics
capitalize on: to get as much advantage out of a situation, event etc as you can
recipient /rɪ'sɪpɪənt/ *n.* someone who receives something
booming /'buːmɪŋ/ *adj.* if business, trade, or a particular area is booming, it is very successful
gadget /'gædʒɪt/ *n.* a small, useful, and cleverly-designed machine or tool
shot /ʃɒt/ *n.* an attempt to do something or achieve something
frown upon/on: to disapprove of something, especially someone's behaviour
interface /'ɪntəfeɪs/ *n.* a connection between two pieces of electronic equipment, or between a person and a computer
simulator /'sɪmjʊleɪtə/ *n.* a piece of equipment used for training people by letting them feel what real conditions are like, for example in an aircraft
wield /wiːld/ *vt.* to hold a weapon or tool that you are going to use

Comprehension Check

1. According to the passage, what is the definition of "e-sports"?
2. List the names of the most important e-sports companies and the games these companies focus on.
3. How did Microsoft help boost the popularity of e-sports?
4. How has new technology helped e-sports?
5. What current and possibly future HIDs are mentioned in the passage?
6. How do you understand "internet streaming" and "live streams" in the underlined sentence in paragraph 7?

Critical Thinking Starters

1. Labelling video games as "sports" is somewhat controversial. While some point to the growth in popularity of e-sports as justification for designating some games as sports, others contend that video games will never reach the status of "true sports". ESPN president John Skipper described e-sports as "not a sport — [they're] a competition." Do you agree that certain video and computer game competitions should be called "e-sports"? Why?
2. In Dota 2's tournament called "The International 2014" a total of around $6 million will be distributed among the teams with winner taking home half of it. And for a Quake tournament called Red Annihilation, its first prize was a red Ferrari. What is your opinion about making money or winning a car in e-sports? Do you think the winners really deserve it? Why?
3. People hold different opinions on the effects of video games. Some think that playing video games over an extensive period of time may cause social withdrawal outside of the gaming realm. And a lack of exercise is a great health risk to which video games often contribute. On a positive note, some think that playing video games online with gamers around the world will allow one to socialize and communicate with various cultures with ease. What's more, many video games focus on team-building exercises and efforts to complete or pass a level. One will learn to direct and to take orders and guidance from other teammates while advancing through various levels and realms with a new set of gamers each round. How do you view students playing video games? Will the advantages overweigh the disadvantages or vice versa?

More to Know

Major League Gaming (MLG), founded in 2002 by Sundance DiGiovanni and Mike Sepso, is a North American professional electronic sports organization, headquartered in New York City, New York. MLG has held official video game tournaments throughout the United States and Canada. Major League Gaming competitions have been broadcast on television, ESPN.com, and other broadband sites. The company has also been involved in television production, and game development. MLG's aim is to elevate computer and console game tournaments to viable competitive and spectator events.

The MLG Pro Circuit roster currently includes *Starcraft II* and *League of Legends* for the PC. *Starcraft II* is currently commentated by DJ Wheat, Day 9, Rob Simpson, Tasteless, Artosis, JP, dApollo, and TotalBiscuit, with other personalities coming on time to time. No *League of Legends* casters have been announced yet.

Expert's View

"After we looked into League of Legends, frankly I was shocked at the scale and the size, and how passionate the community is," Kurt Melcher, associate athletic director at RMU, told IGN. "We give scholarships for a variety of different interests, along with traditional sports like football, basketball, soccer. So we thought, 'Why wouldn't we give scholarships for this?'"

RMU will also be the first university to offer scholarships for recruits based on previous experience with League of Legends. Melcher said that students can receive up to 50 percent off tuition and room and board, which amounts to $19,000. The school is planning on recruiting three teams of nine players each, Melcher said, with a main starter team and two support squads.

Melcher said that he and the athletic director put a proposal together and brought the idea to the president of RMU Illinois, Michael P. Viollt.

"Most presidents would look at this and say, 'Are you crazy? Get out of here,'" Welcher said. "But to [Viollt's] credit he's forward-thinking and saw the potential in this. He thinks there is a differentiation of skill level, and that you can draw a lot of correlation with traditional sports. There's teamwork, there's strategy, [players] have to practice a lot."

Sports in Focus

Table tennis originated in England during the 19th century, where it was played among the upper-class as an after-dinner parlour game. It has been suggested that the game was first developed by British military officers in India or South Africa who brought it back with them. A row of books was stood up along the center of the table as a net（球网）; two more books served as rackets（球拍）and were used to continuously hit a golf-ball.

Competitive table tennis is popular in Asia and Europe and has been gaining attention in the United States. The most important international competitions are the World Table Tennis Championships, the Table Tennis World Cup, the Olympics and the ITTF Pro Tour（国际乒联职业巡回赛）. Chinese players have won the men's World Championships 60% of the time since 1959; in the women's competition, Chinese players have won all but three of the World Championships since 1971. Other strong teams come from East Asia and European countries. Founded in 1926, the International Table Tennis Federation (ITTF) is the worldwide governing body for table tennis. ITTF currently includes 220 member associations. Table tennis has been an Olympic sport since 1988.

Table tennis is a sport in which two or four players hit a lightweight ball back and forth using a table tennis bat（球拍）. Table tennis strokes（击球）generally break down into offensive and defensive categories. Offensive strokes mainly include loop（弧圈球）, flick（挑打）and smash（扣球）. Defensive strokes mainly include push（搓球）, chop（削球）and lob（放高球）. Adding spin onto the ball causes major changes in table tennis gameplay. The major types of spin are backspin（下旋）, topspin（上旋）, and sidespin（侧旋）. Spinning（旋转）the ball alters its trajectory（轨迹）and limits an opponent's options, giving the hitter a great advantage. When doing so the hitter has a good chance of scoring if the spin is successful.

Relevant words and Phrases

body hit	edge ball	penhold grip
shakehand grip	forehand	backhand

Text B

Can Video Games Be Sports?

With millions of fans and millions in prizes, are e-sports living up to their name?

1 The Olympic Games are as ancient a Greek tradition as the Athenian concept of democracy. So long as there's been human culture, sports have been an integral part of it. In their many forms and over their long history, sports have provided relief from the drudgery[1] of daily life and a less bloody way to resolve conflicts than all-out war.

2 A new kind of competition has sprung up in recent years, inciting passion and fervor as sports have for centuries. However these competitions take place not on a court or a field, but inside the world of video games. So-called e-sports are growing rapidly and powerfully: the current Dota 2 tournament offers a rich purse, a huge audience, and plenty of glory for the winners. And it's not the only one. E-sports have devoted fans and famous superstars, huge spectator numbers, and plenty of trash-talking.

3 Professional gaming is established and popular—but is it sports? Vlad Savov and Sam Byford debate the issue.

E-Sports Are Like Email: The Digital Equivalent of Something We' ve Been Doing for Centuries

by Vlad Savov

4 A crowd of thousands erupts in rapturous [2] cheer inside LA's Staples Center while millions more spectate from afar via web streams and TV broadcasts. Only it's not Kobe Bryant and the Lakers electrifying the fans, but the SK Telecom T1 team that's just won the League of Legends (LoL) Season 3 World Championship. In total, 32 million people tuned in to watch them defeat Royal Club in a grand five-on-five battle played out in a virtual[3] arena of mythical creatures and magical superpowers.

5 That LoL final lacked none of the appeal of the basketball games more commonly hosted at

[1]drudgery /'drʌdʒərɪ/ *n.* hard boring work
[2]rapturous /'ræptʃrəs/ *adj.* expressing great happiness or admiratio
[3]virtual /'vɜ:tjuəl/ *adj.* Something that is virtual can be done or seen using a computer and therefore without going anywhere or talking to anyone

the venue. It offered an exhibition of skill, spectacle, and direct confrontation. It's true that owning the competition in a video game is not as physically demanding as running a fast break, but athleticism is actually a secondary feature of sports. Their core appeal is conflict. If sports are a metaphor for war, then e-sports are an even more suitable medium given that most of them are literally about killing the enemy.

6 E-sports are simply games with a finely tuned competitive balance and a passionate group of players who over time have evolved from amateurs to professionals. The rigors of training and staying at the top of your game are identical, whether they be digital or physical.

7 Just like their traditional counterparts, e-sports have teams, star players, jersey[4] sponsorships, and millions of adoring followers producing volumes of fan art.

"E-Sports" Miss the Point of Sports

by Sam Byford

8 As a fan of both sports and video games, I love the concept of e-sports. I agree that athleticism shouldn't be a prerequisite to celebrating competition. I get the appeal of these games' complexity and tactics, but it's disappointing to me that so-called e-sports don't highlight a broader range of skills. The term feels like a desperate grasp for legitimacy[5] by associating with the diverse, inclusive world of traditional sports. Those most passionate about video games should be comfortable with the fact that they are games, not sports.

9 You call these competitions the "logical extreme of online multiplayer gaming." I agree—"e-sports" simply continue what's gone on for decades both online and off, while limiting the focus and potential audience. Meanwhile, no one has any problem talking about "a game of football." So what's in a name?

Instead of Fearing the New and the Unknown, We Should Embrace It

by Vlad Savov

10 The very legitimacy of gaming, the web, and everything you and I hold dear is at stake

[4]jersey /'dʒɜːzɪ/ *n.* a shirt made of soft material worn by players of sports such as football and rugby

[5]legitimacy /lə'dʒɪtɪməsɪ/ *n.* the quality of being legal or acceptable

here. Consider the pride most parents feel when they're able to tell their friends that their child has received an athletic scholarship to a reputable university. Well, you can now get a pro-gaming scholarship at Robert Morris University, but "my son is a gamer" is still something people confess with embarrassment rather than with the beaming joy of a gratified parent. The way we speak of things affects the way we think of them.

There are 35 students on the e-sports team at Robert Morris University in Aurora, the first school to categorize playing video games as a varsity sport, even offering scholarship funds for the "athletes." The team meets every weekday for practice between 4 and 9 p.m., with an hour break for dinner, and competitions are every Saturday, the school's associate athletic director Kurt Melcher told ABC News.

11 Professional gaming feels alien to many people because of the complexity of the games involved, but traditional sports aren't all that simple either. Consider that the most popular sport in the United States (American football) has a rulebook long and complicated enough that even its own referees are not familiar with its full extent.

12 The lack of history for e-sports that you bemoan[6] is the chief reason why they're not as widely accepted. Whereas soccer's offside[7] rule has been passed down through generations and internalized at an early age by most, the concepts and conditions for winning in video games all have to be learned anew. The question you have to ask yourself is, if you were confronted with basketball as a brand-new thing today, would you embrace it as a sport or freak out[8] about the odd scoring system and the arcanery[9] of backcourt passes and traveling violations?

13 To continue to treat e-sports as some obscure and valueless vocation is to continue to treat the web as a pale shadow of "real life." The fact is that every moment spent on the web is an inex-

[6]bemoan /bɪˈməʊn/ *vt.* to complain or say that you are disappointed about something

[7]offside /ˌɒfˈsaɪd/ *adj.* in a position where you are not allowed to play the ball in sports such as football

[8]freak out: to become very anxious, upset, or frightened, or make someone very anxious, upset or fightened

[9]arcane /ɑːˈkeɪn/ *adj.* mysterious and known only by a few people ***arcanery*** *n.*

tricable[10] part of real life. Video games are new and different, but not necessarily inferior to physical ones. All the hallmarks of mental alacrity[11] that grass-based sports exhibit are also present in e-sports. You play with an avatar, but the skill and the thrill of competition are still just as real.

Competitive Gaming Is Nothing New, and "E-Sports" Are Nothing More

by Sam Byford

14 Millions of people will watch Dota players compete for millions of dollars this week. But to apply a label like "e-sports" is optimistic at best and specious at worst. It implies that a substantial paradigm[12] shift has occurred, all the while ignoring the fact that serious gaming tournaments have been going on for decades—and often with games that have much more in common with actual sports than MOBAs. Let's call Dota tournaments what they are: very well-organized video game events. Yes, you can get a scholarship in League of Legends, if you're good enough, but you could have made a living playing Quake in 1996.

15 This weekend sees the Evo 2014 tournament take place in Las Vegas—the largest fighting-game event in the world. It's streamed online, with prize money and sponsorship and so on, and is now in its 18th year. But you won't find anyone calling it an "e-sports" tournament, because much of the fighting-game community recognizes the term for what it is—a pretentious and over-hyped buzzword that rings of insecurity. With its present, narrow remit[13], it does a disservice to the spirit of competitive video games. Why does Dota even need the cachet[14] of games played with balls on fields?

16 Dota and League of Legends are nothing more or less than video game phenomena, following on from others that have been and gone. And that's totally okay.

---

[10]inextricable /ˌɪnɪk'strɪkəbl/ *adj.* two or more things that are inextricable cannot be separated from each other

[11]alacrity /ə'lækrətɪ/ *n.* quickness and eagerness

[12]paradigm /'pærədaɪm/ *n.* a model of something, or a very clear and typical example of something

[13]remit /rɪ'mɪt/ *n.* the particular piece of work that someone has been officially asked to deal with

[14]cachet /'kæʃeɪ/ *n.* if something has cachet, people think it is especially good and desirable

E-Sports Are Too Influential to Be Treated Like A Hobby

by Vlad Savov

17 The people most deeply involved with those games are less concerned with how they're classified and more focused on either developing their skills or expanding the ecosystem to include more players and fans. But that's actually shirking[15] some very real responsibility that comes with the prestige of hosting tournaments that are as well-funded and -attended as the big sporting championships.

18 One of the unsavory[16] parallels that exist between classic sports and their digital brethren[17] is a strong undercurrent of segregation. Whereas athletic sports demand this through their emphasis on physical strength, e-sports can be contested between men and women on a perfectly even footing—in an arena of competitive thinking, the only body part that matters is the player's brain. Unfortunately, that opportunity to define an even more inclusive type of sport isn't being captured and e-sports remain stuck in the ways of the past.

19 A gaming tournament recently elicited a flurry[18] of disapproval for dividing its competitions along gender lines and the atmosphere at elite gaming events is famously unwelcoming to women. But that same tournament reversed its policy in response to the universal outcry and opened its doors to all comers. Taking competitive gaming seriously is the best way to encourage the people who do it to act with the ethics appropriate to a real cultural touchstone, rather than some niche pastime.

20 Ultimately, it doesn't matter whether we regard e-sports as such or not. That's what they are. Players wear jerseys with as many sponsor names as you'll see on a Formula 1 car. The US government is granting athletic visas to League of Legends players. Valve is handing out nearly $5 million to the best Dota 2 team. The most popular live-streaming broadcasts on the internet come from matches fought out in those two games, and their grand finals are being staged in NBA arenas and World Cup stadiums.

21 The competitive spirit is gradually expanding from the physical to the digital, and though resistance to this change may be natural, it will eventually be shown to have been futile.

[15]shirk /ʃɜːk/ *vt.* to deliberately avoid doing something you should do, because you are lazy

[16]unsavory /ʌn'seɪvərɪ/ *adj.* unpleasant or morally unacceptable

[17]brethren /'breðrən/ *n.* (used as a form of address to members of an organization or religious group) brothers

[18]flurry /'flʌrɪ/ *n.* an occasion when there is suddenly a lot of activity within a short period of time

Electronic Sports Will Be a Thing, But Not Today

by Sam Byford

22 What we know today as e-sports will only continue to expand along the present trajectory[19], at least as long as the games themselves remain popular. And that's another serious problem with calling something like Dota 2 a "sport"—how could anyone possibly predict its staying power? The game came out last year. Whether we consider it a sport in a 2014 vacuum or not is going to prove irrelevant.

23 Most modern sports were codified[20] in the 19th century, and much of the emotion we invest in watching them gets its power from that context. Brazil's World Cup humiliation at the hands of Germany is poignant because it could well signal the end of a soccer era. Each new athletic world record is a cumulative achievement that builds on the past efforts of humans who played by the same rules. Andy Murray's Wimbledon victory last year meant the world to the people of Britain because it ended a losing streak[21] that had persisted for close to a century. But it's hard to imagine many caring about Dota 2 a decade from now, never mind 10.

24 Again, though, I like the concept of e-sports and in no way mean to disparage[22] those who are making something out of it. And I do believe the worlds of video games, sports, and technology will someday converge to create truly new and mainstream competitive pastimes. I just think calling League of Legends an "e-sport" is beyond premature.

25 Look at where video games could be headed in the future. Motion control and virtual reality technology improve by leaps and bounds[23] every year. The social infrastructure for players to connect across continents is building up at no less rapid a pace. And the ability for indie[24] developers to publish wonderful titles like Sportsfriends—a collection of completely original games that are informed by the principles of sports—means that there's never been a better time for the next

[19]trajectory /trə'dʒektərɪ/ *n.* the curved path of an object that is fired or thrown through the air
[20]codify /'kəʊdɪfaɪ/ *vt.* to arrange laws, principles, facts etc in a system
[21]a losing streak: a period of time during which you continue to fail
[22]disparage /dɪ'spærɪdʒ/ *vt.* to criticize someone or something in a way that shows you do not think they are very good or important
[23]by leaps and bounds: If someone or something gets better by/in leaps and bounds, he, she, or it improves very quickly
[24]indie /'ɪndɪ/ *n.* a small independent company, especially one that produces records of popular music or television programmes

big thing in competitive gaming to emerge. Maybe we'll even call it a sport.

26 But my personal hope is that it has a lot more in common with real sports than the "e-sports" we know today. True e-sports should be designed as such, using the potential of technology to further the possibilities of competition rather than placing existing video game genres into a tournament context. Going back to the core principles of mainstream sporting competition—simplicity, immediacy, beauty—would be a good start.

Total words: 2060
Total reading time: __________minutes_________seconds

* *The text is based on Can Video Games be Sports? by Vlad Savov and Sam Byford*

Comprehension Check

1. According to the passage, what are the main arguments for calling on-line game competitions "e-sports"?
2. What are Sam Byford's main arguments for not calling on-line competitions "sports"?
3. What is the effect of sponsorship and prize money in on-line tournaments?
4. What does the passage say about the overall future of e-sports?
5. According to the writers, what role does history play in legitimizing a sport?
6. How do you understand "a fast break" in the underlined sentence in paragraph 5?
7. What does the author want to convey by the underlined sentence in paragraph 9?
8. What are the features of "niche pastime" in the underlined sentence in paragraph 19? Use examples to illustrate your point.

Activity Time-Out

Each student will download League of Legends or some other popular multi-player game and compete in the game after class. Then you can discuss together how it felt to play, compete and get fun and decide whether this is sport. You will later make presentations arguing your stance in class.

Pop Culture

Free to Play is a 2014 documentary film by American video game developer Valve Corporation. The film takes a critical look at the lives of Benedict "Hyhy" Lim, Danil "Dendi" Ishutin and Clinton "Fear" Loomis, three professional electronic sports players who participated in The International 2011, the most lucrative video game tournament to date at the time. The central focus of the film is how their commitment to *Defense of the Ancients (DotA)* had affected their lives and how this debut tournament for the sequel, *Dota 2,* would bring more meaning to their struggles. Jeremy Lin, professional basketball player for the Los Angeles Lakers of the NBA, is an avid player of *Dota 2* and makes a guest appearance in the film.

Vocabulary Building

Look up the following words and expressions in reference books and on the Internet.

Words and Expressions	Meaning
footage	
release	
modified	
ghosting	

4

UNIT

Sports and Race

Black or white, we all have football under our skin.

— Eusebio, the Portugese football legend

Pre-reading Thoughts

1. Have you ever wondered why athletes from certain races or ancestry and from different parts of the world seem to be better at one sport than another?

2. Which do you think is more important in athletic performance: genetics or training?

3. What role does an athlete's culture play in the kind of sports he or she may be good at?

Text A

Is Your Sporting Talent Predetermined by Your Ancestry?

1 Let's start with a few safe presumptions. All the sprinters in the men's 100-meter final at the Olympics can trace their ancestry to West Africa. Almost all of the world-class throwers are white, and mostly of Eurasian ancestry. And, Asians flourish in diving, some gymnastic events, judo and table tennis.

2 Over the past 40 years, as equality of opportunity has steadily increased in sports, spreading to vast sections of Asia and Africa, equality of results on the playing field has actually declined.

3 On the one hand, the social and economic barriers limiting participation in sports are crumbling; on the other, the winners in many events are increasingly limited to participants from specific regions of the world.

4 Why is it that every running record from the 100 meter dash to the marathon is held by an athlete of African ancestry? Is it racist to be curious about such phenomena?

Nature Versus Nurture

5 Absolutely not, say a growing chorus of geneticists, anthropologists, and physiologists. "Very many in sports physiology would like to believe that it is training, the environment, what you eat that play the most important roles in sports," states Bengt Saltin, director of the Copenhagen Muscle Research Center.

6 "But based on the data, it is 'in your genes' whether or not you are talented, or whether you will become talented. The extent of the environment can always be discussed but it's less than 20-25%."

7 Too many sociologists, however, even discuss that these trends trivialize the success of all athletes, but most pointedly blacks.

Cultural Factors

8 Do Cultural Factors Matter? Of course: there are no great international cricketers from Texas—black or white! Does that mean that nature—genetically influenced (though not determined) factors such as body size and physiology—are always trumped by nurture—hard work and opportunity?

9 To help answer this question, let's briefly examine the history of distance running. For decades, the "Flying Finns" were the world's best, their wins multiplying in tandem with their growing nationalist tradition of success.

10 By the last decade of the 20th century, the centre of gravity shifted dramatically and decisively toward North and East Africa.

11 According to some, that cycle of history itself suggests that no population has a lock on distance running success. Surely, they say, Kenyan dominance will eventually fade, much as it did for the Finns and Brits, and the trend will shift once again to another nation? Not so fast.

Every day at 9 a.m. sharp in Iten, Kenya, 200 or so runners—most of them unknowns hoping to become champions—train on the dirt roads surrounding the town.

Rethinking Race, Science and Sports

12 Why does the claim that sports success depends in part on genetics get some people so nervous? After all, it's conventional science that different body types have evolved in response to differing environmental conditions in different regions of the world. Fascination about black physicality and black anger about being caricatured as lesser human beings have been part of the unspoken side of the dialogue on race for hundreds of years. The fear is that some might conclude that if blacks are faster on average, they must be weaker mentally. But that's a conclusion not supported by science.

13 What have scientists documented? "Evolution has shaped body types and in part athletic possibilities".

14 The fact that significant differences exist between populations would seem to conflict with a spate of declarations proclaiming that "humans are 99.9 % the same" and "race is biologically meaningless".

15 The paradox revolves around a common misunderstanding about the notion of "race"—in particular, the popular notion that races are discrete groups, each with distinct genetic profiles.

16 Despite its notorious history, racial terminology can be helpful, such as when used in medicine. Many traits are correlated, such as dark skin colour and the presence of the sickle cell gene. But such links are not absolute. Blacks who have evolved in cooler climates are no more likely to contract sickle cell than are non-blacks. Genetic factors help explain the prevalence of any number

of population-specific diseases and physiological responses to drugs. Tay-Sachs is a neurological disease more common among European Jews and their descendants. Northern Europeans are more susceptible to cystic fibrosis. Blacks are genetically more susceptible to sickle cell and heart disease. These are all "racial" differences of a kind, although the interaction of genetic and environmental factors is extremely complex.

17 Today, no credible scientist disputes that evolution, along with local social conditions, has helped shape Kenyan distance runners, white power lifters, with their enormous upper-body strength, and athletes of West African ancestry who are explosive runners and jumpers. In discussing basketball, for instance, the disproportionate representation of African Americans is not because of a lack of socio-economic opportunities, but on account of "the prevalent body shapes of some black African groups".

18 Most scientists are quick to point out that this is not a "black and white" issue, but the consequence of thousands of years of evolution in varying terrains. Although humans share most of their estimated 40,000 genes, there are as many as 500,000 gene components, many of which are more common among people from one geographical region than from another.

19 Each sport demands a slightly different mix of biomechanical, anaerobic, and aerobic abilities. As a result of evolutionary adaptations to extremely different environments that became encoded in the genes, athletes from different insular populations tend to have rather distinct physical and physiological characteristics. As a result, they frequently excel in specific events.

20 Whites of Eurasian ancestry, who have, on average, more natural upper-body strength, predictably dominate weightlifting, wrestling and field events, such as the hammer (whites hold 46 of the top 50 performances). Evolutionary forces in this northern clime have shaped a population with a predilection toward a mesomorphic body type—large and muscular, particularly in the upper body, with relatively short arms and legs and thick torsos. These proportions tend to be an advantage in sports in which strength rather than speed is at a premium.

21 Certain East Asian populations tend to be small with relatively short extremities, long torsos, and a thicker layer of fat. As a result, athletes from this region are somewhat slower and less strong than whites or blacks, but are, on average, more flexible. These characteristics are key poten-

tial advantages in diving, gymnastics, and figure skating. They also have very quick reaction times, which undoubtedly contribute to their success in racket sports. East Asians are very competitive at long distance races, including the marathon, in part because of higher levels of body fat. It should come as no surprise that the world's most remarkable ultra-endurance runners have East Asian ancestry.

22 Genetically linked, highly heritable characteristics such as skeletal structure, the distribution of muscle fibre types, reflex capabilities, metabolic efficiency, lung capacity, and the ability to use energy more efficiently are not evenly distributed among populations and cannot be explained by known environmental factors.

23 "Differences among athletes of elite calibre are so small," "that physique or the ability to fire muscle fibres more efficiently that might be genetically based... it might be very, very significant. The fraction of a second is the difference between the gold medal and fourth place."

24 Although scientists are just beginning to isolate the genetic links to biologically-based differences, it is indisputable that they exist. Such characteristics are not distributed equally among populations. The genetics revolution has decisively overturned the belief that all humans are created with equal potential. Some functional characteristics do differentiate population clusters—most clearly in the proclivity to certain diseases and in body types.

25 In light of recent advances in genetics and the science of human performance, extremists claim that we should not discuss these "racial" or patterned biological differences. Limiting the pejorative use of that problematic concept of race—an admirable goal—is not going to make the patterned biological variation on which it is based disappear. Although people share a common humanity, we are different in critical ways.

26 Athletic competition, which offers a definitiveness that eludes most other aspects of life, is a perfect laboratory for a serious exploration of the complex relationship of genes and culture.

27 "I believe that we need to look at the causes of differences in performance between races in sports as legitimately as we do when we study differences in diseases," says Canadian Claude Bouchard, sports physiologist and geneticist, "I have always worked with the hypothesis that ignorance fosters prejudice. (Critical inquiry) is the greatest safeguard against prejudice."

28 Indeed, if we do not welcome the impending genetic revolution with open minds, if we are scared to ask and to answer difficult questions, if we lose faith in science, then there is no winner; we all lose. The challenge is in whether we can conduct the debate so that human diversity might be cause for celebration of our individuality rather than a source of distrust.

29 Finally, it should never be forgotten that genes are not the ultimate factors in elite performance. While genetics will determine if you have a chance to be an elite athlete, intelligence, dedication, and serendipity are the final arbiters of who wins and loses.

Total words: 1500
Total reading time: __________minutes_________seconds

**The text is based on The Race to Swift: Do You Have the Right Ancestry by Jon Entines*

Vocabulary and Expressions

Eurasian /jʊə'reɪʒən/ *adj.* describes a person with one European parent and one Asian parent

pointedly /'pɔɪntɪdlɪ/ *adv.* in a very obvious way, usually to express criticism or disapproval

trump /trʌmp/ *vt.* to beat someone or something by doing or producing something better

in tandem with: happening at the same time

caricature /'kærɪkətʃʊə/ *vt.* to draw or describe someone in a way that makes them seem silly or stupid

a spate of: a large number of similar unpleasant things that happen in a short period of time

sickle cell: an abnormal red blood cell that has a crescent shape and an abnormal form of hemoglobin

cystic fibrosis /ˌsɪstɪk faɪ'brəʊsɪs/ *n.* a serious disease that causes glands in the lungs and other organs, such as the liver and the pancreas, not to work correctly

anaerobic /ˌænə'rəʊbɪk/ *adj.* not needing or without oxygen

insular /'ɪnsjʊlə/ *adj. Anatomy* of or relating to isolated tissue or an island of tissue

mesomorphic /ˌmesəʊ'mɔ:fɪk/ *adj.* having a robust muscular body-build

reflex /'ri:fleks/ *n.* the ability to react quickly

proclivity /prə'klɪvɪtɪ/ *n.* a tendency to do or like something, especially something bad

pejorative /pɪ'dʒɒrətɪv/ *adj.* disapproving or suggesting that something is not good or is of no importance

serendipity /ˌserənˈdɪpɪtɪ/ *n.* the natural ability to make interesting or valuable discoveries by accident

Comprehension Check

1. According to the passage, what sports do East Asian athletes regularly excel at?
2. How has evolution helped athletes from northern Europe?
3. Why does one population dominate a sport for a period of time and then is replaced by a different population?
4. Why are some people nervous about talking about race in athletics?
5. What is the author's attitude toward further research in the relationship between race and sports?
6. How do you understand "short extremities" in the underlined sentence in paragraph 21?

Critical Thinking Starters

1. Muhammad Ali is a former world heavyweight champion, the fighter of the century and the man they call "The Greatest." Laila, 26, the youngest of Muhammad Ali's seven children, follows in the footsteps of her father. She has been boxing professionally since October 1999 when she defeated April Fowler in 31 seconds. Since then she's won nine more fights convincingly, making her dad, who retired from boxing in 1981, quite proud. "The Intimidator," Ralph Dale was a second-generation racer whose father, Ralph Lee, is a Hall of Famer in his own right. Do you think these instances are coincidences or a person's family history has some effect on his or her athletic ability?
2. There was some controversy to the genetic research on race and sport performance. Some people find it racist to discuss the "racial" or patterned biological differences, while others think athletic competition is a perfect laboratory for a serious exploration of the relationship of genes and culture. Do you think that the relationship of genes and sport performance is a legitimate area of scientific research? Why?

Sports in Focus

跳水 Diving

The history of **diving** is simply from people jumping off things into the water. The earliest forms of diving took the form of people jumping off cliffs, hills or trees. The earliest of competitions in diving history was in the late 1800's. Diving was first introduced into the Olympics at the 1904 event. It wasn't until 1908 that springboard diving（跳板跳水）was invented. Diving is one of the most popular Olympic sports with spectators. Competitors possess many of the same characteristics as gymnasts and dancers, including strength, flexibility, and kinaesthetic（动觉的）judgment. Some professional divers were originally gymnasts or dancers as both the sports have similar characteristics to diving. The global governing body of diving is FINA（国际泳联）, which also governs swimming, synchronized swimming（花样游泳）, water polo（水球）and open water swimming.

Most diving competitions consist of three disciplines: 1 m and 3 m springboards, and the platform（跳台跳水）. Competitive athletes are divided by gender, and often by age group. In platform events, competitors are allowed to perform their dives on either the five, seven and a half (generally just called seven), nine, or ten meter towers. In major diving meets, including the Olympic Games and the World Championships, platform diving is from the 10 meter height.

Divers have to perform a set number of dives according to established requirements, including somersaults（空翻）and twists（转体）. Divers are judged on whether and how well they completed all aspects of the dive, the conformance of their body to the requirements of the dive, and the amount of splash created by their entry to the water. A possible score out of ten is broken down into three points for the takeoff (meaning the hurdle), three for the flight (the actual dive), and three for the entry (how the diver hits the water), with one more available to give the judges flexibility.

The raw score is multiplied by a difficulty factor, derived from the number and combination of movements attempted. The diver with the highest total score after a sequence of dives is declared the winner.

Relevant words and Phrases

diving pool	starting block	balk
clean entry	poise	open tuck

Text B

Racism in Football

Current Situation

1 UK football has moved on a long way from the racist arena it provided in the 1970s and 1980s. When England players received racist abuse in Spain in 2004 it rightly caused outrage across the country and the experiences of footballers from black, Asian and other minority ethnic backgrounds and groups playing at the top level are far removed from the experiences that black footballers such as Luther Blissett, Gary Bennett and Leroy Rosenior, who now work with Show Racism the Red Card, went through during this period. Several factors have influenced this: the increase in number of footballers from black, Asian and other minority backgrounds, the advent of all-seater stadiums, which changed the atmosphere at games and meant that perpetrators[1] were easier to identify, but also the conscious effort that has been made by the FA (Football Association), PFA (Professional Footballers' Association), football clubs and anti-racism campaigns to demonstrate that racism is unacceptable within football stadia; with bans and prosecutions implemented for fans and players engaging in this behavior.

2 However, whilst there has been a change in behavior at football matches, racist attitudes are still widely prevalent because racism remains a widespread problem in society. Show Racism the Red Card delivers programs of anti-racism education to over 50,000 people every year and from our experience we know that many people have not had the opportunity to discuss issues of racism and many are confused and carry misinformation and prejudice. Many football clubs have done great work over the years both independently and with organizations such as Kick it Out and Show Racism the Red Card to help educate against racism and send out messages that the club supports anti-racism initiatives. However, this work is quickly undermined by a lack of action or dismissive words when an incident occurs.

3 There also remain wider issues of racism within football. For example, managers and board members from black and other minority ethnic backgrounds and groups are vastly under-represent-

[1]perpetrator / 'pɜːpətreɪtə / *n.* a person who commits an illegal, criminal, or evil act

ed. There are currently only two black managers across all 92 football clubs, despite the fact that around 25% of professional footballers in the UK are black. There is a perception amongst many that the under-representation of black managers is largely due to racism. Historically, theories were perpetuated that black people were naturally strong and athletic, whilst white people were naturally better thinkers and strategists. Through genetics, it is now clear that these theories are baseless. Humans cannot be divided into discreet categories and a person's skin color tells us nothing about their other abilities. However, many in society still believe this to be the case. Ex-professional Paul Mortimer who now works with the Show Racism the Red Card campaign speaks of managers who wouldn't play him when it was cold as, despite him being born and brought up in South London, they felt that he could only play with the sun on his back. In 1991 Crystal Palace chair Ron Noades stated:

4 "The black players at this club lend the side a lot of skill and flair[2], but you also need white players in there to balance things up and give the team some brains and some common sense."

5 The majority of board members of football clubs are white men and the recruitment processes are not transparent, with new managers sometimes being appointed within days of a previous manager's departure. There may be a conscious or unconscious decision to appoint someone similar to themselves, and similar to coaches who have already achieved success, with well qualified black people being overlooked. Even when black people do secure jobs as managers, they may face racism and a lack of faith in their abilities. For example, when Gary Bennett became manager at Darlington FC he found that he was refused entry to the boardroom[3] as the person on the door would not believe that he was the manager of the club. Once sacked from a position a black manager is less likely to be given another chance somewhere else.

6 Recent statements by several high profile figures have highlighted that there is a lack of awareness and understanding about issues of racism amongst many working in football. For example, the definition of a racist incident as set out by the Stephen Lawrence Inquiry is "*any incident that is perceived to be racist by the victim or any other person*". The purpose of the definition is to remove the onus[4] on the person in charge at the scene determining whether an incident is racist; to include unwitting and unintentional racism, which still has a damaging effect on the target and

[2]flair /fleə/ *n.* a natural ability to do something very well
[3]boardroom /'bɔːdrʊm/ *n.* a room where the directors of a company have meetings
[4]onus /'əʊnəs/ *n.* **the onus** the responsibility for something

to include apparently victimless racism such as racist graffiti[5]. However, many of those working in and around football have immediately dismissed accusations of racism prior to an investigation, issuing defences such as "*I know him and he's not racist*" showing a lack of understanding that it is the action that is racist not the individual, "*What happens on the pitch*[6] *stays on the pitch*". No it doesn't. Football is the most popular sport in the world and is watched by millions of people. Footballers do not have carte-blanche[7] to abuse each other in whatever ways they see fit. Many young people are forced out of grass-roots football because of racist abuse and if we allow people to use racist language on the pitch then there is nothing to stop it from spilling over into other aspects of their lives, affecting their opinions and interactions with others. Another defense is that "*The comment is not that bad and does no harm*". The result is not that simple. Using someone's skin color or ethnicity as an insult has a deeper effect. It implies that it is negative to be of that background and attacks something which is intrinsic to that person. It is an attack not just on the individual, but on other members of their family, community or group. When high-profile people act in this way it gives license for others to copy-cat and creates a society where that behavior is deemed acceptable. If we don't challenge racist language and insults, we are paving the way for some people to go on to commit more serious incidents of hate-crime. People who commit acts of hate crime believe that they are acting on behalf of and with the support of their community; it is up to all of us to demonstrate that this behaviour is unacceptable and not supported. Other defense might be that "*He meant nothing by it. It was just said in the heat of the moment*". We have all had times where we are under pressure or angry and say things that we regret, but that doesn't make them excusable. Even if someone did not deliberately intend to cause harm, this doesn't affect the outcome.

7 The FA's thorough investigation and subsequent decision to impose an 8 game ban and £40,000 fine on Luis Suarez for racially abusing Patrice Evra demonstrates that the issue has been taken seriously by the authorities. However, Liverpool football club's response, with the players wearing T-shirts in support of Suarez and manager Kenny Dalglish visibly backing the player saying he should not have been banned, was regrettable and has had an impact on fans' reactions, with an increase in racist incidents inside the ground and Patrice Evra and other black commentators such as Stan Collymore being racially abused through other forums, such as Twitter.

---

[5]graffiti /grə'fi:tɪ/ *n.* rude, humorous, or political writing and pictures on the walls of bulidings, trains etc.
[6]pitch /pɪtʃ/ *n.* a specially marked out area of ground on which a sport is played
[7]carte-blanche /ˌkɑ:t'blɑ:nʃ/ *n.* complete freedom to do something

Luis Suarez was banned for eight matches for racially abusing Patrice Evra.

8 Since its inception the EDL has sought to organize around football and use football as a vehicle to spread racist and Islamophobic ideology. The EDL seeks to gain credibility by linking the movement with football clubs; using official football club crests[8] without permission in their literature. By utilizing football in this way the EDL is attempting to bring credibility and high profile backing to a dangerous and overtly racist campaign. Show Racism the Red Card has countered the use of club crests throughout this period by working closely with the clubs to ensure that a clear statement is issued to disassociate the club from the EDL and to make clear that the Club does not endorse racism in any way. Upon learning of the unofficial use of the club crest, Swansea City issued the following statement:

9 *"Swansea City abhors racism in any shape or form and would like to make it quite clear that the football club does not support or affiliate itself to this organization, its campaign or any other group of this nature. Permission to use the club crest has certainly not been granted. The club has worked extremely hard over recent years to eradicate any form of racism from within its footballing family—and we will continue to do so."*

10 If organizations such as this are allowed to use football as a base to recruit and assemble, it will create a threatening and racist atmosphere within and around these clubs.

Recommendations for Action

11 Race-equality audits[9] of the policies and practices should be within sporting structures, with action plans developed to overcome areas of imbalance and inequality. There needs to be a

[8]crest /krest/ *n.* a special picture used as a sign of a family, town, school etc.
[9]audit /'ɔ:dɪt/ *n.* a methodical examination or review of a condition or situation

change in the culture of football clubs to ensure that the issue of institutional racism is explored with policies put in place to counter tackle racism and promote equality. It is impossible to develop a strategy to eradicate racism and promote equality within any institution unless there is an understanding of where the inequalities lie and methods to measure improvement once the strategy has been adopted. Therefore all football clubs need to conduct an audit which includes ethnic monitoring of staff and customers across all levels and equality impact assessments on their policies and procedures, both formal and informal. Once this has been conducted action plans can be developed to put processes in place to overcome issues of inequality. The NFL in America adopted the Rooney Rule in 2003. This requires clubs to interview at least one candidate from a black or other minority ethnic background or group for head coaching or other senior management posts. Since the rule's adoption, the league has gone from having two black head coaches to eight and from one black general manager to five. Show Racism the Red Card is in favour of adopting a similar rule in the UK to begin to open doors to black and other minority ethnic managers, which may previously have been denied.

12 Training for all employees from members of the board to players should be implemented, to enable them to be in a position to better tackle racism and promote equality. Educational programs need to be expanded to ensure that everyone working within football: from the chairman, to the manager, to the stewards, receives high-quality and ongoing training which will enable them to:

— Understand the realities of racism and why racist behavior is damaging.

— Learn how to respond effectively to racist incidents.

— Have any myths that they hold about "race" and racism exposed.

— Learn about the correct terminology to use when discussing issues of "race" and racism.

— Learn how to create an inclusive and equitable environment for co-workers, employees and supporters.

13 *Clear, consistent, transparent procedures for dealing with players and fans who commit racially motivated offences.* The footballing authorities need to clearly lay out their procedures for dealing with racism from players and fans. Any punishment needs to be accompanied by education, to ensure that the perpetrator fully understands the impact of their actions and why they were wrong. Punishment without education can just further breed resentment and will not deal with an individual's prejudice and misinformation.

14 *Clear, unambiguous messages from sporting clubs as to the expected behaviour of employees and spectators.* Football clubs need to continue to engage with campaigns such as Show Racism the Red Card and send out consistent messages through messages in the program, actions on the field, to organizing antiracism educational events in order to reach out to fans with the anti-racism message.

15 *Clear, unambiguous messages from government about the importance of promoting race-equality and tackling racism.* Outside of sport, the government needs to ensure that it adopts policy which is underpinned[10] by social justice and does not allow negative false media discourse to dominate public and media debate.

16 *Sporting clubs must clearly show that they reject the ideologies of far-right[11] street movements, such as the EDL which try to use sport as a vehicle around which to organize and recruit.* Clubs must issue statements whenever local far-right groups try to appropriate the club's logo or supporter base in order to recruit and to condemn action which occurs within the vicinity of the ground as well as inside it.

17 *Wider programs of anti-racism education in society, to address underlying prejudice rather than just preventing the expression of this prejudice within the sporting arena.* It is vital that programmes are in place to educate people against racism, counter acquired misinformation and empower people with knowledge and skills to address stereotyping, fear and prejudice picked up from the media, peers, family and friends. It will be impossible to truly rid football of racism, unless the wider societal issues are addressed.

Total words: 2170
Total reading time: __________minutes_________seconds

* *The text is based on Racism in Football*

[10]underpin /ˌʌndəˈpɪn/ *vt.* to give strength or support to an idea, belief etc.
[11]far-right: refers to political groups whose opinions are very extreme

Comprehension Check

1. According to the passage, is racism a major problem in UK football? Give an example to support your view.
2. What did Ron Noades want to express by saying the words in paragraph 4?
3. Should spectators be punished for racist remarks or actions? Why?
4. What advice does the author give for eliminating racism in football?
5. Why does the author refer to the NFL Rooney Rule?
6. Please explain the underlined sentence in paragraph 16.

More to Know

Stephen Lawrence was a Black British man who was murdered in a racially motivated attack while waiting for a bus on the evening of 22 April 1993. The case became a cause célèbre and one of the highest profile racial killings in UK history; its fallout included profound cultural changes to attitudes on racism and the police, and to the law and police practice, before two of the perpetrators were convicted almost 20 years later in 2012.

The case has gone through a range of investigations and trials. The inquiry occurring in July 1997 was conducted by Sir William Macpherson and officially titled "The Inquiry into the Matters Arising from the Death of Stephen Lawrence". Its report, produced in February 1999, estimated that it had taken "more than 100,000 pages of reports, statements, and other written or printed documents" and concluded that the original Metropolitan Police Service investigation had been incompetent and that officers had committed fundamental errors, including: failing to give first aid when they reached the scene; failing to follow obvious leads during their investigation; and failing to arrest suspects.

The report also found that the Metropolitan Police was institutionally racist. A total of 70 recommendations for reform were made. These proposals included abolishing the double jeopardy rule and criminalizing racist statements made in private. Macpherson also called for reform in the British Civil Service, local governments, the National Health Service, schools, and the judicial system, to address issues of institutional racism.

Activity Time-Out

The difficult issues of race and prejudice still linger in international sports. Some athletes face hostility both on and off the field. It's not about their performance—but rather the color of their skin. Read some relevant books and search the Internet to investigate some of the instances of racism in sport and share your findings in class.

Pop Culture

The Unlevel Playing Field is an extraordinarily rich collection of primary sources that charts the significant, intertwining histories of African Americans and sport. This collection contains more than one hundred documents on both pioneering and modern-day athletes, ranging chronologically from a challenge issued by prizefighter Tom Molineaux in the "London Times" in 1810 to contributions from commentators like Frederick Douglass, W. E. B. Du Bois, James Baldwin, and Eldridge Cleaver, as well as contemporary observers such as Nikki Giovanni, Henry Louis Gates Jr., and bell hooks. Introductions and headnotes by David K. Wiggins and Patrick B. Miller place each document in context, shaping a compelling narrative.

Vocabulary Building

Look up the following words and expressions in reference books and on the Internet.

Words and Expressions	Meaning
overrepresentation	
disparity	
segregation	
stereotype	

5
UNIT

Special Populations in Sports

It [Paralympics] has made people realize that athletes are athletes and people are people. It doesn't matter if you're Usain Bolt or in a wheelchair, we're all people. And everyone just wants to talk about the sport now, so that's good.

—Charles Walker, the Paralympic sitting volleyballer of Great Britain

Pre-reading Thoughts

1. Have you ever seen a disabled athlete or an athletic competition for the disabled? What was your reaction?
2. Do you think there is some prejudice in society against people with physical or mental disabilities? If prejudice actually exists, how is it revealed?
3. Do you think sports can benefit people with disabilities? State your reasons.

Text A

Using Sport to Foster the Inclusion and Well-being of Persons with Disabilities

"No country can afford to turn its back on 10% of its population."

—ILO/UNESCO/UNICEF/WHO proclamation, December 3, 1997

1 Disability is any physical or mental condition that limits a person's movements, senses or activities. The term disability is conventionally used to refer to attributes that are severe enough to interfere with, or prevent, normal day-to-day activities. According to the UN Convention on the Rights of Persons with Disabilities, "persons with disabilities include those who have long-term physical, mental, intellectual or sensory impairments which, in interaction with various barriers, may hinder their full and effective participation in society on an equal basis with others." Disabilities can be permanent, temporary, or episodic. They can affect people from birth, or be acquired later in life through injury or illness.

2 Despite great variations in wealth and quality of life across countries, persons with disabilities tend to experience greater social, political, and economic exclusion than persons without disabilities worldwide.

3 In many countries, beliefs and attitudes have evolved to recognize the importance of fully including persons with disabilities. These changing attitudes are largely the result of the leadership of persons with disabilities and their families. As a result, legislation has been enacted to ensure equal rights and efforts are underway to enhance accessibility and inclusiveness in the workplace and community life.

4 The universal popularity of sport, its physical, social and economic development benefits, and its proven success as an education and social mobilization platform, make it an ideal tool for reducing the stigma associated with disability. These characteristics also make sport an ideal tool for fostering the socialization, independence, empowerment and full inclusion of persons with disabilities. In this sense, sport is not a luxury. It is a necessary and complementary approach that can expand the impact of traditional methods of stimulating individual and community development and empowerment.

Using Sport to Educate Stigma

5 In some places, persons with disabilities have succeeded in being seen for their abilities, rather than their disabilities. Elsewhere, people suffer from social stigma associated with their disability. Stigma consists of unfounded stereotypes, inaccurate assumptions, negative perceptions and prejudice. In many communities, stigma is deeply rooted. Many of the discriminatory practices and policies that are barriers to persons with disabilities arise from stigma. Stigma is what causes some children to refuse to play with children with disabilities, teachers to avoid asking what a student with a disability can do, and employers refusing to hire a person with a disability because they believe they are inferior to persons without disabilities.

6 The consequences of stigma can be severe and even fatal. In some cultures merely having a family member with a disability makes it difficult for a woman without a disability in the same family to marry. Mothers may be blamed when a child with a disability is born and then abandoned by their husbands. Often unable to work full-time and care for their child(ren), they may be denied

help by their families because of their child's disability. Parents, driven by shame or fear for their child's safety, may confine a child with a disability in the home. In some cultures, the stigma associated with disability is so severe that it results in infanticide. Because persons with disabilities are sometimes less valued than those without disabilities, they may also be excluded from essential health care. This situation is particularly acute in communities without services and supports for persons with disabilities and their families, such as informal settlements and slums.

7 The more that disability issues are addressed in mainstream society, the more persons with disabilities will be accepted. Sport can help combat stigma because it places persons with disabilities in a position where their skills are highlighted. The focus is not on their disability but their ability to score a goal or make the game-winning assist. This point is underscored by the Office of the High Commissioner for Human Rights:

"For the community, participation by persons with disabilities in sport provides a means of deconstructing disabling images that portray persons with disabilities as passive, inactive and lacking capacities to participate in the wider life of the community. In breaking down stereotypes of disabilities, participation in sport helps build more inclusive communities and therefore greater social cooperation and cohesion."

8 Media coverage of sport events involving persons with disabilities can play a major role in creating more positive and accurate perceptions. For example, the growing profile of the Paralympics has significantly contributed to increasing recognition of persons with disabilities. Over 300 million people watched television coverage of the 2000 Sydney Paralympic Games. This single event significantly increased awareness of the capabilities of persons with disabilities.

9 Using sport, persons with disabilities can work to remove the stigma confronting them in their own communities. In rural Bangladesh, where international NGO Handicap International runs the Sport for Children and Youth with Disabilities Project, staff report a significant change in villagers' attitudes toward persons with disabilities after observing them playing sports alongside their peers.

10 Another example, perhaps one of the best known, is that of Ghanaian Emmanuel Yeboah. Yeboah, who has no lower-right leg, was abandoned by a father ashamed of having a child with a disability. In response to the stigma and negative attitudes he encountered throughout his life, Yeboah decided to cycle across Ghana to draw attention to persons with disabilities and to compel

the national government to address disability issues. Along the way, Yeboah stopped in villages to speak with people about what it means to live with a disability. Eventually, his fight for the rights of persons with disabilities drew international attention, including that of fellow Ghanaian Kofi Annan, then Secretary-General of the United Nations, who became a strong supporter of the cause. Ghana's King Osagyefuo also took interest, inviting the cyclist to meet with him, making Emmanuel Yeboah the first person with a disability in Ghana to receive a royal audience.

11 Stigma is not only an external barrier, preventing persons with disabilities from accessing social, economic and political rights, but it is often an internal barrier, causing persons with disabilities to question their own worth in society. For example, most landmine victims participating in the Cambodian Volleyball League (Disabled) report that they contemplated suicide when they first lost a limb. Based on their own previous notions of persons with disabilities, they had no hope. Through involvement in sports, however, these volleyball players saw that they were capable of far more than they had imagined. Their own views on the limitations arising from their disability were fundamentally changed, giving them a more optimistic outlook and restoring their belief in their future.

12 Stigma presents particular challenges for women with disabilities. Women with disabilities often experience double discrimination—on the basis of their gender and their disability. Studies show that 93% of women with disabilities do not participate in sport or physical exercise and women make up only one-third of athletes with disabilities in international competitions. Many countries still refuse to enter women in these competitions. Access to education and community services, including rehabilitative services, is often affected by gender. This is especially true in countries where it is believed that a woman's primary role lies in the home. As a result of this additional exclusion, women with disabilities have even higher illiteracy rates and lower employment rates than men with disabilities. Women with disabilities are also more likely to be victims of violence, including sexual violence. They are targeted because their reduced status in society makes them vulnerable and because it is difficult or impossible for them to gain justice and redress.

Canada's Diane Roy celebrates winning the final of the women's 5000m T54 at the National Stadium, also known as the Bird's Nest, during the Beijing 2008 Paralympic Games.

13 By providing women with disabilities the opportunity to compete and display their physical ability, sport helps to reduce gender stereotypes and negative perceptions associated with women with disabilities. Sport creates a more equitable and empowering environment for these women, giving them confidence to pursue goals in other areas of their life with the same confidence and belief in themselves.

Sport as an Agent of Socialization

14 Persons with disabilities are generally excluded from education, employment and community life from a young age. Exclusion deprives them of opportunities to engage and develop relationships with others—opportunities essential to their social development and important determinants of health and well-being. As a result, persons with disabilities may have had very little experience greeting people, carrying on conversations and interacting with others.

15 Sport is well suited to helping persons with disabilities acquire social skills they may be lacking. It teaches individuals how to communicate effectively as well as the significance of teamwork and cooperation, goal-setting, self-discipline, respect for others, and the importance of rules. Sport also enables persons with disabilities to take risks and learn how to manage failure and success in a safe and supportive environment. Coaches and teammates provide important role models and can help persons with disabilities to develop skills they can apply in other aspects of their lives, such as employment.

16 Sport's universal popularity makes it ideal for fostering social interaction, even in remote areas. By bringing together people with similar disabilities, sport contributes to normalization en-

abling persons with disabilities to share their experiences and enjoy camaraderie with others who understand their challenges and capacities. Through this peer interaction, persons with disabilities develop a positive sense of self and group identity because they no longer feel set apart—they are like everyone else. Linda Mastandrea, a Paralympic athlete and lawyer says of this effect:

"In the world of wheelchair sports...I realized...I wasn't different, but very much like everyone else out on the floor. Through my years of competition, I found the strength and drive to pursue goals I never would have before. I learned that people with disabilities worldwide had the same struggles I had, trying to fit in, trying to get around, trying to learn, to do, to be."

17 Sport also brings together the parents and families of those with disabilities. Often parents of individuals with disabilities find themselves socially isolated. Social interaction with others who have similar experiences enables families to provide support to one another and empowers them to advocate for positive change to ensure greater inclusion and equality for persons with disabilities.

Total words: 1700
Total reading time: __________minutes________seconds

**The text is based on Sport and Persons with Disabilities: Fostering Inclusion And Well-being by International Network of Sport and Development Consultants.*

Vocabulary and Expressions

instantaneously /ˌɪnstən'teɪnɪəslɪ/ *adv.* happening immediately, without any delay

convention /kən'venʃən/ *n.* a large formal meeting of people who do a particular job or have a similar interest, or a large meeting for a political party

impair /ɪm'peə/ *vt.* to spoil something or make it weaker so that it is less effective impairment /ɪm'peəmənt/ *n.*

episodic /ˌepɪ'sɒdɪk/ *adj.* happening only sometimes and not regularly

stigma /'stɪgmə/ *n.* a strong feeling in society that a type of behavior is shameful

stereotype /'sterɪətaɪp/ *n.* a fixed idea that people have about what someone or something is like, especially an idea that is wrong

assumption /ə'sʌmpʃən/ *n.* something that you accept as true without question or proof

infanticide /ɪn'fæntɪsaɪd/ *n.* the crime of killing a child

underscore /ˌʌndə'skɔː/ *vt.* to emphasize something so that people pay attention to it

profile /'prəʊfaɪl/ *n.* a short description that gives important details about a person, a group of people, or a place

landmine /'lændmaɪn/ *n.* a bomb which is put on or under the ground and explodes when a person steps on it or a vehicle drives over it

rehabilitate /ˌriːhə'bɪlɪteɪt/ *vt.* to return someone or something to a good or healthy condition, state, or way of living **rehabilitative** *adj.*

vulnerable /'vʌlnərəbl/ *adj.* able to be easily physically, emotionally, or mentally hurt, influenced or attacked

determinant /dɪ'tɜːmɪnənt/ *n.* something that controls or affects what happens in a particular situation

Comprehension Check

1. According to the passage, what is the definition of "disabled"?
2. Are disabled people treated differently in different cultures? Why?
3. How can participation in sports help a disabled person?
4. Why is the Paralympics important?
5. How can the media help overcome the misconception and stigma of athletes with disabilities?

Critical Thinking Starters

1. Do you think Paralympic athletes are as equally recognized as Olympic athletes? What measures can be taken to make Paralympic athletes more known to the public?
2. Self-esteem reflects a person's overall subjective emotional evaluation of his or her own worth. It is a judgment of oneself as well as an attitude toward the self. Self-esteem allows people to face life with more confidence, benevolence and optimism, and thus easily reach their goals and self-actualization. Do you think participation in sports helps a disabled person's self-esteem? Why?

Sports in Focus

Squash（壁球）is a growing, global sport played in 185 countries by millions across the world. In 2003, *Forbes* rated squash as the number one healthiest sport to play. It is a racquet（球拍）sport played by two (singles) or four players (doubles) in a four-walled court with a small, hollow rubber ball. The players must alternate in striking the ball with their racquet and hit the ball onto the playable surfaces of the four walls of the court.

The governing body of international squash is the World Squash Federation (WSF). Squash is a medal sport in both the Commonwealth Games and the Pan American Games. The Professional Squash Association sanctions a vibrant professional squash series for both male and female competitors, with events staged throughout the world. Squash is recognized by the IOC and supporters are lobbying for its incorporation in a future Olympic program. The sport has tried to make itself more attractive to the IOC, using all-glass courts, video review systems and a white ball to help make it more spectator-friendly.

The racket (or *Racquet*) is similar to a tennis racket, but it's lighter and smaller. Balls are marked with different colored dots. They are made to bounce（反弹）at different speeds depending on the color of the dots. Balls with two yellow dots are slow, while balls with one yellow dot are a little bit faster. Balls with green or white dots are average. Balls with red or blue dots are fast.

Squash games are played to at least 11 points, and the winning player must win by two points. Games can go on indefinitely until one player gains a two-point lead. Matches are won by the first player to win three games (best of five games). A point is scored（得分）when a player hits a shot（击球）which strikes（击中）the front wall（前墙）of the court and then bounces twice before that player's opponent hits it to the front wall. Every point is started with a serve（发球）, which must be hit from one of the small service boxes（发球框）on either side of the court, must hit the front wall above the service line across the middle of the front wall, and must land in the back quarter of the court on the opposite side from where the serve was hit.

Relevant Words and Phrases

drop shot	stroke	volley
boast	nick	straight drive

Activity Time-Out

Imagine you are playing basketball or football or volleyball with a player who is intellectually impaired in thinking and speech. How would you feel? Would you play as usual? Why or why not? Discuss this with your partners and make a group presentation in class.

Text B

You Know, Eunice, the World Will Never Be the Same After This

1 Special Olympics is an international organization dedicated to providing year-round sports training and athletic competition in a variety of sports for children and adults with intellectual disabilities. Founded by Eunice Kennedy Shriver in 1968, Special Olympics was grounded in her belief that people with developmental disabilities were far more capable than most people assumed, and deserved equal opportunities to demonstrate these capabilities. Today the organization provides programming for 3.3 million children and adults with intellectual disabilities in 30 Olympic-type sports, hosting 32,000 competitions around the world each year.

2 Over the past few decades Special Olympics has been criticized within the academic community for failing to provide inclusive recreational services, reinforcing negative stereotypes, misusing volunteers, and lacking research demonstrating positive impacts for individuals with intellectual disabilities and the larger community. Following the recent passing of Eunice Kennedy Shriver on August 11, 2009 and her husband, R. Sargent Shriver on January 18, 2011, it seems timely to respond to these critics in defense of Special Olympics and the tremendous accomplishments of the

Shrivers. As former Chicago Mayor Richard Daley eloquently[1] stated on the opening day of the first International Special Olympic Games in 1968 *You know, Eunice, the world will never be the same after this.*

A Brief History of Eunice Kennedy Shriver and Special Olympics

3 The Special Olympics movement originally began as a day camp for individuals with disabilities started by Eunice Kennedy Shriver at her home in Rockville, Maryland in 1962. The inaugural[2] camp included 35 children exploring a variety of sports and physical activities. Kennedy Shriver understood from the outset that the young people she invited to her home had many capabilities that were not being recognized and celebrated. Camp Shriver became an annual event and between 1963 and 1968 expanded to more than 300 similar camps across the United States.

4 In response to outreach from the Chicago Park District to identify ways to increase services for people with intellectual disabilities, Eunice Kennedy Shriver harnessed the power of the Kennedy Foundation to plan and fund the first international Special Olympic Games in Chicago's Soldier Field, on July 20, 1968. Over 1000 athletes participated in track, floor hockey, and aquatic[3] sports at the first Games. In her opening ceremony address Mrs. Kennedy Shriver emphasized *...the fact that exceptional children....can be exceptional athletes, the fact that through sports they can realize their potential for growth.*

5 In 1977 Special Olympics expanded to include Winter Games with events in skiing and skating at Steamboat Springs, Colorado. Later Kennedy Shriver, with the help of her husband R. Sargent Shriver, gained approval and endorsement[4] from the U.S. and International Olympic Committee for full recognition of Special Olympics and the authorization to use the name *Olympics*. Over the next few decades Special Olympics established programs in the Far East, Middle East and the countries of the former Soviet Union with R. Sargent Shriver serving as President beginning in 1984 and Chairman of the International Board of Directors beginning in 1990. Internationally, there are now over 226 Special Olympics programs involving 3.3 million athletes.

---

[1]eloquent /'eləkwənt/ *adj.* able to express your ideas and opinions well, especially in a way that influences people **eloquently** *adv.*

[2]inaugural /ɪ'nɔːgjʊrəl/ *adj.* an inaugural event is the first in a series of planned events

[3]aquatic /ə'kwætɪk/ *adj.* involving water

[4]endorse /ɪn'dɔːs/ *vt.* to express formal support or approval for someone or something **endorsement** /ɪn'dɔːsmənt/ *n.*

Eunice Kennedy Shriver is a trailblazer. Her vision has evolved into Special Olympics.

6 On August 11, 2009, Mrs. Kennedy Shriver passed away and a statement from the Shriver family to her Special Olympics *family* in part reads:

> *...it was her unconditional love for the athletes of Special Olympics that so fulfilled her life. As Thomas Merton, the Trappist monk and social activist reminded us:* the beginning of love is to let those we love be perfectly themselves, and not to twist them to fit our own image, lest we love only the reflection of ourselves we find in them.

7 Her love for the athletes of Special Olympics was always just like that. She never hoped that people with intellectual disabilities should be somehow changed into something they were not. Rather, she fought throughout her life to ensure that they would be allowed to reach their full potential so that we might in turn be changed by them, forced to recognize our own false assumptions and their inherent gifts.

8 *She fought the good fight, she kept the faith, and though she knew the race for equality was not finished, she knew that the army of supporters she had hoped for long ago had become a reality that would carry and someday complete her vision...*

9 Fully recognizing that society still holds tremendous misconceptions about the capabilities of individuals with intellectual disability, Eunice Kennedy Shriver and her husband R. Sargent Shriver established a legacy in a movement that will continue to change lives and attitudes for years to come.

Criticisms of Special Olympics

10 A number of scholars have suggested that rather than increasing the quality of life of its athletes, Special Olympics has limited their potential because of the segregated focus of programs and offerings. Storey argues *You can participate only if you have a disability, and as such, you have the major problem facing the program*. Storey, in fact, directly advocates for the discontinuation of Special Olympics in favor of developing more inclusive recreational programs. The scholarly literature on integrated recreational services suggests that these programs should offer opportunities for individuals with cognitive disabilities that include regular interactions with individuals without disabilities, and these services should be designed such that persons with disabilities might enjoy them to the same degree as persons without disabilities.

11 An additional criticism of Special Olympics is that it reinforces the negative stereotypes commonly held toward people with significant learning difficulties. Evidence for this argument is illustrated in media accounts of Special Olympic events wherein athletes are often referred to as mentally retarded[5], handicapped, or *suffering* from a disability. Adding insult to this inappropriate terminology are the comments of famous and highly regarded individuals who, perhaps unintentionally, deride[6] the program with off-the-cuff[7] remarks. One prominent example is the recent comment by President Barak Obama on the Jay Leno show in which he described his bowling skills as ... *like the Special Olympics or something*. A number of scholars have explored the nature of language as it is used to describe undervalued groups. In general, these descriptive labels serve to demean[8] individuals with disabilities, distance them from the larger society, disregard individual differences, and focus attention only on a single aspect or trait of an individual from this group.

12 Closely aligned with this criticism is the concern that Special Olympics often host competitions in which children and adults participate at the same event. Storey suggests that this results in a loss of dignity when adults are denied their age-appropriate status. Storey further emphasizes this issue with examples from the media in which adult athletes are described as children or *kids*, and descriptions of recreational areas at competitions that include juvenile activities *such as clown*

[5]retarded /rɪ'tɑːdɪd/ *adj.* less intelligent than other people because of slower mental development
[6]deride /dɪ'raɪd/ *vt. formal* to make remarks or jokes that show you think someone or something is silly or useless
[7]off-the-cuff: If you speak off the cuff, you say something without having prepared or thought about your words first
[8]demean /dɪ'miːn/ *vt.* to cause someone to become less respected

toss, ring toss, and golf *with plastic clubs and balls*. In effect, these criticisms suggest that Special Olympics promote demeaning perspectives of the broader society toward individuals with severe disabilities.

The Nature and Scope of Special Olympics

13 In order to respond to criticisms against Special Olympics it is first helpful to understand the nature and scope of the movement as defined by its mission, goals, and programs. As articulated in the official SO website, the mission of Special Olympics is to provide year-round sports training and athletic competition in a variety of Olympic-type sports for children and adults with intellectual disabilities, giving them continuing opportunities to develop physical fitness, demonstrate courage, experience joy and participate in a sharing of gifts, skills and friendship with their families, other Special Olympics athletes and the community.

14 The philosophy of Special Olympics is that people with intellectual disabilities can, with proper instruction and encouragement, learn, enjoy and benefit from participation in individual and team sports. Special Olympics believes that consistent training is essential to the development of sports skills, and that competition among those of equal abilities is the most appropriate means of testing these skills, measuring progress and providing incentives for personal growth. Special Olympics believes that through sports training and competition, people with intellectual disabilities benefit physically, mentally, socially and spiritually; families are strengthened; and the community at large, both through participation and observation, is united in understanding people with intellectual disabilities in an environment of equality, respect and acceptance.

15 Special Olympics outlines 11 guiding principles the first of which is to help bring all persons with intellectual disabilities into the larger society under conditions whereby they are accepted, respected and given a chance to become productive citizens.

16 In addition to providing specific sport training and competition, Special Olympics offers a number of other programs focused on integrating sports, developing leadership skills among athletes, promoting the health and well-being of individuals with intellectual disabilities, and improving the perceptions of larger society about the capabilities of this population.

Integrated Sports Programs

17 The Unified Sports program developed over 20 years ago was designed to include equal

numbers of athletes with and without intellectual disabilities on sports teams. This effort has grown to include 150,000 participants in basketball, track and field, soccer, and golf.

Leadership Programs

18 The Athlete Leadership and Global Messenger programs are designed to help athletes explore new opportunities as coaches, officials, public speakers, and board members. These programs assist athletes to become advocates for themselves and their peers and develop skills that lead to more independent living. As a result, there are more athletes serving in leadership roles within the organization.

Health Promotion Programs

19 Special Olympics has become the largest world health organization serving individuals with intellectual disabilities. Under the auspices[9] of the Healthy Athlete program Special Olympics enlists health care volunteers to provide medical screenings[10] and health promotion workshops at competitions. Sports physicals, audiology[11] and vision exams, dentistry, and physical therapy are provided to athletes through this program. Volunteers gather information about the health care needs of individuals with disabilities and train medical professionals about their appropriate care.

School-based Educational Materials

20 The SO Get Into Program provides curriculum resource kits to primary grade teachers of students with and without disabilities. The program learning goals include helping students to understand, accept, and celebrate individual differences. The activities and resources in the Get Into It kit are provided to teachers free of charge through local Special Olympics programs.

Language/Terminology Programs

21 The Special Olympics website offers disability language guidelines that help to inform the media and larger community about the impact of the words they use to describe individuals with disabilities. These guidelines include recommendations for person-first, politically correct, and age-appropriate language. In addition, Special Olympics has organized a campaign to stop the use of the word *retard*. Thousands of individuals and over 200 organizations have joined this movement by pledging their support at http://r-word.org/.

---

[9]auspices /'ɔːspɪsɪz/ *n.* **under the auspices of *formal*** with the help and support of a particular organization

[10]screening /'skriːnɪŋ/ *n.* a test or examination to discover if there is anything wrong with someone

[11]audiology /ˌɔːdɪ'ɒlədʒɪ/ *n.* the area of science and medicine that is concerned with hearing and balance

22 In sum, Special Olympics uses sport and competition as a vehicle to first allow its athletes to change their views of themselves, and second to change the community's understanding and perceptions of people with disabilities. Through SO programming, athletes begin to view themselves as successful, and they begin to learn lessons that carry over into their lives as active participants in the community. Athletes begin to see themselves as individuals worthy of appreciation, and as the larger community witnesses their joy and success they also develop an appreciation and respect for the athletes as people with tenacity[12] and ability. As the President and CEO of Special Olympics New York, Neal Johnson is fond of saying *How can you see an athlete lift 300 pounds over his head and say* he's disabled*?*

Total words: 1900
Total reading time: __________minutes_________seconds

* *The text is based on You Know, Eunice, the World Will Never Be the Same after This by Chandra J. Foote and Bill Collins*

Comprehension Check

1. What is the definition of "Special Olympics"?
2. What criticisms of Special Olympics are mentioned in the passage?
3. How do Special Olympics help change society's perception of intellectually handicapped people?
4. How big is the Special Olympics movement today? List the evidence in the passage.
5. What effects does Special Olympics have in the areas of leadership, health and education?

More to Know

Eunice Mary Kennedy Shriver was a member of the Kennedy family, sister of President John F. Kennedy and Senators Robert F. Kennedy and Ted Kennedy. Eunice Mary Kennedy received a Bachelor of Arts degree in sociology from Stanford University. Following graduation, she worked for the U.S. State Department in the Special War Problems Division. In 1957, Shriver

[12]tenacity /tə'næsətɪ/ *n.* the determination to continue what you are doing

took over the direction of the Joseph P. Kennedy, Jr. Foundation.

The Foundation, established in 1946 as a memorial to Joseph P. Kennedy, Jr.—the family's eldest son, who was killed in World War II—has two major objectives: to seek the prevention of intellectual disabilities by identifying its causes, and to improve the means by which society deals with citizens who have intellectual disabilities. Under Shriver's leadership, the Foundation has helped achieve many significant advances, including the establishment of Special Olympics in 1968.

Recognized throughout the world for her efforts on behalf of persons with intellectual disabilities, Shriver received many honors and awards. In 1984, when President Ronald Reagan awarded Mrs. Shriver the Presidential Medal of Freedom, the nation's highest civilian honor, he said:

With enormous conviction and unrelenting effort, Eunice Kennedy Shriver has labored on behalf of America's least powerful people, those with mental retardation. Over the last two decades, she has been at the forefront of numerous initiatives on behalf of the mentally retarded, from creating day camps, to establishing research centers, to the founding of the Special Olympics program. Her decency and goodness have touched the lives of many, and Eunice Kennedy Shriver deserves America's praise, gratitude and love.

Hot Debate

There are a lot of controversies on Special Olympics. Some claim that it can increase the quality of life of its athletes, while others hold criticisms towards it. For example, they think that Special Olympics reinforces the negative stereotypes commonly held toward people with significant learning difficulties. Which side are you on? Make a debate on whether Special Olympics brings more advantages than disadvantages to the athletes.

Pop Culture

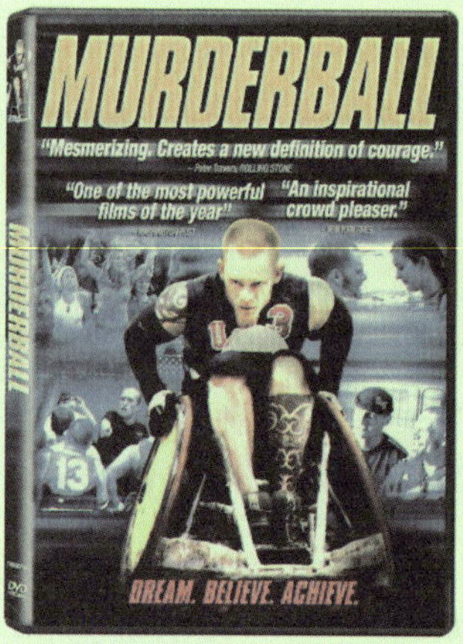

Murderball is a 2005 American documentary film about physically disabled athletes who play wheelchair rugby. Featuring fierce rivalry, stopwatch suspense, and larger-than-life personalities, *Murderball* is a film about tough, highly competitive quadriplegic rugby players. It centers on the rivalry between the Canadian and U.S. teams leading up to the 2004 Paralympic Games. *Murderball* follows the athletes from their training till they make their appearance in the event. The reasons for their disabilities are varied but they are united by the passion for the sport. Having high spirits they go against all odds to attempt victory. *Murderball* is more than a documentary about a single event. Not only does the film pay homage to the players but it also brings to light the issues faced by people suffering from quadriplegia. The film shows different aspects of professional and private lives of the disabled athletes. Highlighted is the courage and zeal of the players who going against the odds learn to live to the max.

Vocabulary Building

Look up the following words and expressions in reference books and on the Internet.

Words and Expressions	Meaning
adaptive sports	
equivalent	
validate	
incorporate	

6

UNIT

Sport Tourism

A travel market focused entirely on participating or watching sport is a unique and exciting concept.

Pre-reading Thoughts

1. People travel for different purposes. What are some of the reasons why people travel? Why do you travel?

2. In what aspects can travel be related to sports? Have you ever traveled for sports?

Text A

Sport Tourism: the Supply Side

1 Tourism lacks a common definition. International organizations, such as the World Tourism Organization (WTO), the World Travel and Tourism Council (WTTC), and the Organization for Economic Cooperation and Development (OECD), have long labored over the task of developing both supply-and-demand-side definitions of tourism. From a demand side, tourists are generally defined according to one or more of the following categories: purpose of trip, time away from home, distance traveled, mode of travel, or geography (domestic, regional, or international travel). From a supply side, both the WTTC and WTO have developed systems for categorizing businesses and organizations depending on whether their revenues are totally or partially derived from tourist spending. To better understand the development of the supply-side of sport tourism, five major areas have been identified: attractions, resorts, cruises, tours, and events.

Attractions

2 Sport tourism attractions are destinations that provide the tourist with things to see and do which are related to sport. Attractions can be natural (parks, mountains, wildlife) or man-made (museums, stadiums, stores). General characteristics represented in this core area of sport tourism include visitations to: (a) state-of-the-art sport facilities and/or unique sports facilities that generally house sports events, such as stadiums, arenas, and domes; (b) sport museums and halls/walls of

fame dedicated to sport heritage and honoring sport heroes and leaders; (c) sport theme parks including water parks, summer ski jumps, bungee jumping; (d) hiking trails developed for exploring nature; and (e) sport retail stores.

3 Aside from the attraction of Broadway shows and shopping on Madison Avenue, over 50,000 New York City visitors tour Madison Square Garden. Likewise, the MCI Center in Washington D.C. is positioned as a year-round tourist destination complete with 100,000 square feet of adjoining shopping, entertainment, and dining facilities, a National Sport Gallery, and the Sportcasters Hall of Fame and Museum.

4 Although retail stores are not frequently considered sport tourism attractions, the Bass Pro Shop in Springfield, Missouri is recognized as the number one tourist attraction in Missouri, accounting for 3.5 million visitors per year. This outdoor sport retail outlet measures 350,000 square feet. Visitors travel from across the globe to explore the vast array of sporting goods, as well as a 34-feet high waterfall and four massive aquariums, the largest being 30,000 gallons complete with bass and other freshwater fish.

Resorts

5 Sport tourism resorts represent well-planned and integrated resort complexes with sports or health as their primary focus and marketing strategy. In many situations, these vacation centers have high standard facilities and services available to the sport tourist. The sport tourism resort category includes amenity and destination spas; golf and tennis resorts; water and snow sport resorts; and nature retreats with a focus on outdoor adventure and exploration. Generally speaking, these resorts are furnished with state-of-the-art sport equipment and facilities and offer visitors various levels of activity opportunities and educational programs led by instructors with a great deal of expertise and personal visibility. These resorts do vary, however, extending from high level international standards specializing in specific and highly developed skills to campground services focusing on recreational sporting activities.

6 Meeting and convention planners have also found sport tourism resorts to be ideal locations. Not only are these resorts attractive to attendees (meeting attendance becomes a sort of reward) but the environment also serves a purpose. For many groups, sport activities have become a very important component of the meeting agenda as they help build camaraderie and team spirit, and

offer excellent networking opportunities. Others believe that the relaxed atmosphere of a resort keeps delegates from getting bogged down or frustrated with the meeting and even allows for more open thinking—bad news or change tends to be accepted more readily.

7 The variety of sports offered at a resort also reduces the stress of a meeting planner in terms of planning free-time activities or events for accompanying family members. In fact, some resorts such as the Marriott's Griffin Gate Resort in Lexington, Kentucky, employ an entire recreational department responsible for customizing sports-based events for meetings of all types. Other resorts such as Saddlebrook Resort in Tampa, Florida, have built extravagant sport facilities.

8 An extension of the sport resort category is sport camps. Sport camps are hosted at resorts, universities, and in the wilderness, and offer organized intensive training sessions in just about every sport imaginable. There are camps for traditional sports such as baseball, basketball, golf, soccer, tennis, as well as more adventurous camps that lead participants down white-water rapids, over rugged canyons, or off steep cliffs. There are also multisport camps such as the Nike sports camps in the United States. Although sport camps are commonly considered an activity for youth, in recent years the number of family and adult camps has been increasing. Fantasy sport camps have been especially successful in capturing the adult market, providing an opportunity for adults to train with their favorite sport stars, with the coach of a popular team, and/or at a famous sport locale.

Cruises

9 The sport tourism cruise category incorporates all boat-related trips that have sports or sporting activities as their principal market strategy. Many ships built today resemble hotels and resorts and have unique sports installations. They also utilize guest sports celebrities as a marketing tool. To further satisfy the sport tourist, cruise ships often arrange special transportation to provide guests opportunities for golf, tennis, snorkeling, waterskiing, etc., in unique and varied water environments. Other planned activities include provision of onboard sport competitions and/or modified games (e.g., a golf driving range on deck), and special presentations or clinics from invited sport celebrities. Cruise-and-drive programs also exist, whereby tourists board private vehicles and are taken to desired sports destinations. Private yachts that sail directly to the sport destination of your choice can also be chartered. The use of watercraft for sporting activities (e.g., recreational and competitive sailing, jet skiing) is another important dimension in this category.

Tours

10 Sport tourism tours bring visitors to their favorite sport event, facility, or destination throughout the world. These tours may be self-guided or organized depending upon access, location, and nature of the activity. For example, many ski tour packages provide air travel, accommodation, local transportation, and ski lift tickets with no special guide or amenities. In contrast, some companies specialize in travel packages that fly fans to an away game, put them up in a hotel for a few nights, provide tickets to the contest, arrange for a cocktail party and pregame briefing with media, schedule a postgame reception with players and coaches, and then return fans safely home. This type of tour is especially appealing to sport aficionados who want to follow their team on the road, take in a major event such as the Super Bowl or Indianapolis 500, and for those who dream of walking the fairways of Augusta National during the Masters golf tournament. Sport tours may include visitations to sport museums and stadiums as well as events or games in multiple locations lasting anywhere from one to two weeks. Some sport tour companies cater to common interest groups while others specialize in corporate incentive programs, educational tours to a specific conference or location, or outdoor adventure challenges.

11 Also included in this category are companies that serve youth teams and professional sports teams, arranging for all their travel and accommodation needs. On average, parents of an elite youth sports participant spend between $1,500 to $5,000 per year on related sport travel. The National Collegiate Athletic Association (NCAA) spends $33.4 million on travel per year ($29.3 million related to sport championships and $4.1 million for business purposes). Each major league baseball team spends approximately $2 million on travel per year.

Events

12 The sport tourism event category refers to those sports activities that attract a sizable number of visiting participants and/or spectators. Visitor types vary depending on the sport event, and some are obviously more spectator driven than others (e.g., Olympic Games versus the National Amateur Shuffleboard Championship). Furthermore, these sport tourism events have the potential to attract nonresident media and technical personnel such as coaches and other sports officials. High-profile sport events such as the Super Bowl, Olympic Games, or World Cup are often referred to as tourism hallmark events and mega events.

13 In some instances, sports tourism events may have a cultural, religious, or even ritual association. According to professor Robert Rinehart, the Super Bowl is "a modern ritual of pilgrimage in which people attend to reunite with their friends and experience the event in concert with others of similar interest". Furthermore, it is found that individuals attend the game "to be seen, to enjoy the hoopla, to support the team, and to continue a ritual." For many, the sport event experience is a recurring, life-shaping experience.

14 As far as economic impact, the sport event category of sport tourism receives the most notoriety as it is increasingly common for organizers to calculate the amount of new dollars or hotel room nights an event generates. Events designed to attract large numbers of spectators can bring thousands, even millions, of dollars into a local economy. However, smaller participatory events, such as tournaments or marathons, can also be advantageous, particularly for smaller cities or less populated regions. Since participatory events often make use of existing infrastructure and volunteer labor, they can be relatively inexpensive to host, thereby yielding high benefit-to-cost ratios. Furthermore, participatory sport events have been shown to be an effective way to attract new visitors and to generate return visits. This is because participatory sport events, similar to sport resorts, target consumers who seek opportunities to share their holidays with others who share an interest in a particular sport.

Total words: 1619
Total reading time: __________minutes_________seconds

**The text is based on An Introduction to Sport and Adventure Tourism by Lisa Delpy Neirotti*

Vocabulary and Expressions

state-of-the-art /ˌsteɪt ɒv ðɪ'ɑːt / *adj.* the highest level of development at a particular time (especially the present time)

amenity /ə'miːnɪtɪ/ *n.* something, such as a swimming pool or shopping centre, that is intended to make life more pleasant or comfortable for the people in a town, hotel, or other place

retreat /rɪ'triːt/ *n.* a place affording peace and quiet

bog / bɒg / *vt.* cause to slow down or get stuck **get bogged down**: to become so involved in something difficult or complicated that you cannot do anything else

rapids /'ræpɪdz / *n.* a section of a river where the water moves very fast, often over rocks

charter /'tʃɑ:tə/ *vt.* hold under a lease or rental agreement (of goods and services)

ski lift /ski:lɪft/ *n.* a machine for taking people to the top of a slope so that they can ski down it

aficionado /əˌfɪsjə'nɑ:dəʊ/ *n.* someone who is very interested in and enthusiastic about a particular subject

participatory /pɑ:tɪsɪ'peɪtərɪ/ *adj.* affording the opportunity for individual participation

Comprehension Check

1. According to the ways of defining tourism mentioned in the passage, can you give a definition of "sport tourism"? What is the focus of your definition, the supply side or demand side?
2. How are the five different facets of sport tourism defined according to the passage?
3. What are the considerations for meeting and convention planners in choosing sport tourism resorts?
4. What can a sport aficionado do during a sport package tour?
5. What benefits can a sport tourism event bring to the host?
6. What does the underlined sentence in paragraph 12 mean? Paraphrase it.

Critical Thinking Starters

1. Sport tourism is one of the fastest growing niche markets in the tourism industry. Several conditions have aided in the increased popularity. The main factors that have contributed to this growth are: economic forces, technological innovations and attitudinal and value changes. In groups, pick one of the following three questions and discuss their key points.
   A. What economic forces drive sport tourism?
   B. What technological innovations influence its popularity?
   C. What attitudinal and value changes have occurred?
2. A sport tourist is regarded as a kind of special interest tourist who has a specific, interest-based motivation for his/her travel to another destination. According to this definition, what are the differences between sport tourists and general interest tourists? Make a chart to show your points.

More to Know

Although some people disagree on how to compute the economic impact of sports travel, everyone will agree that visitors have a beneficial impact. They come, they stay, and they spend. The new dollars entering the local economy benefit local businesses and produce new jobs and taxes.

Some travelers are "day trippers." Though not as great as that of an overnight visitor, their impact on the local economy is still very welcomed.

Communities have learned that visitor expenditures on room nights, restaurant meals, and retailers are good for the economy. Just as cities have competed for decades for meetings, conventions, and traditional tourist travel, they now compete to host sports events or attract the pursuit of favorite sports activities. Cities have also learned that most of the events take place whether the economy is good or in recession. This element of resistance to economic downturns has brought new cities and suppliers to the industry.

Expert's View

World Cup Profile "Can't Be Bought"

Nelson City Council's $1 million investment in the Cricket World Cup will leave a "long term legacy" and attract more visitors, events and money to the region, city leaders say.

But a tourism expert has sounded a cautionary note, saying the international sporting spectacle is unlikely to bring significant economic benefits to the city.

The third and final World Cup match in Nelson last Thursday was potentially viewed by millions of people on televisions, computers and smart phones around the world.

They would all have been introduced to Nelson as a tourist destination and seen images of the region's sunshine, mountains and waters.

They would have heard the commentators fill time by talking about having fish and chips at Mapua and cycling to "beautiful" Kaiteriteri.

International media would have filed stories, all containing the word "Nelson" at least once, in publications and on television channels around the world.

"You can't buy that exposure," Nelson Cricket general manager Richard Hayward said.

And that was the main justification for the council investing close to $1m to bring the sporting spectacle here -- exposure would convert to a tourism boom.

However, University of Waikato tourism professor Chris Ryan said the economic benefits of major sporting events to a country or region were often exaggerated and difficult to measure.

"I have to say, most of the literature on the economic impacts of events anywhere in the world usually indicate that prior to the event there are over optimistic forecasts as to the economic wellbeing that the event will bring."

Sports in Focus

Swordplay has been practised for thousands of years, as evidenced by carvings depicting fencers found in a temple near Luxor dating from around 1190 BC. From the 16th to the 18th century, duels were common, with combatants using a variety of weapons including quarterstaffs（铁头木棒） and backswords（木剑）. Such bouts were bloody and occasionally fatal.

Fencing began from a form of military training to a sport in either the 14th or 15th century. Both Italy and Germany lay claim to its origins, with German fencing masters organising the first guilds in the 15th century, the most notable being the Marxbruder of Frankfurt, formed in 1478.

Three innovations in the 17th and 18th century led to the popularity of fencing as a sport: the "foil"（花剑） -- a weapon with a flattened tip; a set of rules governing the target area; and the wire-mesh（金属网丝） mask. Together, these developments ensured the safety of fencing participants.

Fencing was included for the first time at the 1896 Games in Athens, and has remained on the Olympic programme since then. The women's fencing competition entered the Games in 1924 in Paris. Today, men and women compete in individual and team events, in which three types of weapons are used: foil, epee（重剑） and sabre（佩剑）. The foil was, at first, the only weapon used by women, until the 1996 Games in Atlanta when women's epee was introduced. Women's sabre appeared for the first time on the Olympic programme in Athens in 2004.

Among the figures who have marked this sport, Italy's Nedo Nadi is the only fencer to have won a medal in every weapon in a single edition of the Games. In 1912, at the age of 18, he won in the foil. Then, after being decorated by his country for acts of bravery during the First World War, he won five gold medals in Antwerp in 1920, a historic and unequalled record: in the individual foil and sabre events, and in the team foil, epee and sabre events

Relevant Words and Phrases

piste	rapier	bodywire
foible	hilt	chest guard

Text B

Sustainability[1] Gains Attention in Sport Tourism

1 Over the past five years the concept of sustainable development has become more commonplace. In general terms, sustainability takes the approach of balancing the needs of today with those of the future. Much of the focus has been placed on the environment and the conservation of natural resources. But the environment is only one prong of the three-pronged approach to sustainability, the other two being economics and social (cultural) well-being. The phrase "triple bottom line" is frequently used to describe the interrelationship among the three prongs of sustainability. In the tourism realm, the topic of sustainable development has been receiving a lot of attention in recent years. Without paying attention to the long-term sustainability of a tourism destination, the effects of a large number of visitors can quickly destroy the attractiveness of a destination. In the realm of sport, less attention has been paid to sustainability, and we argue that it is time to start thinking about the long-term sustainability of sport, particularly for those sports that rely on certain climate conditions such as skiing or golf or those that can have negative effects on the environment or local communities, both socially and economically. Thus, as sport tourism continues to grow in popularity, we need to be aware of the potential negative and positive effects of this sector on the sport and tourism industries and to work on the sustainable development of this particular niche. We will now look at each of the three prongs of sustainable development in turn.

Social Dimensions

2 Tourism studies have produced abundant evidence that tourism can have both positive and negative effects on a host community. Some of the positive effects relate to economic benefit or community pride and excitement among residents. This pride in community results in what is called the psychic income associated with hosting an event. Tourism has also been shown to open societies to new ideas and even bring about a liberalization of values in more rigid or closed cultures. Tourism may provide the funding and the impetus to preserve historic buildings, traditional practices (e.g. dances, crafts), and natural settings.

---

[1]sustainability / sə'steɪnəbɪlətɪ/ *n.* the property of causing little or no damage to the environment and therefore being able to continue for a long time

3 In recent years, there has been a growing focus on the social benefits of event sport tourism for communities. Many believe that the social benefits are the true legacy of hosting a mega event. A study of the social impacts of the 2000 Sydney Olympic Games found that despite protests and negative attitudes in the lead-up to the event, during the 16 days of the Games there was "a reason to celebrate rather than protest" and residents reported an increased sense of community. In a similar study of the 2002 FIFA World Cup in South Korea, it was found that although the fervor did seem to diminish after the event, it did not disappear totally.

4 Another social benefit of hosting sport events is the legacy of urban regeneration. Indeed, hosting the America's Cup in 1987 has been credited as being the catalyst for the renovation of the downtown area in Fremantle, Australia. The fears about congestion[2] and crowds were unfounded. Instead, residents thought that infrastructural improvements and potential for increased tourism would contribute to the increased quality of life in the years after the event.

5 Positive outcomes, however, may not always result from sport events. A study of the potential costs associated with the 2000 Sydney Olympics found that a mega event affected different segments of a host community unequally. Low-income residents often suffer the most because they are frequently displaced[3] from their homes by plans to redevelop their neighborhoods with high-priced residences. This displacement of low-income residents has been a common practice in relation to the Olympic Games, as host cities face decisions over where to build stadia, athletes' villages, and so forth.

6 Event sport tourism is not the only type of tourism to have an effect on a host community. The crowding and congestion experienced by small ski towns or golf resort areas such as Myrtle Beach, South Carolina, also need attention. In most tourism regions, host communities experience a love–hate relationship with tourists. On the one hand residents realize that their economic well-being often depends on tourists, yet the high prices, traffic congestion, and sometimes increased crime that accompany living in a tourist destination may lead to resistance and even hostility among community members. All these effects need to be carefully thought through in any proposed tourism development. But as many of us argue, emphasis is too frequently placed on the potential economic benefits. The voices of the community are often unheard, and the social legacies are often

[2]congestion /kən'dʒestʃn/ *n.* the state of being too blocked and crowded
[3]displace /dɪs'pleɪs/ *vt.* force to move

ignored. The sustainability of most events may lie in the social dimensions, particularly enhanced community spirit, increased patriotism, and even an experienced event volunteer labor force that has the skills necessary to help with future events hosted by the community.

Economic Dimensions

7 When community leaders attempt to raise money to build a new stadium, secure a professional franchise, or host a sport event, they often point to the projected[4] economic benefits arising out of these projects. But research has shown, particularly in relation to professional sport, that as many as 70% of spectators come from within the metropolitan area and therefore are not event sport tourists according to any definition of a tourist. Thus, although using sport as a tourist attraction is a valuable strategy for economic and community development, we need to be sure when we read studies about the tourism-related impacts accruing[5] from sport events that locals were not included in the people surveyed or the economic estimates generated.

8 We also need to be clear about how economic impact is measured. At least 11 common mistakes can occur when communities estimate economic impact, including using the wrong multiplier, measuring time switchers and casuals, and including people whose primary motivation was not to attend the event but who happened to be in the vicinity or switched the timing of their visit to coincide with the event. Another phenomenon that appears to be associated with hosting the mega events is the displacement effect. Some potential visitors avoid a host city and region in the years leading up to, and during, the event, dissuaded[6] by fear of congestion, construction-related hassles, and terrorism. There is no accurate way to estimate how many visitors are displaced. But various business owners told that "regular tourism" disappeared in Victoria, British Columbia, when the city hosted the 1994 Commonwealth Games. High prices, the difficulty of obtaining visas, and fears about terrorism were cited as reasons for the downturn in number of visitors. This scenario is more common in the months leading up to most mega events and exemplifies the displacement effect noted earlier, although since 2001 perceived risks associated with mega events appear to have heightened the displacement effect.

9 Studies associated with the 2002 men's FIFA World Cup have documented perceptions of

---

[4]projected / prə'dʒektɪd/ *adj.* planned for the future or calculated based on information already known
[5]accrue / ə'kru:/ vi. to increase in number or amount over a period of time
[6]dissuade /dɪ'sweɪd/ *vt.* to persuade someone not to do something

risk associated with attending an event. As a result of the perceived risks involved, security costs associated with hosting an event have become a major part of an event budget. But in a study of the perceived risks associated with the 2008 Beijing Olympic Games, it was found that among their respondents there was less perceived risk associated with attending the Olympic Games than with visiting China as a regular tourist. Similarly, attendees at the Rugby World Cup in Australia tended to downplay safety and security issues. Thus, the issue of perceived risk and event sport tourism needs more study.

10 Nonetheless, the lure of the potential economic impacts associated with sport tourism will continue to grow as countries around the world rely more heavily on tourism to boost their gross national product. Members of the Cooperative Research Centre for Sustainable Tourism in Australia suggested that conducting a cost–benefit analysis may be more appropriate than emphasizing economic impact. Indeed, some of the preliminary lessons learned from hosting a hallmark event have been not to focus on the effects of an event but to use strategic leveraging to maximize the legacies and thus the sustainability of the event.

Environmental Dimensions

11 As the popularity of sport vacations increases, we must consider the effects on the environment. Over the past 15 years, those in the tourism industry have begun to realize that the environment is the core of the tourism product. The growth in ecotourism has been one outcome of this environmental concern. More recently, however, there has been a push toward extending sustainable development practices to all segments of the tourism industry. This new focus includes adopting a more comprehensive approach to sustainability that not only includes the social and economic dimensions but also recognizes that forces such as global climate change may in turn affect the long-term viability of some tourism activities such as snow sports and scuba diving.

12 Take, for instance, scuba diving. The growing popularity of the sport and recreational activity has resulted in increasing pressure on the environment. Pollution of the water, littering, anchor damage, trampling, and specimen collecting by divers can destroy the natural resource base. Moreover, from the perspective of global climate change, as temperatures increase, the health of the coral reefs is declining because of the increasing intensity and frequency of major storms, coral bleaching events, and other occurrences. Hence, the long-term viability of many diving locations around the world is being questioned.

13 Controversies surrounding skiing provide another example. Tensions have grown between environmentalists and the alpine skiing industry in recent years. In Vermont environmentalists have raised an alarm over the amount of water being taken from rivers for snowmaking. In Colorado an activist group called the Ski Area Citizens' Coalition produces a scorecard that ranks resorts on their environmental friendliness so that skiers can choose to ski at mountains that employ sustainable practices. Yellowstone National Park has limited the use of snowmobiles because of the noise and air pollution that they cause and because conflicts have arisen between snowmobilers and cross-country skiers in the western part of the park.

14 Around the world, ski resort development is causing alarm among environmentalists. Ski resorts are among the most intensive forms of development in mountain regions, requiring tree clearing for ski runs and water for snowmaking and servicing the resorts. A longer season may reduce the economic effects of seasonality, but it leaves little time for grass and plant regeneration and relief from the noise and air pollution caused by the sheer number of people using the mountain roads to access the resorts. From the global climate change perspective, warmer winters and less snowfall may cause many of the lower-elevation ski resorts to close within 30 to 50 years.

15 Some of the same concerns have been raised in relation to the golf industry. Golf courses are land intensive, and the use of chemicals on the greens and the use of water in desert areas have been of particular concern. Some golf courses have adopted strategies to protect the ecological balance of their courses with programs to protect wildlife sponsored by partnerships between the United States Golf Association and the Audubon Society, among others. More needs to be done in this area, particularly in the lesser-developed countries where national governments have identified golf tourism as a source of much-needed foreign currency while ignoring the severe socioeconomic and environmental consequences that golf courses have for their citizens. On a more positive note, it should be noted that some golf courses could benefit from global warming. With less snow and cold weather some golf courses may have longer playing seasons.

16 The IOC has charged host countries with implementing environmentally friendly practices in relation to the Olympic Games. The 1994 Winter Olympic Games in Lillehammer were called the first Green Games. The Norwegian Parliament mandated Project Environment Friendly Olympics to protect the fragile ecology surrounding the small host city. The Lillehammer Olympic Games provided a good example of event sport tourism and environmentalism that future events

could copy to produce a better event. It also satisfied tourists and built a reputation as a clean and attractive destination.

17 Although the Sydney Olympic Games were also called the Green Games, it was contended that Sydney did not keep all its promises, citing the failure to detoxify[7] Homebush Bay, where the main Olympics complex was located. The scholars questioned the traditional approach of using environmental guidelines mandated by sport governing bodies. They suggested that consensus-building approaches in which the local organizing committees and host communities are integrally involved in establishing environmental policies and practices for their events might be more successful.

Total words: 2073
Total reading time: __________minutes_________seconds

** The text is based on Contemporary Sport Management by Paul Pedersen, Janet Parks, Jerome Quarterman, and Lucie Thibault.*

Comprehension Check

1. Why is sustainability getting more attention than before?
2. What social benefits can sport tourism bring? How do you understand the "love-hate relationship" in the underlined sentence in paragraph 6?
3. According to the passage, is sport a good tourist attraction? Why or why not?
4. What kinds of sport events care more about environmental sustainability? Is there a viable solution to the conflicts between socioeconomic benefits and environmental drawbacks of sport tourism?
5. According to the passage, how is "green games" defined?

[7]detoxify /diː'tɒksɪfaɪ/ *vt.* to remove harmful chemicals from something

Activity Time-Out

During the last quarter century the world has witnessed an ever growing concern over economic development and environmental costs. The debate often begins when the saving of "environmental" resources is weighed against the development of the economy. Usual questions arise such as "What will environmental savings cost businesses in time and dollars?" "Is there a fair and equitable breakdown for all parties involved?" What do you think about this issue? Search for related information about it and state your viewpoint in a short essay.

Pop Culture

Everybody knows that Costa Rica is a tourists' paradise. But in the documentary **The Goose with the Golden Eggs**, we hear another side to the story: The industry may be a boon in general, but not every kind of tourist is good for the country. The film examines the impacts of different models of coastal tourism in Costa Rica, from small-scale eco-lodges and a sustainable mid-sized resort to large-scale resorts, vacation homes, and cruise ships along the northern Pacific Coast. The film features interviews with Margarita Penon, Costa Rica's former First Lady and member of Congress, as well as with other government officials, tourism experts, and residents of coastal communities who are affected by Costa Rica's tourism boom.

"It is our hope that this film will stimulate a much-needed public discussion of what types of tourism are most appropriate and beneficial in Costa Rica," says Margarita Penon. "If properly managed, tourism can bring benefits to communities and to conservation, and Costa Rica can choose now to turn the tourism industry into a green and sustainable industry. It can choose not to kill the goose that lays golden eggs."

Vocabulary Building

Look up the following words and expressions in reference books and on the Internet.

Words and Expressions	Meaning
environmental impact assessment	
environmental scanning	
escort tour	
independent tour	

7

UNIT

Sports and Religion

"The mixing of sport and religion has been in place at least since the Greek athletes offered ritual sacrifices to the gods in the hope of enhancing their performance in events. In my Catholic childhood making the sign of the cross before a free throw was fairly common practice. Today the presence of the deity in sporting events seems, dare we say, omnipresent."

— Richard C. Crepeau, Department of History, University of Central Florida

Pre-reading Thoughts

1. Have you ever attended a live sports event? Describe what it was like.
2. What is your impression of followers of a religion? What characteristics would you use to describe them?
3. Can you see any similarities between religion and sport? Have you ever read about a religious fanatic? Have you ever read or heard about a sport fanatic? Do you think they share common qualities?

Text A

Sports and Religion — Is It a Promising Combination?

1 Discussion about sports and religions often are confusing. Some people view sport as a form of religion, or at least "religion-like," whereas others assume that the "true nature" of religion is essentially different from the "true nature" of sport. Still others view sports and religions as two distinct sets of cultural practices, which may be similar or different depending on how people create, define, and use them.

Sports as Religion

2 Attending an NFL game or a World Cup soccer match and being a part of 75,000 or more people yelling, chanting, and moving in unison reminds some people of a religious experience. Some people go so far as to say that sports are religion because they involve passions, dedication,

identities, and ritualistic actions and they are played with bodies made in the image of God. Others stop short of this position and say that sports are simply religion-like because both share some characteristics and can produce similar consequences. In both cases, the following similarities between sports and religions have been noted:

· Both have places or buildings for communal gatherings and special events — sports have stadiums and religions have churches.

· Both have a disciplined search for perfection in body, mind, and spirit — sports emphasize physical performance, and religions emphasize moral purity.

· Both are controlled through structured organizations and hierarchical systems of authority — sports have commissioners, athletic directors, and coaches; and religions have bishops, pastors, and priests/ministers/ rabbis.

· Both have events that celebrate widely shared values — sports celebrate competition, hard work, and achievement; and religions celebrate commitment, community, and redemption.

· Both have rituals before, during, and after major events — sports have initiations, national anthems, halftime pep talks, hand slapping, and band parades; and religions have baptisms, opening hymns, regular sermons, the joining of hands, and ceremonial processions.

· Both have heroes and legends about heroic accomplishments — sports heroes are elected to "halls of fame," and their stories are told repeatedly by journalists, coaches, and fans; and religious heroes are elevated to sainthood, and their stories are told repeatedly by religious writers, ministers, and believers.

· Both evoke intense emotions and give meaning to people's lives — sports inspire players and fans to contemplate human potential, and religions inspire theologians and believers to contemplate the meaning of existence.

· Both can be used to distract attention from important social, political, and economic issues and thereby become "opiates" of the masses — sports focus attention on athlete celebrities, scores, and championships; and religions focus attention on everlasting life and a personal relationship with the supernatural, rather than here-and-now issues and the material conditions of people's lives.

This list helps us understand why some people describe sport as religion or religion-like.

Sport and Religion Are Essentially Different

3 Some people argue that religion and sport each have a unique, separate truth, or "essence." The essence of religion, they believe, is grounded in divine inspiration, whereas the essence of sport is grounded in human nature. People who think this way are called essentialists because they

assume that the universe is governed by unchanging laws and that meaning and truth are inherent in nature. When they study religion and sport, they argue that the fundamental character of religion is essentially different from the fundamental character of sport, and they identify the following differences:

· Religious beliefs, meanings, rituals, and events are fundamentally mystical and sacred, whereas sport beliefs, meanings, rituals, and events are fundamentally clear-cut and secular.

· The purpose of religion is to transcend the circumstances and conditions of the material world in the pursuit of eternal life, whereas the purpose of sport is to embrace material reality and seek victories through physical performance.

· Religion involves faith in one's beliefs, whereas sport involves competition to establish superiority.

· Religion emphasizes humility and love, whereas sport emphasizes personal achievement and conquest.

· Religious services collectively acknowledge the sacred and supernatural, whereas sport events collectively focus on the here-and-now outcome with transitory and secular significance.

Essentialists argue that there are fundamental differences between Super Bowl Sunday and Easter Sunday, even though both are important days in the lives of many people.

Religions and Sports as Cultural Practices

4 Despite important differences between sports and religions, people have combined these two spheres of life in mutually supportive ways. In some cases, people with certain religious beliefs have used sports for religious purposes, and in other cases, people in sports have used religion in the pursuit of performance goals in the following ways.

5 ***To Cope with Uncertainty*** Throughout history, people have used prayers and rituals based on religion, magic, and/or superstition to cope with uncertainties in their lives. Because sport competition involves uncertainty, it is not surprising that many athletes use rituals, some based in religion, to help them feel as if they have some control over what happens to them on the playing field.

6 Wrestler Kurt Angle, a gold medalist in the 1996 Olympic Games, explained that when he had a serious neck injury before his qualifying matches, he prayed to God for guidance. His doctor advised him not to wrestle because he would risk paralysis if he injured his neck again. However, in answer to his prayers, "God said to do it." Thus, he competed using medicine from his doctor to

endure the pain. After he won the gold medal, he said,

I knew my neck was hurt...I knew when I was wrestling in the Olympic Games that He was watching over me. I knew when I won the gold medal that He intended me to win. He wanted someone like me to spread the Word and be a role model for kids.

7 The use of prayers and rituals is not limited to Christian athletes. Former NBA player Hakeem Olajuwon engaged in a regular Islamic prayer ritual as he faced challenges in his life as a professional athlete. He explained that "my religion gives me direction, inner strength. I feel more comfortable. You can take life head on".

8 ***To Stay Out of Trouble*** The late Reggie White was an ordained minister and a retired defensive lineman in the NFL; he was called the "minister of defense". When he was asked about his religious beliefs during his years in the NFL, he said that "studying God's Word helped keep my life on track, even though there were bad influences like drugs and crime all around me". Other athletes say similar things about religion helping them to avoid the risky lifestyles that often exist in the social worlds that develop around certain sports.

9 The fact that religious beliefs may separate athletes from risky off-the-field lifestyles and keep them focused on training in their sports is obvious to coaches. Journalist Andrew Corsello explains that "regardless of their own beliefs, coaches are attracted to the self-control that Christian convictions instill in a man". Furthermore, team owners may see "born-again athletes" as better long-term investments because they believe that religious athletes "are less likely to get arrested".

10 ***To Give Meaning to Sport Participation*** Sport participation emphasizes personal achievement and self-promotion, and it involves playing games that produce no essential goods or services, even though people create important social occasions around sport events. This makes sport participation a self-centered, self-indulgent activity. Although training often involves personal sacrifices and pain, it focuses on the development and use of personal physical skills, often to the exclusion of other activities and relationships. Realizing this can create a crisis of meaning for athletes who have dedicated their lives to personal achievements in sports.

11 One way to deal with this crisis of meaning is to define sport participation as an act of worship, a platform for giving witness, or a manifestation of God's plan for their lives. Many Christian athletes and coaches like to quote Colossians 3:23 in the Bible: "Whatever you do, work at it with

all your heart, working for the Lord, not for men." This enables them to define their sport as a sacred rather than a secular activity. As a result, their doubts about the worthiness of what they do are eliminated because playing sports is sanctified as a calling from God.

12 ***To Establish Team Solidarity and Unity*** Religious beliefs and rituals can be powerful tools in creating bonds between people. When they're combined with sport participation, they can link athletes together as spiritual teammates, building team solidarity and unity in the process. Many coaches know this, and some have used Christian beliefs as rallying points for their teams. For example, Fisher DeBerry, a committed Christian and former head football coach at the U.S. Air Force Academy, used religion to establish an esprit de corps on his team by hanging a sign in the locker room saying "I AM A MEMBER OF TEAM JESUS CHRIST."

13 In conclusion, the combination of sports and religious beliefs offers little promise for changing dominant forms of sport, especially in the United States. Of course, individual athletes may alter their sport-related behaviors when they combine sports and religion in their own lives, but at this time such changes have had no observable effect on what occurs in elite, competitive sports.

Total words: 1532
Total reading time: __________minutes_________seconds

* *The text is based on Sports in Society: Issues and Controversies by Jay Coakley*

Vocabulary and Expressions

chant /tʃɑːnt/ *vi.* to repeat or sing a word or phrase continuously, or to sing a religious prayer or song to a simple tune

inunison together; at the same time

communal /'kɒmjʊnəl/ *adj.* belonging to or used by a group of people rather than one single person

pastor /'pɑːstə/ *n.* a leader of a Christian group or church, especially one which is Protestant

rabbi /'ræbaɪ/ *n.* a religious leader and teacher in the Jewish religion

redemption /rɪ'dempʃən/ *n.* (Christianity) the act of delivering from sin or saving from evil

pep talk /pep'tɔːk/ *n.* a short speech intended to encourage people to work harder or try to win a game or competition

slap /slæp/ *vt.* a quick hit with the flat part of the hand or other flat object

baptism /'bæptɪzəm/ *n.* a Christian ceremony in which a person has water poured on their head, or is covered for a very short time in water, in order to show that they have become a member of the Christian Church

sermon /'sɜːmən/ *n.* a part of a Christian church ceremony in which a priest gives a talk on a religious or moral subject, often based on something written in the Bible

contemplate /'kɒntəmpleɪt/ *vt.* to spend time considering a possible future action, or to consider one particular thing for a long time in a serious and quiet way

theologian /θɪə'ləʊdʒɪən/ *n.* someone who studies the nature of God, religion, and religious beliefs

opiate /'əʊpɪət/ *n.* a drug which contains opium, especially one which causes sleep

secular /'sekjʊlə/ *adj.* not having any connection with religion

transcend /træn'send/ *vt.* to go further, rise above or be more important or better than something, especially a limit

conquest /'kɒŋkwest/ *n.* success in mastering something difficult

transitory /'trænzɪtərɪ/ *adj.* lasting for only a short time

paralysis /pə'rælɪsɪs/ *n.* the loss of the ability to move and feel in all or part of your body

ordain /ɔː'deɪn/ *vt.* to officially make someone a priest or other religious leader, in a religious ceremony

conviction /kən'vɪkʃən/ *n.* an unshakable belief in something without need for proof or evidence

self-indulgent /'selfɪn'dʌldʒənt/ *adj.* allowing yourself to have or do anything that you enjoy

manifestation /ˌmænɪfe'steɪʃən/ *n.* a sign of something existing or happening

sanctify /'sæŋktɪfaɪ/ *vt.* to make an event or place holy

esprit de corps /es'priːdə'kɔːr/ the spirit of a group that makes the members want the group to succeed

Comprehension Check

1. According to the passage, what does the word "essentialist" (in paragraph 3) mean? How would essentialists treat religion and sport?
2. Why is sport participation regarded as a self-centered, self-indulgent activity? And once "a crisis of meaning (in paragraph 10)" has been created, how can athletes find a way out according to the passage?
3. This article shows three different views on the comparison of religion and sport. According to the passage, which view does the author truly believe? Which view do you agree with and why?

Critical Thinking Starters

1. Can you imagine any way that religious belief might interfere with an athlete's performance?
2. In the conclusion, the author states, "The combination of sports and religious beliefs offers little promise for changing dominant forms of sport, especially in the United States." What do you think needs to be changed in sports that religious belief could influence?
3. Imagine winning an Olympic gold medal, receiving death threats from people in your country who brand you as an immoral and corrupt woman, and then being forced to live in exile. At the same time, imagine that you are a heroine to many young women, who see you as inspirational in their quest for equal rights and opportunities to play sports. This was the situation faced by Hassiba Boulmerka, the gold medalist in the 1500 meters at the 1992 Olympic Games in Barcelona, Spain. As an Algerian Muslim woman, she believed that being an international athlete did not require her to abandon her faith or her commitment to Islam. But those who condemned Boulmerka said that although it is permissible for women to participate in sports, it was not permissible to do so in shorts or T-shirts, or while men are watching, or when men and women train together, or when facilities do not permit total privacy or if you are married, unless your husband gives his permission (Beiruty, 2002). What do you think are the dilemmas that Islamic women face in participating in sports?

More to Know

The overlap of religion and sports leaves ample room for controversy, and the history of sports is peppered with many eventful occurrences of religious quandaries.

Sandy Koufax

Nicknamed "The Left Arm of God," Koufax is a Hall of Fame pitcher who played for the Brooklyn (later Los Angeles) Dodgers for the entire duration of his career from 1955 to 1966. In 1965, Koufax, devout in his Jewish faith, caused a stir when he refused to pitch in Game 1 of the World Series against the Minnesota Twins because it fell on Yom Kippur, the holiest day of the year for Jewish people. The Dodgers lost the game 8-2. Koufax returned to pitch in Game 2, which the Dodgers lost, but Los Angeles stretched the Series out to a seventh game, and Koufax took the mound on just two days' rest and threw a three-hit shutout to clinch the Series. Koufax is widely recognized by the Jewish community as a hero for putting his beliefs before his career. President Obama even acknowledged him at the White House's 2010 celebration of Jewish American Heritage month.

Muhammad Ali

Originally known as Cassius Clay, the iconic boxer changed his name after joining the Nation of Islam in 1964, and later converting to Sunni Islam in 1975. During that time, Ali sparked outrage by speaking out against integration of blacks and whites among other controversial topics such as the Vietnam War. Ali gained further notoriety when he refused to enlist after being drafted for the war, citing that it was against his beliefs. He was later charged and convicted of draft evasion and stripped of his boxing titles and license in 1967. The conviction was eventually overturned in 1971 and Ali went on to become the only boxer to be named three-time World Heavyweight Champion by *The Ring* Magazine, World Boxing Council and World Boxing Association. Once considered a controversial athlete, Ali became one of boxing's most renowned fighters and is regarded as an inspiration by many.

Mahmoud Abdul-Rauf

Born Chris Wayne Jackson, Abdul-Rauf was a point guard in the NBA from 1990-2001. He was drafted by the Denver Nuggets in 1990 and converted to Islam a year later. He caused controversy when he began protesting the playing of "The Star-Spangled Banner" before games during the 1995-96 season. After refusing to stand for the song, claiming it was a sign of nationalistic worship that went against his beliefs, Abdul-Rauf was suspended by the league in March 1996. His actions sparked negative attention from fans and fellow athletes, even fellow Muslims. Abdul-Rauf, however, claimed that he was simply exercising his rights of freedom of speech and religion.

Expert's View

Sociologist Steven Overman claims that the Protestant ethic has emphasized a combination of the following seven key virtues in his book *The Influence of the Protestant Ethic on Sport and Recreation* (1997).

1. *Worldly asceticism* — the ideas that suffering and the endurance of pain has a spiritual purpose, that goodness is linked with self-denial and a disdain for self-indulgence, and that spiritual redemption is achieved only through self-control and self-discipline.

2. *Rationalization* — the idea that truth can be discovered through human reason, and that virtue is expressed through efficiency and measurable achievements.

3. *Goal directedness* — the idea that spiritual salvation and the spiritual worth of human action depend on achievement and success.

4. *Individualism* — the ideas that salvation is a matter of individual responsibility, initiative, and choice, and that people control their spiritual destiny by accepting a personal relationship with God/Christ.

5. *Achieved status* — the idea that worldly success is associated with goodness and salvation, whereas failure is associated with sin and damnation.

6. *The work ethic* — the ideas that work is a calling from God and that people honor God by working hard and developing their "God-given potential" through work.

7. *The time ethic* — the ideas that time has a moral quality and that wasting time is sinful and a sign of weak moral character.

Activity Time-Out

The images are everywhere: players pointing skyward after scoring touchdowns, teams gathering for prayer, and coaches praising God following victories. Religion has always been a part of the sports world, and its presence today is hard to ignore. Sometimes religion will cause a disruption in sports, though not often. We usually overlook connections between athletes and their faith, until someone sacrifices one to give priority to the other. Discuss in groups of four the following questions:

When sports and religion collide, which will prevail? Religious rituals and traditions or athletic opportunities?

Sports in Focus

Wrestling is a combat sport (格斗运动) involving grappling techniques (抓手摔技法) such as clinch fighting (扭住对手), throws (摔) and takedowns (摔倒), joint locks (锁关节), pins (压倒对手双肩着地) and other grappling holds (抓手擒拿). A wrestling bout (一场比赛) is a physical competition, between two (occasionally more) competitors or sparring partners (陪练), who attempt to gain and maintain a superior position. There are a wide range of styles with varying rules with both traditional historic and modern styles. Wrestling techniques have been incorporated into other martial arts as well as military hand-to-hand combat (近身格斗) systems.

Wrestling had been contested at the Summer Olympic Games since the sport was introduced in the ancient Olympic Games in 708 BC. When the modern Olympic Games resumed in Athens in 1896, wrestling (in the form of Greco-Roman wrestling (古典式摔跤)) became a focus of the Games, with the exception of the 1900 Summer Olympics when wrestling did not appear on the program. Freestyle wrestling (自由式摔跤) and weight classes (体重级别) both made their first appearance in 1904. The women's competition was introduced in 2004. In February 2013, the IOC voted to remove the sport from the 2020 Summer Olympics onwards. On 8 September 2013, the IOC announced that wrestling would return to the Summer Olympics in 2020. Along with boxing, it is one of only two sports that still require participants to have amateur status to participate in the Olympics.

In Greco-Roman wrestling, the wrestlers use only their arms and upper bodies to attack, and can only hold those same parts of their opponents. As the name suggests, freestyle is a much more open form in which wrestlers also use their legs and may hold opponents above or below the waist. Other wrestling styles include: Collegiate-style (学院式摔跤), which is specific to North America; Chinese wrestling (中国式摔跤); Mongol wrestling (蒙古式摔跤), which is also called "boke (博克)"; Sombo (桑博) and Judo (柔道), etc. There are two ways to win a wrestling match — to pin an opponent or win on technical points. Pinning the opponent's shoulder blades (肩胛) to the mat (垫子) for long as it takes the referee (场上裁判员) to say "tomber (有)" and get confirmation from another judge (侧面裁判员) is one way to win. If a match is not ended by a pin, it is decided by points.

Relevant Words

hammerlock	leg grapevine	fall
near pin	slam	escape position

Text B

Baseball as a Cultural Religion

1 Talcott Parsons, an American sociologist, defined religion "as a set of beliefs, practices, and institutions which men have evolved in various societies, as far as they can be understood, as responses to those aspects of their life and situation which are believed not in the empirical-instrumental sense to be rationally understandable and/or controllable, and to which they attach a significance which includes some kind of reference to the relevant actions and events to man's conception of the existence of the 'supernatural' order which is conceived and felt to have a fundamental bearing on man's position in the universe and the values which give meaning to his fate as an individual and his relations to his fellows". This definition of religion focused on three important elements: beliefs, practices, and institutions. Representing a form of cultural religion in the United States, baseball must include those three elements.

Beliefs

2 Perhaps the most important element of religion is that of belief. Establishing an element of belief in sports, and baseball in particular, is among the most difficult of the linkages to establish.

3 "Sports are religious in the sense that they are organized institutions, disciplines, and liturgies[1]; and also in the sense that they teach religious qualities of heart and soul," writes Michael Novak. In the most literal of ways, words like sacred, devotion, faith, ritual, immortality, and love, which figure prominently in the structure of belief in religion, are also among those found in the language of the national pastime. Harry Edwards, a former sociology professor at the University of California, once identified thirteen other areas where there is overlap as well. They include:

- Sport also has its "saints", or heroes.
- Sport also has its ruling patriarchs[2], or historical leaders.
- Sport has its "gods" — superstar athletes who have great influence over the masses of fans.
- Sport has its high councils who make and interpret the rules of sports involvement.
- Sport has its scribes[3] — the hundreds of sports reports, sports telecasters, and sports broadcasters.

[1]liturgy /'lɪtədʒɪ/ *n.* (a particular set of) the words, music and actions used in ceremonies in some religions, especially Christianity
[2]patriarch /'peɪtrɪɑːk/ *n.* a bishop in particular Eastern Christian churches
[3]scribe /skraɪb/ *n.* informal terms for journalists

- Sport has its "symbols of faith" — trophies; game balls, the bats, gloves, baseballs, and so forth that 'won' this or that game; the clothing, shoes, headgear or socks of immortal personages[4] of sports.
- Sport has its true believers, devotees, and converts[5].

Still, all of these are all literal objects. For these elements to reach a religious level, the followers must believe in the importance of their existence.

4 What these similarities prove, according to Novak, is that "sports are organized and dramatized in a religious way. Baseball claims the devotion, allegiance, indeed fanaticism[6] of millions of persons and it serves as a center of meaning and hope for many players and fans who look to its order to provide a semblance[7] of significance and order in their perhaps otherwise mundane[8], unfocused, or disorganized lives". Seemingly, if an individual believes in the power of baseball, it can develop into a religious devotion.

Practices

5 The practices — or rituals — that make up the game are the second critical element to any understanding of baseball as a form of cultural religion. Religions are organized and structured. Customs develop. Actions are highly formalized. Right ways and wrong ways are plainly marked out; acceptable behaviors are distinguished from unacceptable ones. Baseball has all of the same elements.

6 The game of baseball is perhaps the most structured of all the professional sports. Everything from the core rules of baseball to the exact makeup of the baseball, are all clearly prescribed in the rules of the game. Uniforms for example are monitored by the league and conform to a single design, differing only in color so as to designate[9] city as well as home and away team. Even the breaks become central components in the action — the number of warm-up tosses allowed by a pitcher, the distance a player may move around home plate before being considered out of the batter's box, etc.

7 In short, humans need organizing belief systems, rituals, and places to come together in large

[4]personage /'pɜːsənɪdʒ/ *n.* an important or famous person
[5]convert /kən'vɜːt/ *n.* someone who has changed their religious or political beliefs
[6]fanaticism /fə'nætɪsɪzəm/ *n.* fanatical behavior or the quality of being fanatical
[7]semblance /'sembləns/ *n.* a situation or condition which is similar to what is wanted or expected, but is not exactly as hoped for
[8]mundane /'man'deɪn/ *adj.* very ordinary and therefore not interesting
[9]designate /'dezɪgneɪt/ *adj.* appointed but not yet installed in office

groups for purposes of finding safety, security, and meaning. Baseball and more traditional religions help fill that need.

Institutions

8 In addition to the rules and rituals of the game, the institutions that comprise the game of baseball help qualify the game as a form of cultural religion. In particular, the offices of Major League Baseball which govern the play of the game; the Hall of Fame and similar institutions that recognize that game's history; and the fans and followers that support the teams and the players, provide that element to the sport.

9 The body that governs major league baseball around the world, just like the highest authorities of a religious group, sets the rules, sanctions the playing of games, and awards the winners for their successes. Within each league are individual teams, which represent different congregations. Each has its own stadium or ballpark (house of worship), a unique color of uniform (vestment), and collection of supporters (devoted followers). While still adhering to the rules prescribed by the highest authorities, they do whatever it takes to represent their respective communities and win on their own.

10 Fans show their favorite players respect and support by elevating them to a higher level of recognition. And when their careers come to an end, players' achievements are recognized with records and remembered in baseball's shrines[10]. The thousands of trophy rooms and cases gracing practically every team's headquarters and, of course, the Hall of Fame in Cooperstown, New York, represents the game's most sacred of spaces.

11 What makes baseball most similar to religion, though, is the devotion shown by its fans, the game's congregation if you will. Michael Novak explains that, "in sports cities around the nation, millions of lives are affected by whether in the days of their youth they were privileged to cheer for winners or, good-naturedly, groaningly, grew up with perennial[11] losers". This is a feeling shared by Doris Kearns Goodwin, who writes in her memoirs that, "a sense of camaraderie[12] grew among Dodger fans that made the experience of going to Ebbets Field unforgettable". Later, she explains she "felt part of the invisible community of Dodger fans, linked by shared emotions and experience

[10]shrine /ʃraɪn/ *n.* a place for worship which is holy because of a connection with a holy person or object

[11]perennial /pəˈrenɪəl/ *adj.* lasting a very long time, or happening repeatedly or all the time

[12]camaraderie /ˌkæməˈrɑːdərɪ/ *n.* a feeling of friendliness towards people that you work or share an experience with

to thousands of strangers who, for a few hours, were not strangers at all". Though it is a fictional account, W.P. Kinsella's novel *Shoeless Joe,* offered a similar analogy. Ray, the story's protagonist[13] remarked about the character of the baseball crowd and the virtues of the sport: "We're not just ordinary people, we're a congregation. Baseball is a ceremony, a ritual, as surely as sacrificing a goat beneath a full moon is a ritual. The only difference is that most of us realized that it is a game".

12 For Kearns Goodwin and many others, baseball was not just a spectator sport; it was a crucial catalyst for important life lessons. As Kearns Goodwin explains, through baseball, she discovered the power of a well-told story and the virtue of losing gracefully. Baseball highlighted both the ugliness of racism and the beauty of camaraderie and sportsmanship. And on one unforgettable October afternoon in 1955, when the Dodgers finally captured a World Championship (after years of disappointment), baseball revealed to twelve-year-old Doris Kearns the simple, sweet thrill of a long-awaited victory. Those lessons, she claims, still influence her way of thinking. For Billy Crystal, a longtime baseball fan, "... Baseball fanatics often use the sport to supply the sacred family experiences that religion once provided. Instead of a bar mitzvah[14] or confirmation, seeing Mickey Mantle bat or playing catch with Dad became the seminal[15] experiences of life."

Ballparks as American Sacred Space

13 "Players, managers, broadcasters, memories. All are essential to baseball... and so too are distinctive ballparks." These words by famed sportscaster Bob Costas in the foreword to Curt Smith's Storied Stadiums, makes it clear that the discussion about baseball as a form of religion is not complete without an investigation of the game's sacred spaces. Among the defining characteristics of religious organizations are the churches, synagogues[16], mosques[17], and similar gathering places, which serve as a place for worship and a sacred space. In baseball, stadiums and ballparks serve as "houses of worship spread across the land where millions of congregates come to bear witness to the manifestation of their faith".

14 A ballpark or stadium, as the field on which the game is played, is a site for repeated gath-

[13]protagonist /prə'tægənɪst/*n.* the principal character in a work of fiction
[14]mitzvah /'mɪtsvə/ *n.* a commandment or percept, especially one found in the Bible
[15]seminal /'semɪnəl/ *adj.* containing important new ideas and having a great influence on later work
[16]synagogue /'sɪnəgɒg/ *n.* a building in which Jewish people worship and study their religion
[17]mosque /mɒsk/ *n.* a building for Islamic religious activities and worship

erings of spiritual significance, a place of worship; a cathedral of sorts. The cathedral metaphor for ballparks appears in *Shoeless Joe* as well. The story follows Ray Kinsella, who plows under a field of Iowa corn to build a baseball diamond. During a late-night visit to Metropolitan Stadium in Minneapolis, Ray queries his traveling companions, J.D. Salinger and Archie "Moonlight" Graham, "have either of you spent any time in an empty ballpark? There's something both eerie[18] and holy about it... A ballpark at night is more like a church than a church". Philip Lowry, agrees, writing in the introduction to his celebration of 273 ballparks in the Major Leagues and former Negro Leagues, entitled Green Cathedrals, that "the more I studied (ballparks and stadiums), the more they have begun to resemble mosques, or synagogues, or churches, or similar such places of reverent[19] worship."

15 Ballparks and stadiums offer a connection to the spirit of the past for many fans. It is a place, after all, where the past always shadows the present and where public events melt into our memories, tagging our lifelines with pay-attention-to-this-asterisks. Peter Carino writes that ballparks promise "a spiritual solace[20] that balances the urban and pastoral, links the present and past, and provides a place for a transcendent celebration of cultural identity in the temporary innocence of leisure." In both regards, ballparks and stadiums become sacred sites where memories of the game's most heroic moments and the individuals who perpetrated them, take tangible shape. For fans, it is a place where they can find sanctuary[21] for their spirits.

Conclusion

16 Clearly, sports, and baseball in particular, meet the criteria for cultural religion in America. But the question remains, can sports and baseball in particular, substitute for "religious" ritual in the public realm?

17 A wide variety of columnists, academics, and fans have considered this question. Frank Deford was among the first to identify the kind of religious power that sports exerts on modern Americans. Adapting the critique of Karl Marx, Deford suggested that, if Marx had lived at the end of the twentieth century in the United States rather than in Victorian England, he would have declared that

[18]eerie /'ɪərɪ/ *adj.* strange in a frightening and mysterious way
[19]reverent /'revərənt/ *adj.* showing great respect and admiration
[20]solace /'sɒlɪs/ *n.* help and comfort when you are feeling sad or worried
[21]sanctuary /'sæŋktjʊərɪ/ *n.* protection or a safe place, especially for someone or something being chased or hunted

sports is the opiate of the people, anesthetizing[22] them to the struggles of the classes and focusing their hopes on events that project fulfillment through a vicarious form of participation and through an often delayed form of gratification.

18 But how can baseball satisfy the role that religious traditions once did? Baseball serves as a religious experience because it represents the everyday comfort, guidance, and even entertainment that religion has traditionally provided.

19 In 21st Century America, baseball indeed fulfills the definition of religion as a system of beliefs and practices by which a group of people struggles with the ultimate problems of human life. Religion does not have clear-cut physical properties, nor are its characters readily ascertained and agreed upon. But the game of baseball does, and it serves as a public reflection of, and a catalyst for, the evolution of American culture and society. People look to baseball for entertainment, a sense of community, a sense of structure, and to live out their dreams. They look to baseball to satisfy the role that traditional religion has played in their lives. Play Ball!

Total words: 1967
Total reading time: __________minutes_________seconds

* *The text is based on Gospel on the Mound: Our National Pastime and the Culture of Religion by Brian Reich*

Comprehension Check

1. According to the passage, how can features of sports develop into a religious devotion?
2. What does "congregation" in paragraph 9 mean? Does it hold the same sense with the word in paragraph 11?
3. How do you understand "A ballpark at night is more like a church than a church." in paragraph 14?
4. The last paragraph says, "baseball indeed fulfills the definition of religion as a system of beliefs and practices by which a group of people struggles with the ultimate problems of human life." What do you think of this statement? Does it make sense, in your opinion? Do you think it is exaggerated?
5. The author makes some interesting points about how baseball can be like a religion in a lot of ways. Can you list the ways baseball is NOT like a religion?

[22]anesthetize /æ'ni:sθətaɪz/ *vt.* to make unconscious by means of anesthetic drugs

Pop Culture

Based on a true story, ***Chariots of Fire*** is the internationally acclaimed Oscar-winning drama of two very different men who compete as runners in the 1924 Paris Olympics. Eric Liddell (Ian Charleson), a serious Christian Scotsman, believes that he has to succeed as a testament to his undying religious faith. Harold Abrahams (Ben Cross), is a Jewish Englishman who wants desperately to be accepted and prove to the world that Jews are not inferior. The film crosscuts between each man's life as he trains for the competition, fueled by these very different desires. As compelling as the racing scenes are, it's really the depth of the two main characters that touches the viewer, as they forcefully drive home the theme that victory attained through devotion, commitment, integrity, and sacrifice is the most admirable feat that one can achieve. This powerful film ended up with four Academy Awards: Best Picture, Best Original Screenplay, Best Costume Design, and Best Original Score.

Facing The Giants is the heart-warming story of a downtrodden Christian high school football coach who turns to God when everything seems to be going against him. Trusting God to do the impossible, Coach Grant Taylor and his Shiloh Christian Eagles soon discover how faith plays out on and off the field. When faced with unbelievable odds, the Eagles must step up to their greatest test of strength and courage. What transpires is a dynamic story of the fight between faith and fear.

Vocabulary Building

Look up the following words and expressions in reference books and on the Internet.

Words and Expressions	Meaning
autonomy	
isolation	
protestant	
ideology	

8

UNIT

Language of Sport

An area of human activity that arouses great passions in both participants and spectators is sport, so it is not surprising that this field should have given rise to a rich variety of terms and expressions..

— Elizabeth Potter, lexicographer

Pre-reading Thoughts

1. What kind of sports jargon are you familiar with?

2. Why do you think American baseball language is so common even in international business?

3. If someone uses sports jargon but you don't know what it means, how would you react?

Text A

Do Foreign Executives Balk at Sports Jargon?

1 English may be the international language of business, but foreign executives who are fluent in it find themselves at a loss unless they also master conversational horsehide and the vocabulary of other U.S. sports.

2 Major League Baseball begins Sunday, but in the global world of business the sun never seems to set on the USA's boys of summer. Executives from Qingdao to São Paulo must know what it means to "make a pitch," and if they don't know what it takes to develop a "home-run" product, they had better know how to "manufacture runs". Huh? Business is so rife with the jargon that it makes foreigners wonder what Americans are smoking when they throw around baseball in a business context, like "throwing smoke." Even American women knock around phrases such as "stepping up to the plate" like it's a game of "pepper." It's up to foreigners to "steal the signs" or risk moving

from the "catbird seat" and into the "peanut gallery." From there, they could attempt a "Hail Mary pass," but now the conversation requires a working knowledge of football—American football.

3 The Hail Mary doesn't make sense anywhere that isn't football mad. You can establish your American centricity and risk a religious offense at the same time.

4 United Kingdom native Paul Roscoe is president of Sentillion, a technology company near Boston. He has lived in the USA for eight years, long enough to develop a taste for Red Sox and Patriots games, and he understands what others at his company mean when they say "red-zone selling," because in football the stakes get higher when a team gets inside the opponent's 20-yard line. In business the stakes get higher when a sale is about to close.

5 Arrow Electronics is a *Fortune* 500 company in Melville, N.Y., that does business in 53 countries. CEO William Mitchell remembers wanting to change the agenda at a global leadership meeting in Fiuggi, Italy. He stood up and announced, "I'm calling an audible." Americans understood. "The Europeans hadn't a clue," Mitchell says.

6 The list of sports jargon seems endless. Nicola Sanna, the Italian CEO of American software company Netuitive, has a Ph.D. in economics and is fluent in English, French, German, Italian and Spanish. But he had to learn the terminology of golf to know that "we're under par" meant the company was exceeding its target, even though it sounds quite the opposite. There is plenty of golf played in Europe, but only Americans seem to speak it in a business context.

"Jump-ball Scenario"

7 Alan Guarino, CEO of executive recruiting firm Cornell International, offers a basketball anecdote. He was meeting with executives of an Indian company in London when one of his colleagues tried to talk the Indians out of a clause in a contract by insisting on a "jump-ball scenario" where neither side would stand to gain an unfair advantage.

8 "We talked about this for 10 minutes, when one of the executives from India says, 'I'm not quite clear what you mean by the jumping ball,' " Guarino says.

9 So pervasive is the use of U.S. sports in a business context that Australian Barry Thomas, an executive at Cook Medical, the American maker of health care devices, assumes that "the whole

nine yards" is about football, though he wonders why it isn't the whole 10 yards. An Internet search indicates that the origin of the saying probably has nothing to do with football, but the theories of where it does come from range from the contents of a concrete truck to the amount of material in a kilt to the length of a machine-gun ammo belt.

10 DaimlerChrysler appears destined to break up nine years after their merger. No one is suggesting baseball has anything to do with it. But when those from Stuttgart mix with the Tiger fans of Detroit, a baseball influence is not out of the question.

11 Dieter Zetsche, CEO of DaimlerChrysler, is a German born in Istanbul who is fluent in English. When he came to USA TODAY in 2004 for a wide-ranging interview, a reporter warned Zetsche that he was about to get a question "from left field." Zetsche paused, then responded in his dry, Henry Kissinger accent: "That's OK, as long as you don't throw me a curve ball."

12 If you really want to confuse, toss Yogi-isms—amusing quotes from former New York Yankee Yogi Berra—into the mix. Yogi-isms are legend in U.S. business circles but will make a foreigner's head spin. Examples of Yogi-isms are: "When you get to a fork in the road, take it," and "Ninety percent of the game is half mental."

Yogi Berra at 90

13 Pace Micro Technology has offices in the U.K., the USA, Hong Kong, Germany and France. But more than half of the company's sales are to U.S. customers, perhaps due in part to its advertising slogan, "Bringing Technology Home," the brainchild of British CEO Neil Gaydon after he had spent five years in the USA. How did Gaydon come up with the slogan, which is a double entendre to the baseball literate? He's not really sure, but were he to say that the idea came from "out

of left field," Americans would understand.

14 However, even baseball fans aren't sure why "out of left field" is a synonym for something off-the-wall. Internet sites suggest that it could be that in many ballparks the left field wall is deeper and more remote than in right field. Or, it could be because there used to be a mental hospital beyond the third-base side at Chicago's old West Side Park. Some suggest that it refers to the left field seats at Yankee Stadium, where fans sat a bit miffed because Babe Ruth played in right.

Ruth in his New York Yankees uniform, in 1920

15 Whatever the origin, there is no European equivalent nor is there a sports term that helps Europeans understand "manufacturing a run." However, some baseball terms have international synonyms. For example, a "googly" is not a search engine, but a bowl (pitch) in cricket that bounces in front of the batter's feet. Now, American executives might see this as an opportunity for the batter to "take one for the team," but the cricket batter must defend the wicket at all costs and, therefore, swing at balls that baseball players would let go. Americans, therefore, who hear the word googly at a business meeting can translate it into a curve ball.

"In the Bleachers"

16 Lock has lived in Germany and Japan in addition to his native U.K. During the 1990s, he was CEO of Triumph Motorcycles USA in Atlanta, so he spent enough time watching the Braves to become baseball literate. That helped him to understand what it meant when Triumph sales agents who worked in remote parts of the USA were said to be "in the bleachers," terminology Europeans don't comprehend, he says.

17 Similarly, few Americans understand that an "own goal" is kicking or deflecting the ball into your own net in soccer and is commonly used in European business for messing up due to no fault but your own. Latin American business discussions can include the phrase "*parar la pelota*," or "to stop the ball," which means to pause and assess before deciding the next move.

18 Roscoe says he has wasted 45 minutes in meetings trying to explain "sticky wicket" and other cricket terms such as "hitting a six" to confused Americans. "They will never get the rules of cricket. You have to be born and bred," Lock says.

19 How do American executives react when confronted with foreign sports terminology they don't understand? Wright says he learned to pretend he understood when the British tossed around terms like "the pit," which refers to rugby. He says he had 1,500 people working for him who might lose confidence if he seemed confused, "So I figured the best thing to do was to nod and move on."

"All the Bases Covered"

20 Johan Eliasch, the Dutch CEO of Amsterdam-based ski-maker Head, says sports jargon is universal to business because both feed on competition. But Roman Stanek, founder of Web services company Systinet, who was raised in the Czech Republic, says he searched the local Czech Internet sites and talked to friends, yet couldn't come up with an example of Czech sports jargon used in business. Stanek says Czechs enjoy sports such as soccer but never discuss it at the office. He says you're more likely to hear "home run" at a Czech business meeting because of the influence of American movies.

21 The Japanese would know what "all the bases covered" means in baseball, but they don't seem to be able to translate it into business.

22 Baseball hasn't caught on in the U.K., but baseball jargon is increasingly understood because of the airing of U.S. TV shows such as *Friends* and *Desperate Housewives*.

Total words: 1470
Total reading time: __________minutes__________seconds

* *The text is based on Do Foreign Executives Balk at Sports Jargon? By Del Jones*

Vocabulary and Expressions

balk /bɔːk/ *vi.* to not want to or refuse to do something that is difficult, or frightening

jargon /'dʒɑːgən/ *n.* special words and phrases which are used by particular groups of people, especially in their work

rife /raɪf/ *adj.* **rife with sth** full of something unpleasant

scenario /sɪ'nɑːrɪəʊ/ *n.* a situation that could possibly happen but has not happened yet

recruit /rɪ'kruːt/ *vt.* to persuade someone to work for a company or become a new member of an organization, especially the army

kilt /kɪlt/ *n.* a skirt with many folds, made from tartancloth and traditionally worn by Scottish men and boys

ammo /'æməʊ/ *n. informal* (=**ammunition**) objects that can be shot from a weapon such as bullets or bombs

toss /tɒs/ *vt.* to throw something, especially something light, with a quick gentle movement of your hand

double entendre /ˌduːblɑːn'tɑːndrə/ *n.* a word or phrase that might be understood in two ways, one of which is usually sexual

literate /'lɪtərət/ *adj.* having knowledge of a particular subject, or a particular type of knowledge

off-the-wall *adj. informal* a little strange or unusual

miffed /mɪft/ *adj.* slightly annoyed or upset

wicket /'wɪkɪt/ *n.* in cricket, a set of three vertical sticks with two small pieces of wood balanced across the top of them, at which the ball is aimed. There are two wickets on a cricket field.

deflect /dɪ'flekt/ *vt.* to cause to change direction

Comprehension Check

1. According to the passage, what is the perceived relationship between sports and business?
2. Why should a businessman learn sports language?
3. How do you understand "home run" in line 3 of paragraph 2?
4. Why is "googly" in line 3 of paragraph 15 a negative term in American business language?
5. Why does American sports language seem to be more common in business language?

Critical Thinking Starters

1. What sports language do you use in your daily life? Give some examples.
2. What are the popular sports that have added idioms to the modern language in China? What kind of language comes from those sports?
3. Jargon bears the cultural imprints characteristic of the country or region, so it differs from culture to culture. How can you learn to understand sports jargon from other cultures?
4. What should you do if you use sports language but you see that your friend doesn't know what you mean?

More to Know

Lawrence Peter "Yogi" Berra is a retired American Major League Baseball (MLB) catcher, manager, and coach. He played almost his entire 19-year baseball career (1946–65) for the New York Yankees. He is widely regarded as one of the best catchers in baseball history. He was elected to the Baseball Hall of Fame in 1972.

Berra, who quit school after the eighth grade, was also known for his pithy and paradoxical quotes, such as "It ain't over 'til it's over", while speaking to reporters. Simultaneously denying and confirming his reputation, Berra once stated, "I really didn't say everything I said."

Berra is also well known for his pithy comments and witticisms, known as **Yogiisms**. Yogiisms very often take the form of either an apparently obvious tautology or a paradoxical contradiction.

Examples

- As a general comment on baseball: "90% of the game is half-mental."
- On why he no longer went to Ruggeri's, a St. Louis restaurant: "Nobody goes there anymore. It's too crowded."
- "It ain't over till it's over." In July 1973, Berra's Mets trailed the Chicago Cubs by 9½ games in the National League East. The Mets rallied to win the division title on the final day of the season.
- When giving directions to Joe Garagiola to his New Jersey home, which was accessible by

two routes: "When you come to a fork in the road, take it."

- On being the guest of honor at an awards banquet: "Thank you for making this day necessary."
- "You can observe a lot by watching."
- "Always go to other people's funerals, otherwise they won't go to yours."
- His stock answer to a writer's cruel nickname, "The Ape": "It doesn't matter if you're ugly in this racket. All you have to do is hit the ball, and I never saw anyone hit with his face."

Berra appeared as himself in an AFLAC commercial. In a barber shop, he told another customer, "They give you cash, which is just as good as money," a reference to his "Yogiisms."

Sports in Focus

Boxing is one of the most popular games, especially in Europe and the Americas. It was earlier known by the name Pugilism, meaning sweet science. The game evolved from 16th- and 18th-century prize-fights（酬金拳击赛）, largely in Great Britain, to the forerunner of modern boxing in the mid-19th century, again initially in Great Britain and later in the United States. We have three world-acclaimed boxing organizations today—the World Boxing Council (WBC), International Boxing Federation (IBF) and the World Boxing Association (WBA). The International Amateur Boxing Association was formed in 1946 and it is the first international body for amateur boxing.

Boxing is a martial art and combat sport（格斗项目）in which two people engage in a contest of strength, speed, reflexes, endurance and will, by throwing punches（击打）at each other, usually with gloved hands. Historically, the goals have been to weaken and knock down the opponent.

Amateur boxing became an Olympic sport in 1908. Olympic and other amateur bouts（场）are typically limited to three or four rounds（回合）, scoring is computed by points based on the number of clean blows landed, regardless of impact, and fighters wear protective headgear, reducing the number of injuries, knockdowns（击倒）, and knockouts（击倒获胜）. Professional boxing remains by far the most popular form of the sport globally, though amateur boxing is dominant in Cuba and some former Soviet republics. For most fighters, an amateur career, especially at the Olympics, serves to develop skills and gain experience in preparation for a professional career.

In amateur boxing competitors wear protective headgear and gloves with a white strip or circle across the knuckle（指关节）. A punch is considered a scoring punch only when the boxers connect with the white portion of the gloves. Each punch that lands cleanly on the head or torso（躯干）with sufficient force is awarded a point.

Professional bouts are usually much longer than amateur bouts, typically ranging from ten to twelve rounds, though four-round fights are common for less experienced fighters or club fighters. Headgear is not permitted in professional bouts, and boxers are generally allowed to take much more damage before a fight is halted. At any time, the referee may stop the contest if he believes that one participant cannot defend himself due to injury. In that case, the other participant is awarded a technical knockout win. A technical knockout would also be awarded if a fighter lands a punch that opens a cut on the opponent, and the opponent is later deemed not fit to continue by a doctor because of the cut. In contrast with amateur boxing, professional male boxers have to be bare-chested.

Relevant Words and Phrases

deadlock	hook	footwork
bob and weave	stance	uppercut

Text B

Why Does Boxing Give Us More Language for Our Lives Than Any Other Sport?

1 I've been boxing for a few years, but it was only recently that I began noticing that most of the sports metaphors I used or heard during the course of a regular week or month came from boxing.

2 You might think that is because I'm a boxer, that I'm attuned[1] to *those* expressions more than others.

3 But then I started trying to come up with everyday metaphors and idioms from other sports, and I found there was a notable imbalance. There seems to be far more boxing expressions than phrases drawn from any other sport.

4 I can think of a few idioms and metaphors from basketball (slam dunk, home court advantage), baseball (bring it home, major league, threw me a curve, struck out, hit one out of the park), golf (par for the course, below par), wrestling (no holds barred, take it to the mat), horse racing (neck and neck, by a nose, chomping at the bit, free reign, home stretch)...

5 But when it comes to boxing, there seems to be a much longer list.

6 **Why are there so many boxing expressions in our everyday language?** Why are so

[1]attuned /ə'tju:nd/ *adj.* familiar with the way someone thinks or behaves so that you can react to them in a suitable way

many phrases and common metaphors drawn from a sport that simply doesn't have the kind of widespread adoration that baseball, basketball, or soccer has? (Why can I come up with more *horse racing* metaphors than football metaphors?)

7 Is it because our lives are a fight? Because the world is a contentious[2] place filled with opposing forces? That doesn't seem to fit, since *most* sports are about opposing teams or players.

8 **There IS something gritty[3] and painful and dark about boxing that I just don't see in other sports.** Many famous fighters came up from the poorest, most dire situations. And boxing puts us in a gut-wrenching, heartbreaking, bone-crushing kind of place at times. It publicly exposes our bodies and our vulnerabilities. It requires both the basest human physical violence as well as a sharp mental acumen[4], along with truckloads of courage and heart.

9 It's more stripped down than football, more messy and violent than basketball, volleyball, or soccer.

10 **It is certainly filled with more extremes...** Boxing is both brutal and graceful, painful and glorious, terrible and triumphant; more so than any other sport I can think of.

11 I wanted to compile a list of common metaphors and expressions derived from boxing and explain them from a boxer's experience and viewpoint to affirm just how clear, common, and predominant these words and expressions are.

In Your Corner

12 The corner refers not only to the spot where you can stand or sit down and rest between rounds, but also the person who is in that spot taking care of you. When someone's in your corner, they're thinking, strategizing, cheering for, and supporting you.

13 A good corner (person) is critical in boxing because you need an outside perspective, someone thinking for you when you are too physically engaged to be able to work the mental game. A corner can call the shots for you (another metaphor you hear used in many sports), give you an idea

[2]contentious /kən'tenʃəs/ *adj.* causing a lot of argument and disagreement between people
[3]grit /grɪt/ *n. informal* determination and courage **gritty** /'grɪtɪ/ *adj.*
[4]acumen /'ækjʊmən/ *n.* the ability to think quickly and make good judgements

of your opponent's weaknesses, keep you on strategy, calm you down, and even take care of your injuries.

Down (or Out) for the Count

14 If you go to the canvas after a hard punch, you automatically get a 10-count from the referee. If you can't get back up and continue the fight, you're down for the count.

15 Related is "take a knee," which is from old-school boxing, where a fighter voluntarily goes to one knee to concede the fight. You don't hear that much in everyday language (although coaches might do it to call everyone into a huddle), but once in a while someone will take a knee to beg off doing something they really don't want to do, like attend a long graduation service or a family reunion.

Pull Your Punches[5]

16 When you are in an actual fight, you wouldn't not put your full weight, power, and reach behind a shot. But in sparring[6] and everyday boxing you don't necessarily want to punch with your full power. Training is different than competing, and if you hurt your training partner you won't have anyone to train with.

On the Ropes

17 There are some boxers who are awesome at fighting while pressed up against the ropes, but for the most part it's a position you don't want to find yourself pinned in.

18 Being on the ropes means your opponent is controlling the game, and they are keeping you in position and racking up points punching you relentlessly because you can't get away from them. It typically means you're tired, not thinking clearly, and your opponent is actively winning the fight.

Roll with the Punches

19 When I first started boxing I thought defense was all about completely *avoiding* being punched. In fact, a slip or roll is just a way to defuse some of the power of a shot that is most likely going to land. In other words, you're probably going to take the shot. But you don't want to take it full on, in all its power. Instead, you slip quickly an inch or two to the left or right, or roll under or

[5]punch /pʌntʃ/ *n.* a quick strong hit made with your fist (=closed hand)
[6]spar /spɑː/ *vi.* to practise boxing, without hitting hard

to the side.

20 It's how a sailor might walk on the deck of a ship that's pitching and yawing[7] in high seas; they aren't avoiding the swells, but rather moving in concert with them so that they aren't tossed to the deck.

Knockout[8]

21 Obvious, right? But by the sheer prevalence of usage I'd say it points to one of the reasons we viscerally[9] identify with boxing over other sports. It's about power, winning, and losing, and we connect it to sex, life, and death.

Take it on the Chin / Lead with Your Chin / Glass Jaw

22 In the ring, you keep a tight guard, or you slip and roll in order to *not* take punches to your face or chin. Of course you DO take shots to the nose, chin, jaw, cheek, ears, and forehead; it's part of the game.

23 But most people use the phrase to describe being brave in the face of adversity, or courageously taking the full brunt[10] of a bad situation.

24 In boxing, it's stupid to voluntarily take it on the chin—you can get your head snapped back, and you can be knocked out.

25 Related is "glass jaw," which is used to refer to someone easily knocked out when hit on the chin. Most boxers aren't going to go very far in the ring if they have one of these.

Toe to Toe / Infighting

26 In today's boxing, this is used to describe inside fighting, where your toes are likely to touch. Sometimes you even step on each other's feet when you're fighting close and inside.

[7]yaw /jɔː/ *vi. technical* if a ship, aircraft etc. yaws it makes a turn away from its proper course

[8]knockout /'nɒkaʊt/ *n.* an act of knocking your opponent down in boxing so that he cannot get up again

[9]visceral /'vɪsərəl/ *adj. literary* visceral beliefs and attitudes are the result of strong feelings rather than careful thought *viscerally adv.*

[10]brunt /brʌnt/ *n.* **take the brunt of sth** to receive the worst part of an attack, criticism etc.

27 It's NOT, however, standing squared up and face to face (which seems to be the common usage); that's just poor fighting position. You box with one foot forward and one to the rear, your lead shoulder in front. So you're slightly sideways to each other, and presenting the smallest possible target.

28 The only other time you'd be toe to toe with your opponent is when you greet each other at the start of the fight. The ref calls you in from the corners, you listen to your instructions and agree to the match, bang gloves and return to your corners to wait for the bell.

Square Off

29 Presumably this is derived from the shape of the modern boxing ring (which is a square, but we call it a ring because of how a circle forms around fighters). You wouldn't actually face an opponent "square on" or face to face in boxing today, as mentioned above.

Saved by the Bell

30 This was a boxing reference long before it was an internet hoax about people in the 1500s being buried with strings and bells to protect against being buried alive. Being saved by the bell does not necessarily mean you don't lose the fight, only that you get a few seconds' rest to try and recover to go another round if there is one. It might mean you narrowly avoid being knocked out if you took a bad shot and were about to go to the canvas or were being counted out when the bell rang.

Beat Them to the Punch

31 This is a beginner's fundamental strategy in the ring, and one of the main uses for a jab[11], the first punch you learn in boxing. A jab is primarily used to keep your opponent at bay or to interrupt their shots. Very effective, very basic, and part of the bread and butter of every boxer's work.

Low Blow

32 The thing you may not know about it is that in amateur boxing, you can't score from any shot below the waistband of your opponent's trunks. The reason is obvious.

33 And sometimes if a boxer is wearing the same color tank and shorts, the officials will re-

[11] jab /dʒæb/ *n.* a sudden hard push, especially with a pointed object or your fist (=closed hand)

quire them to wrap a band of athletic tape around their waists to mark the scoring boundary. This is why you'll see most boxing trunks with contrasting waistband colors.

Throw in the Towel

34 I read somewhere that this one used to be "throw in the sponge"—or at least, that was how a corner could end a fight and thus save damage when his or her boxer was clearly losing. These days we use towels, of course.

35 It's not all that uncommon in amateur boxing (although it's more likely that you'll see a ref call off a fight), but I rarely see it in pro fights.

Keep Your Guard Up / Taken Off Guard

36 This is another fundamental of boxing, just as in life. When you see a boxer's gloves begin to drop below the chin, you're seeing a boxer who is tired and open for full-face shots. If you're in a boxing gym you're likely to hear the phrase "Gloves up!" repeatedly called by coaches. It's so important that many of our non-boxing-specific exercises—like squats, for example—are performed with our guard up, too.

Heavyweight / Lightweight

37 I find it interesting that weight categories are so standard and equal in boxing, but in life people only want to be heavyweights.

38 The only time you see issues of inequality in weight categories in boxing is during sparring, where you might find a featherweight working with a welterweight[12], or when a fighter who is naturally one weight class has cut or gained an enormous amount of weight to get into a different class.

Take a Dive

39 It sounds like a swimming phrase to me, but it comes from the boxing tactic of going to the canvas and intentionally losing a fight. Typically it's used when a boxer (illegally) loses for money. They threw the match by taking a dive.

[12]welterweight /'weltəweɪt/ *n.* a boxer who is heavier than a lightweight but lighter than a middleweight

In the Clinch[13]

40 This could originate from wrestling, I'm not sure. But in boxing, your performance in the clinch is critical because you get in one either to stop your opponent's flurry[14] of shots, or to rest while also leaning on and tiring your opponent.

41 Clinches happen all the time and are a basic part of every fighter's strategy, but they're technically illegal, and referees break them up pretty quickly because the object of the round is to fight, not rest.

Fight Until the Bell Rings / Go the Distance

42 I had to put this one last, for effect. Rocky taught the world about going the distance—all 15 rounds—in the ring with Apollo Creed; it wasn't about *beating* Creed, it was about finishing the fight. But boxers have been fighting to make it through their scheduled rounds since long before then, whether they were "bums from the neighborhood" or not.

Total words: 1980
Total reading time: __________minutes_________seconds

** The text is based on Why does Boxing Give Us More Language for Our Lives Than Any Other Sport? by Lisa Creech Bledsoe*

Comprehension Check

1. List and explain five idioms or expressions you have learned from watching English language sports programs.
2. Why is "lightweight" used as a negative expression in life?
3. What does "throw in the towel" mean in boxing and daily life?
4. How do you understand "keep your guard up" both as a boxing idiom and an everyday expression?

[13]clinch /klɪntʃ/ *n.* a situation in which two people hold each other's arms tightly, especially when they are fighting

[14]flurry /'flʌrɪ/ *n.* an occasion when there is suddenly a lot of activity within a short period of time

Activity Time-Out

Make a complete sentence out of sports idioms and recite to your partner. See if he or she understands what you mean. Example: *I really struck out in that exam and now I'm about ready to throw in the towel.* Then report the sentences of your group to the whole class.

Pop Culture

Rocky (1976) is a popular film. The character Rocky Balboa is a small-time boxer who seems to be going nowhere in life, as he works day-in and day-out as a collector for a loan shark and fights in sleazy clubs for low-paid reward, to which Rocky is mocked and told that he's nothing but a "bum", especially by gym trainer Mickey Goldmill. But when heavyweight champion of the world Apollo Creed chooses Rocky at random as his opponent in a title fight, Rocky realizes he now has the chance to prove he is not worthless and strives to go the distance for his self-respect.

When the match actually takes place, Apollo is in a jovial mood until Rocky knocks him down in the first round with a single uppercut, the first time Creed has ever been knocked down in his career. He then endures a gruelling 15-round fight with the game Balboa, who manages to get to his feet after Creed takes him down with an uppercut in the 14th round in what appears to be the end of the match. This was the first time anyone had ever taken the champion the full 15 rounds.

Both fighters are beaten, bloodied, and bruised by the end of the bout—Rocky with severe eye damage and Apollo with internal bleeding. Apollo gains a controversial split decision victory, and neither fighter wants a rematch, at least for that very moment...

Vocabulary Building

Look up the following words and expressions in reference books and on the Internet.

Words and Expressions	Meaning
semantic field	
circumlocution	
outgroup	
ingroup	

9
UNIT

Sports and Politics

To create national strength through sports training, and international harmony through sporting competition.

— Pierre de Coubertin

Pre-reading Thoughts

1. In what ways do you think sports can be related with politics? Do you think this relationship is beneficial to the development of sports?

2. Recall the opening ceremony of one mega sports event. Where were political elements seen? What would it be like without these political elements?

Text A

Government in Sports —Example: the United States

1 Many governments around the world have established ministries of sports which aggressively promote sport participation, financially support high-performance athletes who represent their country in international competition, and help fund public athletic facilities. No such agency exists in the United States. Instead, the U.S. Congress designated the United States Olympic Committee (USOC) to develop and conduct amateur sport and to train and support Olympic and Paralympic athletes.

Safeguarding the Public

2 The U.S. government helps provide safety for its citizens. Sports that are dangerous or involve cruelty to animals are outlawed or discouraged. Bullfighting, cockfighting, and other so-called sports that abuse animals are punishable by fines or imprisonment. Sports that are inherently

dangerous to participants, such as boxing, bungee jumping, skydiving, and auto racing, are carefully monitored and controlled by government regulations.

3 The U.S. government also regulates sports that may be reasonably safe within a controlled environment. Activities such as boating, fishing, hunting, using firearms, water sports, and bicycling have certain rules, require training for instructors and participants, and require certain protective equipment. The government also regulates outdoor activities that may affect the natural environment or endanger species. For example, the U.S. government regulates where, when, and how fishing can be done.

4 The U.S. government also strives to protect the public in sports when unruly fan behavior is a risk or when a terrorist attack threatens the staging of large events. For many Americans, the first wake-up call to terrorism in sport came in 1972 when a Palestinian terrorist group took Israeli athletes hostage during the Summer Olympics in Munich, Germany. After a daylong standoff and a failed rescue attempt, eleven Israeli athletes, one German police officer, and five of the eight kidnappers were killed. Nearly 25 years later, at the Atlanta Olympics, a bomb went off in the Olympic Park and killed two people while injuring over 100 others. Panic set in, events were suspended, and spectators feared for their safety. Ever since then, security plans have been a major priority.

Protecting the Rights of Citizens

5 The government can play a key role in protecting the rights of its citizens in sports. In 1972 the U.S. Congress passed Title IX, which declared that women and girls should have equal access to sport. In 1990, U.S. President George H.W. Bush signed the Americans with Disabilities Act (ADA), which protected the rights of athletes with physical or mental disabilities. Public facilities, including sport facilities, now meet certain standards to accommodate people with physical disabilities; and the USOC provides sport competition and training for athletes with physical disabilities. Other U.S. laws protect the rights of children through child labor laws and protect the rights of athletes to play as professionals and to represent a specific country. Some laws regulate performance-enhancing drugs in sport.

6 Civil rights acts decree that discrimination against persons of various racial, ethnic, and class preferences is illegal by governments who support regulated access to sport programs. Although private clubs continue to have some leeway in determining their membership, any public facility

or program must provide equal access for all persons. National governing bodies for specific sports are expected to develop policies that ensure equal access to all athletes. People who take issue with the conduct of any organization or facility can seek redress in a court of law and protection from discrimination based on race, creed, national origin, religious preference, or sexual orientation.

Protecting the Financial Interests of the Public

7 Sports are a huge economic engine in the United States, and the money wrapped up in sport affects every citizen either directly or indirectly. In the past, the U.S. government sometimes stepped in to direct and control the expansion of sports as they grew in power and significance. For example, in cities where proposals were advanced to use public monies to build stadiums or arenas that would benefit the owners of professional franchises, governments stymied the proposals or put them to a public vote.

8 Historically, laws have been passed exempting professional sport leagues from antitrust laws. Major League Baseball, the NFL, and the National Basketball Association have a virtual monopoly on their sports and wield tremendous influence over their athletes, ticket prices, television rights, and the sharing of revenue between teams and cities. The point to be taken here is that when government decides what is in the public interest, those who have economic power and influence are more likely to affect government decisions than those who have little power or influence. Also, owners of professional sport franchises are often able to further their business interests by claiming that their success will benefit the community and other local businesses such as hotels and restaurants.

9 Local governments often give huge tax incentives to owners of professional franchises in order to convince them to locate or keep their franchise in a certain city. When an owner loses money due to mismanagement, excessive player contracts, or changes in the economy, he may ask the city for a better tax deal or threaten to leave town for a more attractive financial package. For example, the Oakland Raiders football team relocated to Los Angeles in 1982 only to move back to Oakland in 1995 when they could not agree on a deal for a new stadium in Los Angeles. Oakland offered the team some $63 million in upfront incentives, loans, and other benefits to return.

Promoting Identity and Unity Among Citizens

10 Local, city, and state governments have long used sport to promote pride, identity, and unity among their citizens. By attracting a professional franchise, city leaders expect to capitalize on their financial investment by providing entertainment to residents and creating a bond among people of all backgrounds forged by a common interest in the home team.

11 For example, the performance of the local professional football team can be a hot news item on any given day. Strangers use the fortunes of their local team to break the ice in conversations with others. If the team performs beyond expectation, fans feel a little bit prouder to be a part of their city and just a bit better about life. In contrast, an entire populace can be cast into gloom due to a seemingly unimportant detail such as a flubbed field goal in the waning seconds of play.

12 Even very large metropolises such as New York, Chicago, and Los Angeles rally around their home team. In strikingly diverse race and ethnic groups, the city residents and suburban dwellers join to support their teams. Although most residents never actually see a professional game, they form strong opinions concerning the team's performance and learn the details through the print media, radio, and television. Team jerseys and hats appear throughout the city, and at every turn the team logo is displayed on billboards and auto stickers.

13 A particular type of fan support grows around pro teams that are cast in the image of their city and its historic ethnic groups. The Broad Street Bullies emanated from their rough-and-tumble approach to the game of ice hockey that resulted in a world championship. The pride of the City of Brotherly Love has been the Flyers, Iggles (Eagles), and Phillies. In this city dominated by ethnic enclaves of immigrants, fans are unique in their approach to sport, fanaticism, and impatience with their heroes. This is a city that cheered the triumph of Rocky on the steps of the Philadelphia Art Museum and booed Santa Claus at an Eagles game.

14 Special sporting events also can unify a city. Hosting the Super Bowl, the National Collegiate Athletic Association (NCAA) basketball play-offs, baseball's All-Star Game, the Olympic Games, the Pan American Games, various collegiate championships, and even youth national championships can draw communities together, uniting businesses, media, and fans. The economic benefits the host cities accrue often more than compensate for the expenses of staging the event. Local volunteers often spend long hours helping operate the event in exchange for perks such as ac-

cess to tickets.

15 A notable example of a city using sports to build an identity is Indianapolis, which labels itself the "amateur sports capital of the world." Through the entrepreneurial activities of a local sport commission, the city aggressively bids to host every imaginable amateur sport championship and has staged over 250 national and international sporting events. The city is also home to collegiate sports (NCAA) and high school sports (National Federation of State High School Associations) and the American College of Sports Medicine. A dozen national sport organizations have their national headquarters located in Indianapolis. The city's business community has been steadfastly supportive, and the financial bonanza to the city's economy has enabled the government to improve the downtown and add sports and recreation facilities that are the envy of similar cities.

16 Even smaller cities use sports to build unity. They may focus on a particular sporting event, on a local college, or even on the local high school. State universities located away from large metropolitan areas usually garner tremendous fan support because they have no competition from professional sport events or teams. In a state like Texas where fans take their high school football seriously, the local football team is a source of town pride.

Total words: 1523
Total reading time: __________minutes________seconds

**The text is based on Social Issues in Sports by John Wood*

Vocabulary and Expressions

standoff /'stændɒf/ *n.* a situation in which neither of two opposing groups or forces will make a move until the other one does something, so nothing can happen until one of them gives way

decree /dɪ'kriː/ *vt.* to officially decide or order that something must happen

leeway /'liːweɪ/ *n.* freedom to act within particular limits take issue with to disagree strongly

stymie /'staɪmɪ/ *vt.* to prevent something from happening or someone from achieving a purpose

upfront /'ʌpfrʌnt/ *adj.* speaking or behaving in a way that makes intentions and beliefs clear

flub / flʌb/ *vt.* to fail or make a mistake, especially when performing

rough-and-tumble /rʌfən'tʌmbl/ *adj.* characterized by disorderly action and disregard for rules

enclave /'enkleɪv/ *n.* a part of a country that is surrounded by another country, or a group of people who are different from the people living in the surrounding area

boo /buː/ *vt.* to make an expression of strong disapproval or disagreement

perk /pɜːk/ *n.* an incidental benefit awarded for certain types of employment (especially if it is regarded as a right)

bonanza /bə'nænzə/ *n.* a situation from which large profits are made

Comprehension Check

1. According to the passage, what are the situations in which sports are considered dangerous? What can be done to keep the public safe?
2. What rights can a citizen of the United States have in sports?
3. Why can professional sport leagues be exempted from antitrust laws?
4. What does "City of Brotherly Love" in paragraph 13 refer to? Why does the author mention it?
5. According to the passage, in what ways can the government fulfill certain purposes through sports?

Critical Thinking Starters

1. Why do you think there is no ministry of sports agency in the United States since much of sports can be tied to government?
2. Prior to the beginning of a game or sports event, it is not uncommon to see everyone stand up to listen to and/or sing the national anthem. Why do people do this and what does it mean within the world of sports? How would the atmosphere be different if there was no playing of the national anthem?

More to Know

Whatever the initial motivators for government involvement in sport, most countries in the world have some form of sport policy which include the following objectives:

Social cohesion

- health education focusing on certain values through physical education
- management of at-risk groups (e.g. young people)
- promotion of national unity

Economic development

- construction of sports facilities
- encouragement of private sponsorship
- position in international competition

Promotion of foreign policy

- diplomatic pressure (boycotts, etc.)
- bringing nations together and co-operation (e.g. Commonwealth Games)
- promotion of a country's international image

Social development, welfare and health

- promotion of sport as an instrument for promoting good health
- reduction in inequality of access to sports facilities
- promotion of equity (male/female, minority groups, etc.)

Activity Time-Out

On average, the President of the United States honors roughly seven championship teams each year with an invitation to visit the White House and celebrate their achievement. This has included high school teams, collegiate athletes, professional franchises, and even Olympic gold medalists, who relish the opportunity to visit with the nation's "number one fan." At the ceremony, the President offers a customary set of remarks about the coach, players, and organization and he is then presented with a #1 jersey from the team's primary representative.

Yet what would happen if a player decided to turn down the invitation of the President? Find one such case and discover why the player refused. Share your findings with the class.

Sports in Focus

Archery, one of the oldest sports still practiced, is closely linked to the development of civilization. As a cultural advance, it was comparable to the discovery of fire and the invention of the wheel.

In 1200 BC the Hittites and Assyrians shot their bows from chariots, becoming fearsome opponents in battle. They made their bows with tendon（腱）, horn and wood and also developed a new re-curved shape. This made their bows shorter and more powerful, making them easier to handle for an archer on horseback.

Archery was the favourite sport of the Egyptian pharaohs during the 18th dynasty (1567-1320 BC). Many centuries later, some of the earliest recorded archery tournaments took place during the Zhou dynasty (1027- 256 BC) in China. Such events were attended by Chinese nobility. Much later, English writers honoured the longbow（长弓） for famous contributions to their country's victories in the battles of Crécy, Agincourt and Poitiers.

Archery first appeared in the Olympic Games in 1900, was contested again in 1904, 1908 and 1920, then again, after an absence of 52 years, from 1972 to the present.

Competitive archery involves shooting arrows at a target for accuracy from a set distance or distances. The most popular form of competitive archery worldwide is called target archery（标靶射箭）.

There are five types of bow used in target archery: recurve（反曲弓）, compound（复合弓）, barebow（裸弓）, longbow and American flat bow（美式平板弓）.

There are also four main disciplines: target（室内射箭）(set rounds shot indoors in winter and outdoors during summer), field（野外射箭）(a combination of different targets and faces at different distances in mixed terrain and elevation), clout（地靶射箭）(where the target is marked out on the ground with a coloured flag; the arrows closest to the flag score the highest points) and flight（射远射箭）(where the archer tries for the furthest distance an arrow can travel).

Relevant Words and Phrases

armguard	chestguard	fletching
quiver	nock	stabiliser

Text B

Moving Beyond the Ping-Pong Table: Sports Diplomacy in the Modern Diplomatic Environment

1 Since antiquity, well aware of the reach and power of the opiate of the masses, governments have long been drawn toward sports and sporting festivals. Diplomacy, the conduct of relations between sovereign states with standing in world politics by official agents and by peaceful means, and sports have become increasingly compatible. Today sports diplomacy is associated with governments employing sportspeople to amplify a diplomatic message, or with states using sporting events to enhance their image among global publics, to cool tensions in flagging[1] diplomatic relationships, or simply to test the ground[2] for a possible policy change. Sports diplomacy transcends cultural differences and creates opportunities for alternate avenues for overcoming hostilities, offi-

[1]flagging /'flægɪŋ/ *adj.* becoming weaker
[2]ground /graʊnd/ *n.* a rational motive for a belief or action

cial dialogue and people-to-people relations, uniting separate nations through a love of sports. More specifically, sports diplomacy involves representative and diplomatic activities undertaken by sports people on the behalf of, and in conjunction with, their governments. The practice is facilitated by traditional diplomacy and uses sports people and sporting events to engage, inform and create a favourable image among foreign publics and organisations, and to shape their perceptions in a way that is conducive to the sending government's foreign policy goals. If traditional diplomacy is the means to a state's foreign policy ends[3], sports diplomacy is one of the means to the means of those ends.

2 More and more diplomatic institutions are turning toward sports. There are at least four reasons behind it. First, sports and sportspeople can amplify and complement a nation-state's diplomacy. Since the early 1970's, for example, China's re-emergence and acceptance into the international community has been closely linked to international sports. The most famous instance is of course the "ping heard around the world" where an opportune[4] series of matches between Chinese and American ping-pong players paved the way for the restoration of China's seat on the United Nations Security Council, Richard Nixon's visit to China in 1972, and the normalization of Sino-U. S. diplomatic relations. Since then, China has continued to develop a sporting prowess to match its economic rise, whether as host of the 2008 Beijing Olympics, or through its support of the basketball player Yao Ming as a global spokesperson and representative of Chinese culture, modernity, and progress. The U.S. State Department typifies a rallying call[5] "to aggressively use sports as a diplomatic tool" through several programs with American diplomatic partners that promote cultural awareness, discipline, teamwork, leadership, persistence, respect for rules and other players. The State Department regularly employs "Sports Ambassadors" such as figure skater Michelle Kwan and baseball star Cal Ripken Jr. to engage in sports diplomacy. As recently as August 26th 2012, a team of four professional basketball players and coaches visited Burma as part of a State Department sponsored program "to emphasize the importance of sports, cooperation and respect for diversity" and to conduct a number of workshops and sporting clinics. For governments, these sports diplomacy exchanges are an attractive means of promoting international understanding and friendship as well as dispelling stereotypes and prejudices. Not to mention they are also "low-risk, low-cost and high profile."

[3]end /end/ *n.* the purpose for which something is done or toward which you are working
[4]opportune /'ɒpətjuːn/ *adj.* happening at a time that is likely to produce success or is convenient
[5]rallying call /'rælɪŋ kɔːl/ something such as a word or phrase, an event, or a belief which encourages people to unite and to act in support of a particular group or idea

3 Second, sporting mega-events can offer the host nation significant public diplomacy opportunities. The right to host such an event is a confirmation of good international citizenship, and if the diplomatic posture, image and message is thoughtfully crafted and aligned to positive sporting values, broad swathes of foreign publics can be schmoozed[6]. Globally, some one billion people tuned in for the opening ceremony of 2012 London Olympic Games, 4.8 billion watched throughout and at its closing three hundred million witnessed Jacque Rogge, the President of the International Olympic Committee, telling the organizers that they had "shown the world a happy and glorious Games…the best of British hospitality and earned the respect and admiration of a global audience." Using sports, it is likely that Brazil will proselytize[7] an image of a rising, modern South American regional leader and economic powerhouse on the back of the 2014 FIFA World Cup and 2016 Olympic Games.

4 Third, sports are no longer a niche or backwater institution below governments. While governments traditionally thought of sports as beneath them, these days they cannot afford to be so aloof. In the twenty-first century the scope, power and omnipotence of sports is remarkable. While in 1990 Appadurai identified five dimensions of globalization-- ethnoscapes, technoscapes, finance capes, mediascapes and ideoscapes--Manzenreiter in 2011 proposed the missing element of "sportscapes", which "emphasize the significance of sports as another landscape of global dimensions, as well as its autonomy. Sportscapes are characterized by the transnational flows of physical culture, ideologies and practices centering on the body."

5 Set free by globalization and driven by increasingly visible non-state actors such as Fédération Internationale de Football Association (FIFA), the International Olympic Committee and sporting demi-gods like Leo Messi, David Beckham and Roger Federer, sports matter today and governments are keen to tap in. In the post-modern information age, foreign publics are more likely to be engaged by soft power overtures[8] from nations such as cultural or sporting exchanges.

6 Fourth, sports diplomacy allows governments considerable flexibility in testing the strengths or weaknesses of a diplomatic relationship beyond official policy positions. Sports diplomacy exchanges are a soft method of exploring a possible policy change. They create alternate channels for

[6]schmooze /ʃmuːz/ *vt.* to talk informally with someone, especially in a way to win some advantage for yourself

[7]proselytize /'prɒsəlɪtaɪz/ *vt.* to try to persuade someone to change their religious or political beliefs

[8]overture /'əʊvətjʊə/ *n.* a communication made to someone in order to offer something

dialogue between so-called estranged peoples and nations and in some cases, can be employed as tool to punish, express disdain or provoke another nation.

7 In 2012, for example, the Argentinian government expressed its opinion of the host of the London Games and its claim to the Falklands Islands by producing a controversial television advert showing an Argentine Olympian athlete training at sensitive sites in the contested islands. The advert, which finished with the slogan "To compete on English soil we train on Argentine soil," provoked outrage in Westminster with Philip Hammond, the UK Defence Secretary, calling it "tasteless, very insulting and disrespectful propaganda."

8 Arguably, sports multiply the channels through which a government can disseminate a diplomatic message to a much wider audience and to test whether the public of the two countries would be accepting of less or more formal diplomacy. Clearly sports diplomacy has potential.

9 So why has it not been done before? Most of the reasons why sports diplomacy has to date been limited, sporadic[9], and practiced and written about on a case-by-case basis, concern the sacrosanct[10], bizarre and at times downright violent nature of international sports: a darker realism to the aspirational idealism that its advocates are consistently trumpeting.

10 For most of the direct participants in sports–the fans, players and coaches–the sporting realm borders on sacred. Any encroachment by the "suits" (diplomats, politicians or sporting administrators, for example) is often viewed with derision. Intrusions to the temple by charlatans[11] are nothing more than a gimmick, sham or photo op, a powerful figure pretending to have a common interest with their subjects in order to secure a few votes in the next election. Talking up sports as a diplomatic tool, exploiting sports as a means to an end, confusing sports-as-a-tool for political or diplomatic purposes with sports-as-sacred is anathema[12] to the pure sporting public. Both the practitioner and scholar need to be aware. Words and messages that have some meaning in international relations can be nothing more than "empty sounds...after passing through the gates of sport."

11 Such intrusions can also backfire. The October 2012 award of the Australian Order of Merit

[9]sporadic /spə'rædɪk/ *adj.* happening sometimes; not regular or continuous

[10]sacrosanct / 'sækrəusæŋkt/ *adj.* thought to be too important or too special to be changed

[11]charlatan /'ʃɑːlətn/ *n.* a person who pretends to have skills or knowledge that they do not have, especially in medicine

[12]anathema /ə'næθəmə/ *n.* something that is strongly disliked or disapproved of

to legendary batsman Sachin Tendulkar by Australian Prime Minister Julia Gillard provides a case in point. While visiting India on a state visit, Ms. Gillard said of the award "this is a very special honour, very rarely awarded to someone who is not an Australian citizen...Cricket is of course a great bond between Australia and India. We are both cricket-mad nations." Many in the Australian cricketing fraternity were not so enamoured. Tendulkar had been accused of lying to an International Cricket Council following the suspension of a team mate during a Sydney test in 2008, and his standoffish[13] behaviour during his last and final tour to Australia in the summer of 2011 lost him enormous respect. Tendulkar's recent unsavoury behaviour and the shunning of his fans illustrate one limitation of sports diplomacy: not every sports person is a capable of diplomacy.

12 Moreover, sports are often associated with war, tribalism, conflict, division, separation and violence – the antithesis of good diplomacy. For Fischer, sports "imitate" war, "a sampling of the daily sports page reveals conquest, battle, war, destruction, victory...the taking of manhood, honour and prestige." These are hardly the sort of values that the advocates of sports diplomacy champion. Virtues, values, and "humanitarian gestures," Redeker writes, "have no place in sports" in that they "blatantly contradict sportive logic."

13 The positive rhetoric which suggests that sporting encounters can act as a pressure release to simmering conflicts in international relations by conducting the "metaphorical battle in the stadia" is only partly true. Sports are not always a substitute for war, a symbolic, non-violent way to enhance international relations. Just ask any of the residents of towns and cities across Europe who were unlucky enough to host an England football match in the past twenty years. English hooligans frequently took "the war metaphor too far and acted like invading armies on the continent of Europe." Players too struggle with diplomacy. When Holland beat Germany in a memorable but ill-tempered European Cup semi-final in 1988, one of the Dutch players "ostensibly[14] wiped his bottom with a German shirt." Thus the relationship between violence, nationalism and sports may be greater than any diplomatic undertones in international sports.

14 Just as a state actor can employ sports and sporting events to amplify a diplomatic message, so too can recalcitrant[15] non-state actors. Perhaps the most egregious case concerns the 1972 Mu-

[13]standoffish /ˌstænd'ɒfɪʃ/ *adj.* behaving in a slightly unfriendly and too formal way
[14]ostensible /ɒs'tensɪbl̩/ *adj.* appearing or claiming to be one thing when it is really something else
[15]recalcitrant /rɪ'kælsɪtrənt/ *n.* (of a person) unwilling to obey orders or to do what should be done, or (of an animal) refusing to be controlled

nich Games tragedy where eleven Israeli athletes were kidnaped and murdered by Black September, a radical Palestinian terrorist organisation. Writing a week after the tragedy a spokesman for the group issued the following statement:

A bomb in the White House, a mine in the Vatican, an earthquake in Paris could not have echoed through the consciousness of every man in the world like the operation at Munich...the choice of the Olympics, from a purely propagandistic viewpoint was 100 percent successful. It was like painting the name of Palestine on a mountain that can be seen from the four corners of the earth.

15 These words confirm a negative aspect of sports diplomacy: just as sports can disseminate positive sporting values, there is a "strong underlying connection" between sports and the publication of undiplomatic messages.

16 Animosity, war and violence are manifest in sports. Therefore, when a Department of State official says that "sports diplomacy is not really about competition at all. It is about respect for diversity, leadership, teamwork and dialogue," it can sound idealistic. If sports diplomacy is to have a sustainable, meaningful future then it is important for its advocates – both theorists and practitioners – to be mindful of the folly of pretending sports are something they are not.

17 The pressure to win at all costs - the harsh reality of international sports - produces dopers and cheaters, as well as match-fixers, gamblers, a cast of unsavoury characters, and other elements that are distinctly anti-diplomatic in their moral physiognomy[16]. Who could forget, for example, the South Korean and Indonesian badminton players that were banned from the London 2012 Olympics for "conducting oneself in a manner that is clearly abusive or detrimental to the sport" and "not using one's best efforts to win a match"? Not surprisingly, the institute of sports parodies the relations between states: just as there are Herculean moments of unifying idealism there is a Hobbesian aspect to sports, a bleak yin to its aspirational yang.

18 Bearing these and other realities in mind, sports diplomacy should have a positive future in the modern diplomatic environment. As a method of demonstrating comity between estranged peoples and nations it has a proven track record. It is topical and malleable[17] depending on its particu-

[16]physiognomy /ˌfɪzɪˈɒnəmɪ/ *n.* the outward appearance, taken as offering insight into its character

[17]malleable / ˈmælɪəbl/ *adj.* easily influenced, trained or controlled

lar circumstances and immense in terms of the scope and reach of the globalized sportscape. In the plural, modern and dynamic diplomatic environment, sports diplomacy offers people and nations a chance to showcase their best in ways other than politics, warfare and global one-upmanship[18].

Total words: 2021
Total reading time: ________minutes________seconds

** The text is based on Moving Beyond the Ping-Pong Table: Sports Diplomacy in the Modern Diplomatic Environment by Stuart Murray*

Comprehension Check

1. What is sports diplomacy? Give some examples from the passage.
2. How do you understand "one of the means to the means of those ends" in the underlined sentence in paragraph 1? What relationship is there between diplomacy and sports diplomacy according to this sentence?
3. According to the passage, what makes sports diplomacy so attractive to governments?
4. What is the new dimension of globalization? Why can it be the new dimension?
5. What does "the temple" refer to in the underlined sentence in paragraph 10? What does "photo op" mean?
6. According to the passage, what are the reasons for sports diplomacy not being practiced?

[18]one-upmanship /ˌwʌnˈʌpmənʃɪp/ *n.* when someone does or says something in order to prove that they are better than someone else

Pop Culture

Many people say sports and politics don't mix. One sportswriter disagrees with that. In fact, he would argue that professional sports has always been political and has been a positive force in shaping American society.

Dave Zirin is the sports editor for the magazine *The Nation* and a columnist for *SLAM Magazine*, *The Progressive*, and *Sports Illustrated Online*.

In the documentary ***Not Just a Game: Power, Politics & American Sports***, Zirin argues that far from providing merely escapist entertainment, American sports have long been at the center of some major political debates and struggles. Zirin first traces how American sports have glamorized militarism, racism, sexism, and homophobia, then excavates a largely forgotten history of rebel athletes who stood up to power and fought for social justice beyond the field of play. The result is as deeply moving as it is exhilarating: nothing less than an alternative history of political struggle in the United States as seen through the games its people have played.

Vocabulary Building

Look up the following words and expressions in reference books and on the Internet.

Words and Expressions	Meaning
game-changer	
straight bat	
stickhandle	
fakery	

10

UNIT

Sport Psychology

"When Bernard Hinault (5-time winner of the Tour de France) was in New York years ago, a magazine editor asked him, 'what psychological psych-ups do you use before a race? Do you imagine the race or hear voices telling you to psych up?' Hinault rolled on the bed—I'm not kidding you—for twenty minutes just laughing".

— Greg LeMond quoted by Bill Strickland in *The Quotable Cyclist*

Pre-reading Thoughts

1. What is sport psychology? What do sport psychologists do? Write down 2 questions about sport psychology that you'd like to have answered after learning.

2. How do psychological factors impact sport and exercise? Do you think athletes need a psychologist? Why?

3. How do sport and exercise influence psychological development? Do young athletes learn aggression from participating in youth sports?

Text A

Sport Psychology

1 For over 25 years the field of sport psychology has been trying to answer the question: Who is a sport psychologist? Confusion still exists regarding who is a sport psychologist (or sport psychology consultant, mental coach, mental skills trainer, etc.) because the field has not fully answered the question"What is sport psychology?"

The Origins of Sport and Performance Psychology

2 Coleman Griffith is often credited as the first person to apply psychological principles systematically to improve sport performance when he was hired by the Chicago Cubs in 1938. His primary focus was psychomotor skills, motor learning and the connection between personality variables and physical performance. Although he was a psychologist, his study of athletic performance

was more attractive to sport academics so it became part of sport studies.

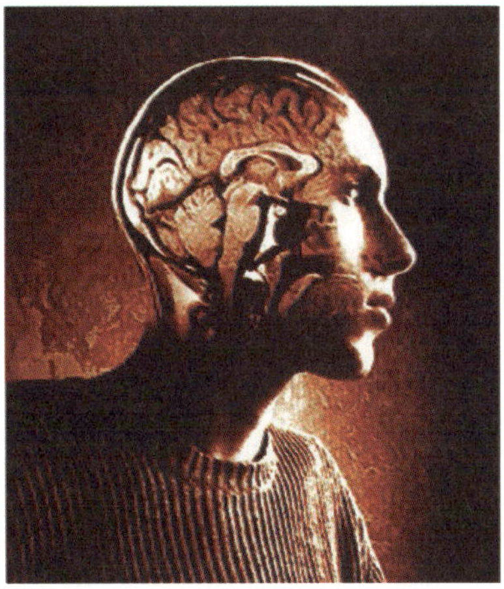

3 At that point in history, sport psychology was strongly connected to performance, particularly physical performance. Indeed, its early members could have called the field "performance psychology". Somewhere along the way, two major shifts happened that have left the field in a state of confusion. The first was the inclusion of exercise in the title of the discipline. Many professional organizations began referring to the field as "sport and exercise psychology," which implicitly and explicitly connected them and perhaps even suggested they were the same profession. This created some confusion because sport and exercise each have a different focus.

4 The second issue has been the growing interest in sport psychology by those with primary training in the practice of clinical or counseling psychology. The first book examining sport from a psychological standpoint was Ogilvie and Tutko's (1966) *Problem Athletes and How to Handle Them*. The initial forays into the sport world by psychologists were, understandably, limited to what the field of psychology was focused upon at that time: psychopathology. These psychologists did not focus on developing theories of performance, but rather stuck to their theories of personality. This trend continues today as psychologists with training in psychotherapy focused on psychopathology and addressing general life issues often refer to their treatment of athletes as "sport psychology." These psychologists fall prey to the old adage "you don't know what you don't know." Because they do not have the appropriate training in sport psychology and performance principles, despite being well-intentioned, they end up calling the therapy they give an athlete as sport psychology when it is just regular counseling not related to sport. The end result is that athletes, teams, and coaches who are seeking sport psychology services to improve their performances are commonly disappointed when they discover the "sport psychologist" they hired is only proficient in mental health therapy and not in understanding performance. These misunderstandings on both the practitioner's and the client's parts are the result of the ongoing lack of clarity regarding what sport psychology is. Unfortunately, the end result is often (and understandably) coaches and athletes giving up on sport psychology because they can see that the profession lacks a consistent identity.

Definitions: Performance Psychology and Sport Psychology

5 From the history of the field it is evident that the core application of sport psychology has been focused on performance excellence. As mentioned above, the discipline could have been referred to as performance psychology. Recently, Hays (2006) described performance psychology as helping people learn how to perform better and more consistently in endeavors where excellence counts. Her definition accurately characterizes the context of athletics and sport psychology. In this sense, sport psychology is really a domain within performance psychology; it is the study of performance psychology principles and interventions in the context of competitive athletics (rather than other types of performance). We can clear up confusion by first precisely defining performance psychology. Building on Hays' description, we propose the following definition of performance psychology:

> *Performance psychology is the study and application of psychological principles of human performance to help people consistently perform in the upper range of their capabilities and more thoroughly enjoy the performance process. Performance psychologists are uniquely trained and specialized to engage in a broad range of activities, including the identification, development, and execution of the mental and emotional knowledge, skills, and abilities required for excellence in performance domains; the understanding, diagnosing, and preventing of the psychological, cognitive, emotional, behavioral, and psychophysiological inhibitors of consistent, excellent performance; and the improvement of performance environments to facilitate more efficient development, consistent execution, and positive experiences in performers.*

Differentiating Performance Psychology from Other Specialties of Psychology

6 It is important to distinguish performance psychology from other specialties of psychology. We will compare and contrast performance psychology with exercise and health psychology, clinical and counseling psychology, positive psychology, and consulting psychology. As all of these are subfields within psychology, they will have some overlap and commonalities. However, just because they have these commonalities does not mean they should be grouped together.

Exercise and Health Psychology

7 Exercise and sport are differentiated for good reasons. What makes sport something other than exercise is the element of performance and competition. Although exercise may include elements of performance at times (e.g., recreational runners entering road races), there is a qualitative shift when moving from exercise to performance. The clients in these fields are both involved in movement, however, the goals, purposes, and contexts of the movement are quite different. Exercise psychology has as its major goal positive health outcomes (i.e., encouraging the adoption of healthy exercise behaviors or using exercise for health outcomes, including psychological functioning) instead of performance outcomes.

8 Exercise psychology and sport psychology have been connected due to their inclusion in Physical Education/Kinesiology/Exercise and Sport Science academic programs, however, in practice they are distinct fields. Exercise psychology is connected to health psychology whereas sport psychology is part of performance psychology.

Clinical and Counseling Psychology

9 Performance psychology shares a great deal with counseling and clinical psychology, such as using psychologist's interviewing skills, and understanding how we can change our behavior. However, counseling and clinical psychologists use theories about personality development in their work, whereas performance psychologists' work should be based on theories about performance excellence. Thus, the focus of each field varies significantly and cannot always be compatible. Fortunately, efforts are being made to correct this situation.

10 Generally speaking, counseling psychology focuses on helping people work through normal developmental issues in life, whereas clinical psychology focuses on helping people with serious mental health issues. But, as described before, "Doing therapy with a person who happens to be an athlete is not sport psychology". Another general distinction is that performance psychologists often address environmental, organizational, and systemic issues (e.g., coaches, team dynamics) in addition to working with individuals. Although clinical and counseling psychologists may sometimes work with families and systems, the performance environment requires different roles and responsibilities as practitioners have to work with many people within a sport organization. This requires additional training to be competent to work effectively with coaches, teams, and organizations. Despite these differences, the fields of clinical and counseling psychology provide a good foundational basis for a general understanding of people and for the challenges in building a strong

working alliance within helping relationships.

Positive Psychology

11 Performance psychology also shares many elements with positive psychology. The main focus of positive psychology is about people finding happiness and meaning in life, which is an important part of developing performance excellence. Although important, it is one of many foundational elements and does not address the core issues of performance. Finding happiness and meaning in life do not always equate with optimal performance. Positive psychology is focused on day to day functioning in life. It is limited though because there is much more to the development and execution of performance KSAs than the discipline of positive psychology addresses.

Consulting Psychology

12 The Society of Consulting Psychology defines consulting as:

> *a helping relationship that assists people, groups, or organizations in meeting their mission, goals, or objectives. Consultation is typically multi-dimensional, often with multiple concurrent clients and inter-related factors. Consultants can be change agents, facilitators, collaborators or experts in the working relationship with clients. A consultant's work focus includes people, processes, and/or organizational structures.*

13 Consulting psychologists typically work in a business context helping people become more productive at their jobs. Performance psychologists often use a consultation model in working with clients; however the issues addressed are typically different. Performance psychologists emphasize the development and execution of KSAs at a discrete time and in a public fashion. Although consulting psychologists may work to help "performance," this is primarily related to ongoing functioning or productivity, as opposed to the type of discrete performance described earlier. Despite the different issues, the field of consulting psychology has a tremendous amount to offer performance psychology with respect to research and scholarship regarding interventions and ethics.

Total words: 1453
Total reading time: __________minutes_________seconds

** The text is based on Defining the Practice of Sport and Performance Psychology by Division 47 (Exercise and Sport Psychology) of the American Psychological Association*

Vocabulary and Expressions

psychomotor /ˌsaɪkəʊ'məʊtə/ *adj.* of or relating to or characterizing mental events that have motor consequences or vice versa

foray /'fɒreɪ/*n.* an initial attempt (especially outside your usual areas of competence)

psychopathology /ˌsaɪkəʊpə'θɒlədʒɪ/ *n.* the study of mental disease

kinesiology /kɪˌniːsɪ'ɒlədʒɪ/ *n.* the branch of physiology that studies the mechanics and anatomy in relation to human movement

concurrent /kən'kʌrənt/ *ad/.* occurring or operating at the same time

discrete /dis'kriːt/*adj.* constituting a separate entity or part

Comprehension Check

1. What causes the confusion about "What is sport psychology?" And what are the results of that confusion?
2. Based on the name of their book, what was the focus of Ogilvie and Tutko's work in sport psychology? How did this negatively influence the field of sport psychology?
3. The author describes some psychologists with the adage "you don't know what you don't know" (paragraph 4). Paraphrase the sentence and explain what they didn't know?
4. How does the definition given separate performance psychology from other types? What phrases and ideas clarify it?

Critical Thinking Starters

1. Using a visual aid can help in understanding a text. Make a chart or Thinking Map to show the differences between the types of psychology listed in the article. Show the similarities and differences to sport psychology.
2. Think of the career you would like to pursue (e.g., sport and exercise psychology, coaching, athletic training, sport journalism). Describe how the knowledge and the practice of sport psychology can affect you in that career.

More to Know

Some of the research methods used in sport psychology

• **Experiment**: involves comparing people's responses or performance under two or more artificially created conditions. For example, we might set up two conditions in which basketball players are either punished or rewarded as they train, and thus measure the effect punishment and reward has upon their motivation and performance.

• **Quasi-experiment**: involves comparing two or more naturally occurring groups. For example, we might be interested in comparing the personality characteristics of athletes in individual and team sports, or comparing men's and women's attitudes to boxing.

• **Survey**: involves asking questions or asking for responses to suggestions. This can be done verbally (interview) or on paper (questionnaire). Surveys are useful in investigating attitudes and motives.

• **Observation**: involves systematically watching people's behaviour in particular circumstances. We might use observation, for example, to see how frequency of aggression changes in response to losing in a contact sport.

• **Correlation**: involves measuring two or more variables and seeing how they are related. In a positive correlation, as one variable increases, so does the other. An example of such a correlation is that between physical size and hostility. In a negative correlation, as one variable increases, the other decreases. An example of this is the relationship between experience as a martial artist and hostility—as experience increases, hostility declines.

Activity Time-Out

"When the crowd gives to the athlete, the athlete gives back to the crowd." Perhaps no social-psychological effect is more important to athletic performance and outcome than the audience, or spectator, effect. The evidence is clear, for example, that there is significant advantage to playing at home in baseball, football, basketball, ice hockey, and soccer. However, playing at home sometimes can be a disadvantage which would make athletes get so charged up that they lose focus of what they have to do. As a sport psychologist, how would you suggest working with an athlete who suffers from self-attention in front of the home crowd? And how can the home team best take advantage of the home court advantage or the visiting team best prepare for an away contest when playing a team of equal quality and ability? Devise a game plan in your favorite team sport.

Sports in Focus

Judo is a martial art that was born in Japan, and it is now known around the world as an Olympic sport. The term judo actually comes from two Japanese characters. "Ju" means gentleness, yielding or flexibility. "Do" means way, path, or teaching. The fundamental principle of judo is "Maximum Efficient Use of Mind and Body (精力善用, 自他共荣)". The hand-to-hand combat sport puts the emphasis on getting the advantage in both offensive and defensive position. It is not about using power to subdue opponents, but about using technique to control them. The main element in this pursuit is balance. The judoka (柔道运动员) gains control by unbalancing opponents and throwing them the proper way.

Adapted from a traditional Japanese martial arts form known as jujitsu (柔术), judo was established as a modern sport in 1882 in Japan by Professor Jigoro Kano (嘉纳治五郎). Kano combined a range of techniques and formulas from various jujitsu schools and built a new system which put the emphasis on three major disciplines with the new sport throwing (投技), groundwork (寝技) and striking (当身技), which together became the modern form of Judo.

A judoka can score one point and win the bout by performing a good throw, immobilizing the opponent with a legitimate hold for 30 seconds for forcing an opponent to submit to a hold, such as a chokehold (封喉) or armlock (锁臂). A victory by scoring one point is called an ippon (一本). Yuko (有效) and koka (效果) are the other two levels of scoring, although neither results in points. Judo has traditional rules that must be upheld in competition. For instance, before and after each bout (回合), the two judoka must bow to each other in the contest area. Then there are other rules that have to do the hygiene. For example, judokas must be clean, have dry skin and short finger nails and toe nails. A high degree of technical skill and understanding of strategies may help determine the outcome of a judo game.

Relevant Words and Phrases

tatami	judogi	hajime
soremade	matte	kyu

Text B

Sport Psychology in Combat Sports

1 Psychological issues play a major role in optimizing health and improving performance of athletes in combat sports. Understanding psychological principles will help in maintaining motivation for grueling[1] training regimens[2] over long periods of time, dealing with pre-competition preparation and stress during competition, and redefining goals and objectives after competition. Coaches and athletes at all levels realize the importance of all of these issues.

Stress and Coping

2 Managing stress before, during, and even after competition is a most important battle which all athletes face. While this is true for all sports, it is especially true in combat sports, because the "usual" stress of athletic performance is compounded by the fact that one is in actual combat with others who can produce pain and injury. These aspects of combat sports increase the amount of stress during competition, and thus make psychological issues more actual.

Pre-Competition Stress

3 Given that athletes have an optimal level of stress at which they will perform their best, one important issue concerns how to prepare them appropriately to be at that level prior to competition, and not have too little or too much stress. One of the first things coaches and athletes must do, therefore, is to determine exactly what that optimal level is.

4 How can that be done? One method is based on the link between anxiety and heart rate; the more anxious (stressed) a person is, the faster the heart will beat. Measuring heart rate, therefore, is a quick, unobtrusive[3] way to gain a glimpse of the athlete's level of anxiety at any one time. The next question is, then, when would one measure it? There are many possible times when this measurement can be taken, but perhaps the period most directly applicable to pre-competition is the pre-workout stage, after warm-ups. If athletes are warmed up, report that they are"feeling good,"

[1]grueling /'gruəlɪŋ/ *adj.* extremely tiring and difficult, and demanding great effort and determination

[2]regimen /'redʒɪmən/ *n.* any set of rules about food and exercise that someone follows, especially in order to improve their health

[3]unobtrusive /ʌnəb'truːsɪv/ *adj.* not noticeable; seeming to fit in well with the things around it or them

and are about to engage in strenuous sparring[4] which mirrors competition, that may be an optimal time at which to measure heart rate to gauge[5] that athlete's optimal level of stress. If that value is known, then it can be compared against the value when heart rates are measured immediately before competition. If it is too high prior to competition, the athlete may need to be de-stressed. If it is too low, the athlete may need to be "pumped up".

5 Although too much and too little pre-competition stress are both problems for athletes, in our experience the more common problem is too high stress. Too much stress prior to competition may lead to less-than-optimal performances during actual competition, possibly because one's emotions are too strong and/or one's body just cannot adapt to changing combat situations in an optimal fashion. Thus coaches and athletes need to be aware of this potential problem, and, if recognized, engage to reduce (but not eliminate) the stress.

6 One very successful technique to regulate one's emotional reactions involves deep breathing. Breathing, in fact, is a part of many healing arts. It fosters the development of self-awareness, which is an aspect of emotion regulation that is important if one is to be able to monitor and manage one's emotional reactions. However, breathing needs to be practiced. Breathing can be introduced as a way of fostering centering and self-awareness for athletes in many ways, such as the beginning and end of practice. It can also be introduced in the middle of practice, especially during tough rounds. Once well practiced, individuals can often derive the benefits of deep breathing even by just starting the procedure. This can be useful for athletes in the few seconds prior to matches, or even in the breaks during matches, and coaches can keep their athletes focused by having them breathe.

7 Clearly, each athlete is different, and deals with stress in his or her own way. Some prefer to stay in a corner by themselves thinking; others prefer to listen to music and walk. Some prefer to be in groups and chat away; others prefer to lose themselves in a vigorous warm-up routine. Athletes should not be pigeonholed[6] into a standard routine for everyone because there is no routine that is the best for everyone, especially in individually-based combat sports. However, coaches and athletes can bring some clarity to this process by understanding optimal stress levels, and helping find ways in which their athletes can achieve that optimal stress level prior to competition.

---

[4]sparring /'spɑ:rɪŋ/ *n.* making the motions of attack and defense with the fists and arms; a part of training for a boxer

[5]gauge /geɪdʒ/ *vt.* to calculate an amount, especially by using a measuring device

[6]pigeonhole /'pɪdʒɪnhəʊl/ *vt.* treat or classify according to a mental stereotype

Competition Stress

Dealing with High-Intensity Stress in High-Stakes Environments

8 Judo competition, like all combat sports, is difficult because athletes constantly need to make motor decisions to adapt their tactics and techniques to their opponents and the flow of the matches in a highly stressful environment. While this is true for all sports, the difficulty inherent in this process is compounded by the fact that judo is a combat art, and athletes are not just competing, but are fighting as well. For these reasons — competition, combat, and the flow of the match — judo competition is highly stressful, and thus the athlete's ability to deal with this high level of stress becomes a major factor in winning.

9 Although this psychological ability to handle stress is important, we strongly believe that the priority in supplemental training for high-level judo competition is first in strength and conditioning. (The priority in primary judo training is the development of judo skills and technique.) The reason for this is that judo competition at the highest levels — Olympics, world championships, union championships, international tournaments, and many national championships — include the strongest and best conditioned athletes in the world. Judo competition requires enormous aerobic and anaerobic conditioning, and judo athletes at the highest levels train to achieve these. They also develop extraordinary strength, both through normal judo training and supplemental weight training. If they are not physically prepared, it makes little difference how well they are prepared mentally, nor how much ability they have to regulate their stress during competition.

10 Achieving strength and conditioning necessary for high-level competition brings with it, in fact, many psychological benefits. Athletes who are stronger and who can go more rounds at high intensity will develop more self-confidence in competition. Judo, unlike many other combat sports, involves gripping the other opponent, and, when doing so, often athletes gauge the strength of their opponent when they grip. Athletes at their peak of strength and conditioning will know, at the time of the grip, that they are stronger than their opponents, and that can lead to a boost in confidence during a match. Athletes who are stronger can also break the grips of their opponents. Thus, these psychological benefits are positive side effects of an emphasis on strength and conditioning in

supplemental training.

11 If athletes can match the strength, conditioning, experience, and talent of their opponents, then psychological factors during matches are crucially important. Of course, athletes must be motivated to win, and, if they are not motivated to win in the first place, then no amount of strength, conditioning, experience, or talent will help them. Assuming they are motivated to win at all costs (or, equally important, not to lose), then one important psychological variable that must be considered concerns the degree to which athletes can manage the high intensity stress that is inevitable in competition, and especially during matches.

12 The ability to regulate or cope with stress is known as emotion regulation. It refers to the degree to which an individual can monitor, manage, and modify one's emotions to achieve constructive outcomes. Emotion regulation is a key skill in adjusting and adapting constructively to many changing life circumstances. Athletes with high degrees of emotion regulation will be able to manage the high intensity stress associated with high-level competition in order to adapt and adjust well during matches. They will be able to keep their emotions in check, even when they are behind or put under pressure, so that they can think clearly, rationally, and rapidly about the adjustments in their performance necessary to win. Athletes with low degrees of emotion regulation, however, are slaves to their emotions, overcome by their feelings, and unable to think clearly. They might freeze or panic, or do things they would not normally do. Differing ability to regulate emotion is one reason why players who are strong in practice may lose to those with less talent in actual competition.

Training Emotion Regulation in a High-Stress Environment

13 One of the difficulties of sport psychology in the combat sport arena is the fact that one needs to make psychological principles applicable to this very specific area of competition. In practice, it is one thing to mentally train athletes when they are out of competition in a non-stress environment. It is, however, a completely different thing to train athletes mentally in a high-stress, emotionally-wrung environment, which is precisely the environment of high-level competition. Skills in a stress-free environment are often not applicable in a high-stress environment, which is why we believe many mental imagery tasks, a commonly used sport psychology task with athletes, may not be as successful in judo. These tasks are often conducted in a stress-free environment, so athletes who may be able to imagine success in competition in that environment may find it difficult

to perform them in a high-stress environment if their emotions are in control of their behavior, and not vice versa.

Post-Competition Stress: Interpreting Winning and Losing

14 Once a competition is concluded, athletes are flooded with a range of emotions, whether they win or lose. The emotions of athletes who win may range from ecstasy, achievement, pride, and joy to tears for all of the hard work and sacrifices they and all those around them have made throughout years of grueling training. Athletes who lose may experience sadness, despair, dejection[7], anger, shame, contempt, disgust, and even fear. Clearly, athletic competition, especially in combat sports, can be associated with strong, raw emotions for all involved.

15 When athletes experience these strong emotion after competition there is little that others can do except to share the emotion with the athlete. Emotions have their own life course, and they need to run their course. Attempts to prematurely block or change the course of an emotion will be futile. Coaches, friends, and family members, despite their good intentions, often do not realize that this is the case, and attempt to intervene[8] when athletes have just completed the competition, when emotions are too raw to allow that to occur.

16 Thus, there is an appropriate time to intervene, and every individual athlete is different on exactly when that time is. Coaches and athletes can work by noting when that is through time spent together. Once athletes and coaches are in the proper frame of mind, then one of the most important jobs of coaches is to find out the way in which winning or losing is interpreted to the athlete. In psychology, the interpretation of the causes of events is known as attributions, and the study of attributions is a major part of social psychology. Most individuals, regardless of culture or gender, have a self-serving[9] bias when they make attributions about successes and failures. In practice, people have a tendency to attribute their own successes to stable, internal factors ("I am intelligent", "I am a hard worker"), and their own failures to unstable, external causes (referee mistake, "my opponent was lucky"). Also, people have a tendency to attribute other people's successes to unstable, external factors ("they were lucky", "they had a good draw"), and other people's failures to stable, internal factors ("they don't work hard enough", "their technique is terrible"). All of these

[7]dejection /dɪˈdʒekʃən/ *n.* a feeling of sadness that you get, for example, when you have just been disappointed by something

[8]intervene /ɪntəˈviːn/ *vi.* to intentionally become involved in a difficult situation in order to improve it or prevent it from getting worse

[9]self-serving /ˈselfˈsəːvɪŋ/ *adj.* working or acting for your own advantage

are ways in which we protect our own sense of self, regardless of our socio-cultural background. However, this way of thinking does not help improve long-term success in performance, or growth as an individual. Instead it is better attribute both successes and failures to controllable internal factors (e.g., effort, thinking styles, planful actions, etc.) This will help athletes and coaches identify what their strengths and weaknesses are, and focus on overcoming those. Focusing on what one can do to improve future outcomes will most likely lead to improved future outcomes.

Total words: 2178
Total reading time: __________minutes_________seconds

* *The text is based on Sport Psychology in Combat Sports by David Matsumoto*

Comprehension Check

1. Why is managing stress extremely crucial in combat sports?
2. In paragraph 4, there is a metaphorically used phrase "pumped up". What does it mean? What are the usual ways for athletes to pump up?
3. Is there a standard routine for all athletes to perform in combat sports? Why or why not?
4. For judo athletes, especially the strongest and best conditioned athletes, which will take the priority, stress controlling or skill training? Why? Under what condition, do psychological factors play a more crucially important role?
5. How can we help athletes and coaches interpret winning and losing?

Expert's View

How do you begin to build traits that successful athletes possess into your life? How do you turn these qualities into useful behaviors that will make a difference in the way you train and race? Below JoAnn Dahlkoetter has offered suggestions that have helped many clients tremendously toward excelling in their sport.

• Generate a positive outlook: Direct your focus to what is possible, to what can happen, toward success. Rather than complaining about the weather or criticizing the competition, the mentally trained athlete attends to only those things that he or she can control. You have control over your thoughts, your emotions, your training form, and how you perceive each situation. You have a choice in what you believe about yourself. Positive energy makes peak performances possible.

• Visualize your goals daily: Put yourself in a relaxed state through deep abdominal breathing. Then, as vividly as possible, create an image in your mind, of what you want to achieve in your sport. You can produce a replay of one of your best performances in the past. Then use all those positive feelings of self-confidence, energy, and strength in your mental rehearsal of an upcoming event. See yourself doing it right. Then use your imagery during the event itself.

• Build a balanced lifestyle: Create a broad-based lifestyle with a variety of interests; strive for a balance between work and fun, social time, personal quiet time, and time to be creative. Develop patterns of healthy behavior. Eat regularly, get a consistent amount of sleep each night, reduce your work load at times if possible, and allow time to relax and reflect between activities. Develop a social support network of close friends and family, some who are sports oriented, and some with other interests. Learn to communicate openly; resolve personal conflicts as they occur, so they don't build to a crisis on the night before an important race.

• Vary your workouts: Train at a new, scenic place at least once a week. Change your normal training schedule, even if only for two days. Try "active rest" by doing a different sport for a few days (e.g. hiking, swimming, inline skating, cycling, or cross-country skiing). You'll get a tremendous psychological boost and probably not lose any of your fitness level. Put new spark in your training schedule by doing interval work, tempo work (fast 20-30 minute training), varying your speed and doing endurance work, rather than slogging along at the same old pace.

• Enjoy and take the pressure off: Make a deliberate effort each day to create enjoyment in your sport, renewing your enthusiasm and excitement for training. Don't try to force your physical improvement. Lighten up on your rigid training schedule and exercise according to your feelings each day. Remove the strict deadlines and race dates which have been cast in stone. Let your next breakthrough occur naturally, at its own pace, when the internal conditions are right. Use setbacks as learning opportunities. Do the best that you can do, draw out the constructive lessons from every workout and race, and then move on. Look for advantages in every situation, even if the conditions are less than ideal.

JoAnn Dahlkoetter, Ph.D., author of *YOUR PERFORMING EDGE*, is an internationally recognized sports psychologist, past winner of the San Francisco Marathon and 2nd in the Hawaii Ironman Triathlon.

Hot Debate

Having a strong psychological foundation will allow athletes to achieve the greatest execution of a skill during a performance. When the competition level of an individual increases the pressure to succeed intensifies, hence the importance of a solid mental core. This pressure of being successful has led to the development of psychological skills training and an attitude towards athletes being mentally tough. Current studies suggest that coaches and athletes believe that being mentally tough is vital to success in their sport. However, what mental toughness actually is? The issue of nature vs. nurture, the notion whether people are born with mental toughness or develop this psychological edge through years of hard work, which enables them to, generally, cope better than their opponents, is highly debatable. Work with your partners and hold a debate in your class.

Pop Culture

Sanshiro Sugata is about a young, inexperienced man named Sanshiro Sugata who comes to the city to apprentice at a jujitsu school. His first night, he sees Yano, a master of judo, in action; he is impressed by this more spiritual form of martial arts and he begs to be Yano's student. As the youth learns technique, he realizes he also must learn to accept the spiritual dimension of strength and control. Sanshiro's true education isn't just the learning of judo; it's the growth and maturity of his mind and soul. But his journey is fraught with obstacles, embodied by jujitsu's finest master, the implacable Higaki, who vows to kill Sanshiro in a midnight fight on a windswept mountainside.

Vocabulary Building

Look up the following words and expressions in reference books and on the Internet.

Words and Expressions	Meaning
imagery training	
motor learning	
reinforcement	
arousal	

11

UNIT

Philosophy of Sport

The dilemma of sport is that it brings the active person nearer to the truth of being and offers him the choice of authentic existence, but at the same time encourages conformity to conventional rules, flight from freedom and from the "creative will", and the "objectification" of man who thus becomes a mere means to an end.

Pre-reading Thoughts

1. Greeks defined philosophy as the "love of wisdom" and philosophers as "lovers of wisdom". But what do philosophers do?

2. Art in its various forms (including sport) add fullness, variety, beauty, and flavor to our lives. Science makes discoveries that contribute to our health and comfort. While we often take these things for granted, have you ever thought of what life would be like without them?

3. How could philosophy be related to sport? Upon further consideration: such questions are often not so easily answered…
   · What counts as a sport? Why?
   · Does sport affect or reflect social norms and values (both in individuals and in society)?
   · Is sport an "art form"?
   · What place does winning have in sport?

Text A

Philosophy of Sport

1 Sport is a significant human activity. Its origins reach back into the depths of history and its contemporary practice reaches across cultures and continents. Sport, furthermore, is a meaningful human activity. Some people devote large portions of their lives to it, many people practice it on a regular basis, and most people at least watch it on television — especially when the Olympic Games come around. It is surprising, given the importance so many people attribute to sport, that philosophers have more or less neglected it as a subject of serious inquiry. Despite sport's metaphysical relationship with art and play, despite its ethical association with virtue and fairness, despite its political connection with education and democracy, and even despite Socrates's comparison of himself to an Olympic athlete, serious philosophical discussion of sport did not take hold until the latter part of the twentieth century.

2 In 1961, Allen V. Sapora and Elmer D. Mitchell published *The Theory of Play and Recreation*, which applied the theory of play to the administration of sports and recreation programs. Meanwhile, Eleanor Metheny began publishing theoretical articles such as "This 'Thing' Called Sport" in physical education journals. In fact, Metheny's work inspired so many others, she might be considered the mother of modern philosophy of sport. It was also during the 1960s that philosophers began to inquire into the role of sport in human life. In 1964, James W. Keating published "Sportsmanship as a Moral Category" in the philosophy journal *Ethics*, perhaps marking the first time since Plato that mainstream philosophy took sport as a subject for moral speculation.

3 Arguably, however, Paul Weiss's 1969 book *Sport: A Philosophic Inquiry* represents the real emergence of sport as a subject within academic philosophy. Weiss's membership in the philosophy department of Yale University and his prominence within the field of metaphysics brought almost instant credibility to the philosophical study of sport. Weiss, neither an expert on nor a practitioner of sport, begins his book with the words "1 am not an athlete." Nevertheless, his exceptional research and reasoning skills combined to establish a style for philosophy of sport that reached back to its ancient Greek roots and applied itself directly to modern athletic practices. The book considers not just the metaphysical nature of sport but also "the challenge of the body" and the educational potential of athletics. The book marks the beginning of modern philosophy of sport, not least because of Weiss's ancestral role in the forming of the first academic society dedicated to the philosophy of sport.

4 It is, of course, people rather than books that create an academic field—more specifically, the desire of a group of people to better understand something, in this case, sport. December 28, 1972, is the official birth date of the International Association for the Philosophy of Sport (IAPS), then called the Philosophical Society for the Study of Sport (PSSS). This group was busy throughout the late 1960s and early 1970s teaching courses, organizing conferences, and publishing books and articles on the philosophy of sport. The first issue of the *Journal of the Philosophy of Sport* (JPS) appeared in 1974.

5 The philosophical perspective on sport originated in Ancient Greece, having experienced a revival in the latter part of the 20th century. It is an area of philosophy that seeks to conceptually analyze issues of sport as human activity. These issues cover many areas, but fall primarily into four philosophical categories: metaphysics, epistemology, ethics, and aesthetics.

Metaphysics

6 The most general branch of philosophy is concerned with answering the question: What is reality? A metaphysical position in an overall philosophic system, pragmatism, for example, usually sets the tone and serves as the basis for further reflections on epistemology, ethics, and aesthetics. Within metaphysics is a subdiscipline, ontology, which concerns itself with the general nature of existence. Ontology examines the nature of being and man's relationship to God and nature. It also relates to inquiry and investigation about the nature of self, mind-body relationships, and the nature of man's freedom and necessity.

7 With regard to sport, metaphysics and ontology examine such diverse topics as dualism and embodiment and the impact of these concepts on how the body and its activities are viewed. In addition, religious overtones, man's relationship to others, his search for a meaningful existence via the sport experience, and the quest for freedom from deterministic necessity or the seeking of the personal freedom to be creative and self-determined fall within the metaphysical/ontological branch of philosophy. Questions and examinations related to the nature of sport and human movement and their potential as a medium of expression, harmony, and communication with self and others become metaphysical concerns. Kleinman summarizes:

> *For the theorists in physical education, the questions concerning body and mind have always posed a distinct problem. Is mindful activity separate and distinct from physical activity? Is it the responsibility of the physical educator to develop minds as well as bodies? Are bodies subservient to minds? It becomes obvious that the familiarity with the problems of metaphysics will enable the physical educator to establish better grounds for his beliefs about his own discipline.*

Epistemology

8 As the study of the nature of knowledge, epistemology directs its attention to examining the origin, limitation, and acquisition of knowledge. The various ways of knowing include: reason, i.e., inductive and deductive logic; experience; intuition; problem solving; and divine revelation.

9 Relative to the sport experience, epistemology is concerned with the learning potential that the sport experience provides, with how some people learn, with the kind of self-understanding sport

may foster, and with what we can come to "know" about the world around us and about other people as a result of our playing. Knowledge acquired as a result of direct experience, observations, and reflection is the concern of epistemology. Theories about the nature of knowledge can aid us in more effectively learning skilled movement as well as the ways in which sport is a medium for acquiring knowledge.

Ethics

10 Within the broader category of axiology, which considers the general nature of value, ethics relates to a variety of judgments concerning moral behavior: right/wrong, good/bad, moral/immoral. Ethics is the study of criteria and potentiality as they relate to moral conduct. Our actions and preferences are indications of an underlying ethical framework. Ethics assists in establishing principles which will guide decision-making based not on actuality—what is—but on potentiality—what *should* be.

11 Many ethical questions are directly related to sport. As a rule-bound activity in many instances, breaking written and unwritten rules and codes of behavior are the most obvious ethical concerns. The nature and intensity of competition, which is part of sport, often leads to ethical questions related to the appropriate emphasis on ends versus means. Sportsmanship, winning, gambling, player and owner rights, and coaching techniques all fall to ethical scrutiny in the sport setting.

Aesthetics

12 A second subdiscipline of axiology, aesthetics, relates to concerns about the nature and form of beauty as it is present in a variety of art forms. In addition, it is the branch of philosophy which attempts to establish criteria for making aesthetic judgment. Its function is synthesized as studying the form, content, and subject matter of the arts; the role of intellectuality (contemplation) and emotionality (feeling) in the arts; the nature of the aesthetic experience and pleasure; the moral, social, political, didactic, and cultural significance of the arts; the relation of the art product (work of art) to the process by which it is created; the role of technique and expression (creativity) in the arts; the role of the artist, performer, and audience in the arts.

13 In the sport context, attention to sport as an art form, creativity, audience and performer

perceptions of aesthetic experiences have all been viable topics. Criteria for judging forms, technique, style, and beauty in a variety of sports requiring criticism have also employed application of the aesthetic dimension of philosophy.

14 From what have been mentioned above, we can see that the role of philosophy and philosophical inquiry is to force reflection on those things we believe and to aid in the development of a sound and systematic basis for our behavior. It encourages speculation about what may seem intuitive or emotional and aids us in organizing our thoughts and ideas about what we know and what is beautiful in our lives. These "truths" may be related to our moral conduct, to the nature of things and ideas, or directed inward toward potential self-understanding. When you question the behavior or actions of yourself or others, you are at the threshold of philosophy and starting the quest for understanding.

Total words: 1441
Total reading time: __________minutes________seconds

**The text is based on The Scientific View of Sport: Perspectives, Aspects, Issues by O. Grupe, D. Kurz and M. Teipel*

Vocabulary and Expressions

metaphysics /metə'fɪzɪks/ *n.* the philosophical study of being and knowing
ancestral /æn'sestrəl/ *adj.* of or belonging to or inherited from an ancestor
epistemology /ɪˌpɪstɪ'mɒlədʒɪ/ *adj.* the theory of knowledge, especially the critical study of its validity, methods and scope
pragmatism /'prægmətɪzəm/ *n.* (philosophy) the doctrine that practical consequences are the criteria of knowledge and meaning and value
ontology /ɒn'tɒlədʒɪ/ *n.* the metaphysical study of the nature of being and existence
dualism /'djuːəlɪzəm/ *n.* the belief that things are divided into two often very different or opposing parts
embodiment /ɪm'bɒdɪmənt/ *n.* a concrete representation of an otherwise vague or abstract concept
overtone /'əʊvətəʊn/ *n.* something that is suggested, but is not clearly stated
deterministic /dɪˌtɜːmɪ'nɪstɪk/ *adj.* believing that everything that happens must happen as it does and could not have happened any other way, or relating to this belief
subservient /səb'sɜːvɪənt/ *adj.* the thing is less important than the other thing
inductive /ɪn'dʌktɪv/ *adj.* using a particular set of facts or ideas to form a general principle

deductive /dɪ'dʌktɪv/ *adj.* to reach an answer or a decision by thinking carefully about the known facts

axiology /ˌæksɪ'ɒlədʒɪ/ *n.* the study of values and value judgments

scrutiny /'skruːtɪnɪ/ *n.* the careful and detailed examination of something in order to get information about it

synthesize /'sɪnθəsaɪz/ *vt.* to combine so as to form a single idea or impression or a more complex product

emotionality /ɪˌməʊʃə'nælətɪ/ *n.* emotional nature or quality

didactic /daɪ'dæktɪk/ *adj.* (mainly disapproving) intended to teach, especially in a way that is too determined or eager, and often fixed and unwilling to change

viable /'vaɪəbl/ *adj.* capable of doing what it is intended to do

threshold /θreʃˌhəʊld/ *n.* the starting point for a new state or experience

Comprehension Check

1. Why is it unusual that sport has not got much attention from philosophers?
2. What does "the challenge of the body (in paragraph 3)" mean?
3. What is epistemology? How do you understand "sport is a medium for acquiring knowledge (in paragraph 9)"?
4. Paraphrase the underlined sentence in paragraph 10 to illustrate the nature of ethics.
5. What is axiology? What two categories does it contain? How are these related to sport?

Critical Thinking Starters

1. Research the term "dualism" and "embodiment" to find out what they refer to and explain how they are related to sport?
2. Compare your experience playing sports with your experience creating art. How are the experiences similar? How different? Give some examples from sport to show how aesthetics are related to sport.
3. What best describes your approach to competition: demonstration of competence, mastery of technique, dominance over opponent, self-testing, or meeting challenges? How do the games you play allow you to compete to meet these needs? Can you see yourself changing your focus now or in the future?

More to Know

Ten Intrinsic Values of Sport

Autotelicity—the notion that it is (at least ideally) an end in itself, done for its own sake, without the need of external purpose or justification. In sport, match-fixing scandals, or similar cases in soccer and cricket, are condemned not because players profit; they are already professionals. The problem is that such scandals bring profit making inside the game, selling out its internal principles for the sake of external goods. A true professional, one who values and identifies with a particular activity, will not reduce that activity to mere means toward other ends. Like art, poetry, and staring at sunsets, sport is an activity that should be valued primarily for its own sake.

Boundaries—a transgression of the limits that mark it off from everyday practicalities and of the rule-based constraints that carve out a space dedicated to open responsiveness. Real boundaries, like whistles and court outlines, act like theater curtains or temple doors, as signals to adopt a particular attitude or to "frame" the upcoming experience—whether as an athlete, an official, or a spectator—in a special way.

Freedom—a paradox derives not from the absence of constraints; to play a sport we must subject ourselves to an intricate network of rules. Because we voluntarily accept these rules, however, we gain the psychological feeling of freedom. Because we collectively accept these rules, furthermore, the community of sport achieves the liberty identified by John Stuart Mill as foundational to creativity and thriving.

Challenge—Many of sport's internal benefits derive from the challenges it presents. It is challenge that produces such goods as enjoyable absorption in the game and the cultivation of virtues. Valuing challenge in sport entails a sincere effort to win because competitors provide much of the challenge for their opponents. It is the process of training and hard work that gives the faster swimming time its worth.

Fairness—Equal opportunity and reward according to merit—the basic principles of fairness—are inscribed into sport's rules and logic. Winning can only imply athletic superiority if the contest itself was fair and no potentially superior athlete was excluded from it. It is for this reason that competition classifications according to social categories like race, gender, and disability can challenge sports' fairness. Such categories are not essential to sport, which reminds us that fairness is also a property of human beings and communities.

Uncertainty—Uncertainty of outcome is a primary quality of good contests. Furthermore, it is what absorbs us in sport and makes it a welcome relief from everyday predictability. Sincere doubt about the outcome was a key innovation of Olympic-style sport in ancient Greece—one that might have inspired the advent of philosophy. Crowds often leave stadiums once the outcome of a game seems decided; insofar as the aesthetic value of the event depends on a sense of possibility, that value diminishes as the predictability of outcome increases.

Learning—Sport itself is a kind of truth-seeking process, but we also learn things through the experience of sport. In sport, we learn experientially, in a holistic way that integrates mind and body. Ethical concepts are manifest in behavior, giving sport the educational potential to function as a moral laboratory. The world is even learning from sport about globalization.

Community—We acquire virtue through sport not so much by training and improving our individual performances but rather by participating actively and thoughtfully in sports communities with histories, traditions, and shared standards of excellence.

Beauty—Beauty in sport is not just a matter of aesthetic pleasure, but derives at least partly from a philosophical understanding of sport. In a sense, all of the values listed above relate to beauty in sport. Athletic beauty is not merely skin deep but ideally a reflection of the virtues demanded by training and competition.

The philosophical study of sport can not only help us to learn and explain important concepts in metaphysics, ethics and social-political philosophy but also give us a better understanding of a significant human activity.

Expert's View

In the article "The Paradise Lost? Mythological Aspects of Modern Sport" published in *Sport, Ethics and Philosophy* in 2011, Raphaël Massarelli and Thierry Terret attempts to answer two questions: (i) what has been the influence of doping and sponsorship on contemporary sport; and (ii) how (if at all) have both influenced the symbolic contemporary forms of the sportsman/woman myth.

Sport, in modern times, finds its roots in the mythological sources of ancient Greece, where it was born as a sacred game to be performed in the honour of Zeus in Olympia or of other gods elsewhere during the Panhellenic games. Since the beginning of the twentieth century and until the 1970s sport was mythogenic (Barthes 1975). But is sport still mythogenic in the twenty-first century? They argue that modern sport has become increasingly dependent upon the industrial and entertainment worlds, thus losing along the way the imprinting of symbolic innocence that the myth conferred in the recent past. Moreover, the contemporary perception of sportsmen/women by the general public has changed in so far as it concerns the symbolic aspect of the performer. If their function as social link appears to be intact, sportsmen seem to have lost the classical Olympic symbolism that was generally accepted among spectators until a few decades ago. It does not appear that the mythical aura of sport has been lost but rather the symbols that it has previously carried. Popular admiration is nowadays more concentrated on the sportsman's capacity to acquire fame and fortune by means that appear to be in everybody's reach, including doping. Consequently, the commoner identifies himself/herself with the sportsman/woman but does not see him/her any longer as a hero carrying classical moral values.

Activity Time-Out

Task 1

Select a sport in which you have a good background of experience and observation. In terms of this sport, what kinds of knowledge can be acquired from observation either as a participant-observer or as a spectator? What kinds of knowledge are gained from direct participation? Is it possible that some things are best known through observation or best known through experience? Explore these means of gaining knowledge.

Task 2

The "fitness boom" of the past five years—jogging, health clubs, commercial racquetball and tennis centers—may or may not be here to stay. What health or social factors may be influencing the general population to exercise? What has been the "turn-off" to physical fitness over the years? Make a survey and write a report with your group mates.

Sports in Focus

Rhythmic gymnastics is a unique blend of the dance, art and sport. It combines elements of ballet, modern dance, basic acrobatic skills and manipulation of five hand apparatus (轻器械): rope (绳), hoop (圈), clubs (棒), ball (球) and ribbon (带). The essence of rhythmic gymnastics is its ability to allow you to express yourself through elegant and graceful movements. This elegance and grace shines from the rhythmic gymnast in many ways. Their precision, choreography (编舞), flexibility and presentation awe the viewer like few other sports.

Rhythmic gymnastics is a woman-only event, and its benefits on female development are endless. Girls enrolled in a rhythmic gymnastics program will demonstrate progress in a number of key developmental areas. Some of these areas include flexibility, grace, balance, strength, agility and hand-eye coordination.

The sport is governed by the Federation Internationale de Gymnastique (FIG) (国际体操联合会), which designs the Code of Points (评分规则) and regulates all aspects of international elite competition. The largest events in the sport are the Olympic Games, World Championships, European Championships, World Cup and Grand-Prix Series (大奖赛系列).

Rhythmic gymnastics grew out of the ideas of I.G. Noverre (1727–1810), Francois Delsarte (1811–1871), and R. Bode (1881–1970), who all believed in movement expression, where one used dance to express oneself and exercise various body parts. Peter Henry Ling further developed this idea in his 19th-century Swedish system of free exercise, which promoted "aesthetic gymnastics", in which students expressed their feelings and emotions through bodily movement. This idea was extended by Catharine Beecher, who founded the Western Female Institute in Ohio, United States, in 1837. In Beecher's gymnastics program, called "grace without dancing", the young women exercised to music, moving from simple calisthenics (健身操) to more strenuous activities.

During the 1880s, Émile Jaques-Dalcroze of Switzerland developed eurhythmics, a form of physical training for musicians and dancers. George Demeny of France created exercises to music that were designed to promote grace of movement, muscular flexibility, and good posture. All of these styles were combined around 1900 into the Swedish school of rhythmic gymnastics, which would later add dance elements from Finland. Around this time, Ernst Idla of Estonia established a degree of difficulty for each movement. In 1929, Henrich Medau founded The Medau School in Berlin to train gymnasts in "modern gymnastics", and to develop the use of the apparatus.

Competitive rhythmic gymnastics began in the 1940s in the Soviet Union. The FIG formally recognized this discipline in 1961, first as modern gymnastics, then as rhythmic sportive gymnastics, and finally as rhythmic gymnastics. The first World Championships for individual rhythmic gymnasts was held in 1963 in Budapest. Groups were introduced at the same level in 1967 in Copenhagen, Denmark. Rhythmic gymnastics was added to the 1984 Summer Olympics in Los Angeles, with an Individual All-Around competition (个人全能比赛). However, many federations from the Eastern European countries were forced to boycott by the Soviet Union. Canadian Lori Fung was the first rhythmic gymnast to earn an Olympic gold medal. The Group competition was added to the 1996 Summer Olympics in Atlanta.

Relevant Words and Phrases

backbend	body wave	circumduction
flip toss	free spin	hop

Text B

How the Arts Were Manifested in the Modern Olympic Games

1 Sculptor Robert Graham was commissioned to create a monumental "Olympic Gateway" in front of the Los Angeles Memorial Coliseum[1]; 10 Los Angeles artists were commissioned to paint murals[2] alongside downtown freeways; 16 American artists received commissions to create a poster art series; and 20 exhibitions were held as part of the 1984 Los Angeles Olympic Arts Festival. These are but a few examples of the cultural arts presented in conjunction with the Los Angeles Games. The history and conceptual development of the Olympic Games has always acknowledged

[1]coliseum /ˌkɒlɪˈsiːəm/ *n.* an oval large stadium with tiers of seats; an arena in which contests and spectacles are held

[2]mural /ˈmjʊərəl/ *n.* a painting that is applied to a wall surface

that the arts are a significant part of this worldwide event.

2 The manifestation of the arts in the modern Olympic Games began in Paris (1906) when Pierre de Coubertin and the International Olympic Committee discussed the particulars concerning the role of the arts in the modern Games. First on the agenda was to define the arts and examine:

to what extent and in what form the Arts and Letters could take part in the celebration of the modern Olympiads, and in general associate themselves with the practice of sports in order to benefit from them and ennoble them.

3 The Committee ultimately defined the arts as architecture, sculpture, painting, literature and music. Competitions in these mediums were proposed and accepted with the stipulation[3] that all works be "directly inspired by the idea of Sport." Other artistic mediums considered to reflect and enhance the Olympic atmosphere included open-air performances, choreographed[4] processions with "masts[5], escutcheons[6] [coat of arms], garlands[7], draperies[8], sheaves[9]" and the torchlight as props[10] and special effects. Reflecting upon the results of the 1906 conference, de Coubertin in 1910 wrote:

Three Olympiads having been celebrated with success; thought might now be given to endowing them with refinement and beauty....

4 De Coubertin's quest to incorporate the arts as an integral part of the modern Games was influenced by the concept of eurythmics[11] developed by Émile Jaques-Dalcroze. Eurythmics is a system of rhythmic exercises utilized to teach children to hear and distinguish rhythms, pitches, speed and other elements of music; a conscious linking of varied experiences. De Coubertin interpreted eurythmics as the mutual interaction between arts; this supported his idea that both art and sport are equally dynamic in producing an aesthetic response. <u>A person's aesthetic appreciation of one form</u>

[3]stipulation /ˌstɪpjʊ'leɪʃn/ *n.* a restriction that is insisted upon as a condition for an agreement
[4]choreographed / 'kɔ:rɪəgra:ft/ *adj.* well-designed, recherche
[5]mast /mɑ:st/ *n.* a tall pole on a boat or ship that supports its sails
[6]escutcheon /ɪ'skʌtʃən/ *n.* a shield; especially one displaying a coat of arms
[7]garland /'gɑ:lənd/ *n.* a circle made of flowers and leaves worn around the neck or head as a decoration
[8]drapery /'dreɪpərɪ/ *n.* hanging cloth used as a blind (especially for a window)
[9]sheaf /ʃi:f/ *n.* a package of several things tied together for carrying or storing
[10]prop /prɒp/ *n.* a support placed beneath or against something to keep it from shaking or falling
[11]eurythmics /juə'rɪðmɪks/ *n.* the interpretation in harmonious bodily movements of the rhythm of musical compositions; used to teach musical understanding

of "beauty" (i.e. art) heightens the enjoyment of the respective experience (i.e. sport) and vice versa.

5 De Coubertin felt that this source of aesthetic interaction was dynamic, and that such an interaction could be consciously motivated by creating a suitable environment. Once produced, the interaction would lend an aesthetic and spiritual aura to any occasion. De Coubertin's viewpoint is expressed in this statement:

Sport must be seen as producing beauty and as an opportunity for beauty. It produces beauty because it creates the athlete, who is a living sculpture. It is an opportunity for beauty through the architecture, the spectacles, and celebrations which it brings about.

6 His strong belief in the aesthetics formed de Coubertin's desire to create a solid link between art and sport in the Olympic Games; changing it from a simple athletic contest to an aesthetic-spiritual celebration. As provocative as his theory was, the International Olympic Committee would perpetually be faced with the problem of successfully fulfilling de Coubertin's Olympic ideal. The inclusion of the arts in the modern Games would take form in events such as art competitions, art exhibitions, and would eventually lead to the Olympic art festivals of today.

7 After hesitant beginnings, the International Olympic Committee implemented art and design competitions as one of the artistic aspects during the Olympic Games of 1912 through 1948. Artists competed in such areas as architecture, city planning, sculpture, painting, music, literature, poster design and the like.

Olympic Posters: a Link Between Art and Sport

8 The influence of posters as an art form has increased significantly over the years. Like music, poster art can be enjoyed and appreciated without a great deal of technical knowledge. Yet to have an idea of how and why this medium has developed and flourished can only increase the observer's enjoyment. The term poster art implies a practical purpose, but also one that appeals to the mind and emotions in a way that extends beyond the pragmatic. This idea is illustrated in the Olympic posters in this exhibition. The development of poster art, like much of our material culture, has its roots deep in the past and is bound up with history.

9 Pictorial imagery has been documented as dating back to 40,000 B.C.E., but the more com-

mon practice of combining recognizable figures with text on transportable surfaces has only been in evidence since the Chinese perfected the process of papermaking shortly after 100 C.E. Most of the earliest printmaking processes were limited to woodcut impressions of sacred images. Similar practices in woodcut imagery and text reproduction spread from China to Spain around 1150, then to Italy in the next hundred years, and finally to Germany in 1390. Techniques for reproduction remained relatively simple throughout Europe until the early 1500s when the process of engraving was developed, allowing for more refined and detailed printed images. In addition, due to the enhanced durability of metal plates, larger numbers of reproductions were made possible. Popular applications included the reproduction of holy pictures, travel souvenirs, book plates, maps, book illustrations, and handbills[12]. The introduction of image copyright laws in 1526 was brought about by the growing popularity of specific reproductions with artists' signatures.

10 Another advancement in technology that set the stage for modern poster art was the invention of lithography (derived from a Greek word meaning "stone writing"). This 1798 invention by young actor, writer and playwright Alois Senefelder (1771-1834) was used mainly for ordinary printing purposes, but its potential for original artwork soon became apparent. By 1848, lithographic prints could be reproduced at a rate of 10,000 per hour. However, all lithographs were printed in black and white until 1858, when Jules Cherét (1836-1933) produced the first color lithograph (using three separate stones) at his workshop in France. Additional improvements in color lithography, a growing interest in Japanese woodblock prints, and a proliferation of art movements stimulated greater intellectual and artistic expression in poster art and design during this period.

11 Over time, and in tandem[13] with technological and societal changes brought about by the Industrial Revolution, poster art became a practical and more profitable means of gaining the attention of a public ready for world travel and new experiences. The Olympic posters in this exhibition reveal much about the aspirations and values of their eras. By examining particular Olympic posters from different decades, it is possible to identify individual design decisions such as composition and choice of imagery, contrasts in color and texture, and the integration of typography[14] as well as the political or social context in which those decisions were made.

---

[12]handbill /'hændbɪl/ *n.* an advertisement (usually printed on a page or in a leaflet) intended for wide distribution

[13]in tandem: If two pieces of equipment, people, etc. are working in tandem, they are working together, especially well or closely

[14]typography /taɪ'pɒgrəfɪ/ *n.* the style, size and arrangement of the letters in a piece of printing

12 Consider, for example, the first poster designed to promote the modern Olympic Games. For the 1912 Olympic Games in Stockholm, Sweden, landscape and portrait artist Olle Hjortzberg created a visually elaborate lithograph depicting a dominant, centrally situated athlete in a striking and heroic pose, proudly waving his national flag in sweeping, gestural motions. The stoic[15] facial expressions on other figures in the composition supported the underlying message that a few chosen athletes possessed, in addition to physical perfection, a moral resolve that qualified them to be appropriate representatives of an international society captivated by the fruits of progress and expansion. The addition of richly saturated[16] colors and an exuberant rendering of billowing[17] fabric symbolic of national flags added to the highly emotional feeling of prosperity and invincibility[18] in competition. The dynamic visual impact is apparent, and many of the Olympic poster designers who followed during the next two decades, Jean Droit, Paris 1924; Joseph Johannes Rovers, Amsterdam 1928; and Ludwig Hohlwein, Garmish-Partenkirchen 1936, used similar artistic devices to promote the Olympic Games through the veneration[19] of the resolute athlete.

13 In the late 1940s, however, a more subtle approach was incorporated into Olympic poster design. The poster by graphic designer Walter Herz, promoting the 1948 Olympic Games in London, England, is a prime example of this trend. While Europe embarked upon its recovery from the economically devastating effects of World War II, a renewed increase in tourism was thought to be part of the restoration equation. This designer's approach to imagery and text communicated the requisite "what, where and when" without the potentially offensive warlike connotations. Borrowing from the idea of a traditional travel poster, he used familiar historic images and restrained block lettering in a visually balanced layout. His incorporation of four equally

[15]stoic /'stɒɪk/ *adj.* determined not to complain or show your feelings, especially when something bad happens to you

[16]saturated /'sætʃəreɪtɪd/ *adj.* (of color) being chromatically pure; not diluted with white or grey or black

[17]billow /'bɪləʊ/ *vi.* to spread over a large area, or (especially of things made of cloth) to become filled with air and appear to be larger

[18]invincibility /ɪnˌvɪnsə'bɪlətɪ]/ *n.* the property being difficult or impossible to defeat

[19]veneration /venə'reɪʃən/ *n.* a profound emotion inspired by a deity

dominant components title, architectural rendering, classical athletic figure and the five-ring Olympic symbol as well as the restrained use of color, contributed to this poster's subdued[20] appeal for renewed travel after the war. The introduction of this poster signaled a trend in Olympic poster design that attempted to deemphasize political influences. This stylistic trend is effectively illustrated by Ilmari Sysimetsä's design for the 1952 Olympic Games in Helsinki.

14 The 1960s, in contrast, witnessed a dramatic change in poster art and design. Designers returned to the use of bold, fully saturated colors in imagery. However, a new economy of line and the deliberate application of logographic forms guaranteed instant recognition on an international level. These concepts were epitomized[21] in Japanese graphic designer Yusaku Kamekura's poster promoting the 1964 Summer Olympic Games in Tokyo, Japan. His design integrated symbols, flat color and typography to "poster-art perfection," excluding all unnecessary elements. This design came to serve as a unifying graphic element on other posters in the accompanying photographic series, and established "design unity" (theme and variation) in all the graphic components of the Olympic Games that year. Kamekura continued his influence on Olympic poster art by successfully designing three posters for the 1972 Winter Olympic Games in Sapporo, Japan.

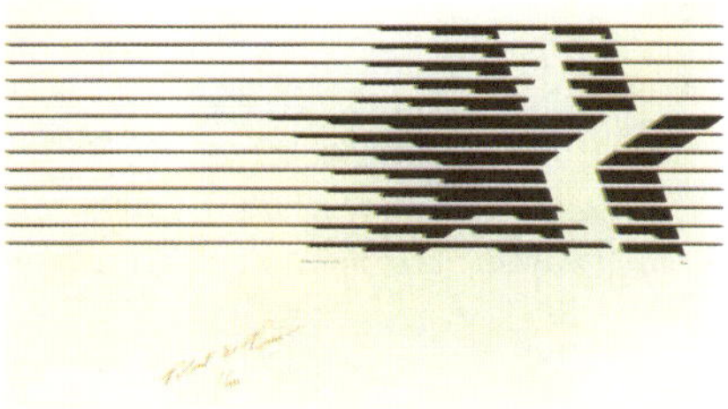

15 With the establishment of the design unity concept for all Olympic Games, designers were able to explore other ways to illustrate the energy and drama of sport. By using the logo as the "heralding[22]" element, designers and artists could employ more innovative and expressive mediums (photography, collage[23], or mixed media) to communicate the emotional, kinetic[24] and spellbinding[25] aspects of the Olympic events. This concept is clearly illustrated by the selection of Robert Miles Runyan's Stars in Motion design for the 1984

[20]subdued /səb'dju:d/ *adj.* in a soften tone; restrained in style or quality
[21]epitomize /ɪ'pɪtəmaɪz/ *vt.* embody the essential characteristics of or be a typical example of
[22]herald /'herəld/ *vt.* to be a sign that something important, and often good, is starting to happen, or to make something publicly known, especially by celebrating or praising it
[23]collage /kə'lɑ:ʒ/ *n.* (the art of making) a picture in which various materials or objects, for example paper, cloth or photographs, are stuck onto a larger surface
[24]kinetic /kɪ'netɪk/ *adj.* involving and producing movement
[25]spellbinding /'spel'baɪndɪŋ/ *adj.* attracting and holding your attention completely

Olympic Games in Los Angeles. His image became a logo attached to all posters in the Art Series that year, including poster imagery by artists such as Billy Al Bengston; Carlos Almaraz and John Baldessari.

16 With minimal reflection, it is easy to appreciate the practical and artistic merits of poster art. Poster imagery helps to connect people with ideas and events. Today, an international audience becomes caught up in anticipation of each Olympic Games, stimulated in part by the blending of "art and sport" made familiar by the designers of Olympic posters. Since 1928, the image of the five-ring Olympic symbol on Olympic posters has served to herald the coming of the Games. As described by Juan Antonio Samaranch, President of the International Olympic Committee:

Created to announce an event, a poster possesses the astonishing and fascinating quality of becoming with the passage of time, the symbol and the indelible[26] mark that will be engraved forever in the collective memory of mankind.

17 The enduring power of Olympic poster art lies in its combined capacity to inspire and to celebrate worldwide participation and international goodwill. It is certain that the arts will continue to play a significant role in the modern Olympic Games. And in conjunction with athletics, the cultural events will continue to express and encompass a total cultural presence and international unity as once perceived by Pierre de Coubertin.

Total words: 2434
Total reading time: __________minutes_________seconds

** The text is based on How the Arts Were Manifested in the Modern Olympic Games by Lisa Anne Escovedo and Olympic Posters: a Link Between Art and Sport by Constance B. and Cheryl Anne Bailey*

Comprehension Check

1. How did the original idea of eurythmics inspire the joining of sport and art?
2. Paraphrase the underlined sentence in paragraph 4. Explain it in your own words.
3. Explain how sport reflects aesthetics apart from obvious sports which combine music and dance such as gymnastics and figure skating. Use the expressions from the passage.

[26]indelible /ɪn'delɪbəl/ *adj.* (before noun) Indelible memories or actions are impossible to forget, or have a permanent influence or effect

4. List the ways that art and the Olympics are combined. Can you think of some specific ways that you have noticed in your observations of sport activities?

Pop Culture

FOREVER STRONG is inspired by the real-life sports/self-help philosophies of coach Larry Gelwix, of the rugby team of Highland High School in Salt Lake City. Hotshot Arizona rugby star Rick Penning (Sean Faris) is on his way to greatness, even when his Flagstaff team loses, surprisingly, to the unconventional, well-disciplined Highlanders. Then the hard-partying, drug-using Rick injures his girlfriend in a car crash. It's not his first such offense, and Rick, practically disowned by his victory-obsessed coach father, gets sentenced to juvenile prison. The compassionate warden (Sean Astin) arranges for the sulky Rick to practice on the Highland team, where the athlete gradually learns the spirit of real teamwork, sobriety, spirituality, and honor on and off the playing field.

Vocabulary Building

Look up the following words and expressions in reference books and on the Internet.

Words and Expressions	Meaning
multiculturalism	
utilitarianism	
social practice theory	
ethos	

12

UNIT

Sports Industry

Branding professional athletes has often been overlooked by people, but often this process is referred to as one of the most important elements to scoring endorsements, sponsors and partnerships. Too often players are seen to excel on the court, but fail to manage their lives off the big stage. The field of sport marketing is an exciting and fast-moving part of the sports industry that presents new challenges requiring innovative and effective solutions.

Pre-reading Thoughts

1. What are some famous logos or slogans associated with sports or sport products?

2. Can you think of some commercials you have seen recently for sports or sport related products?

3. When you think of the term "sport marketing" what do you imagine? What do you think is involved in sport marketing? How would you describe the job of a sport marketer?

Text A

Sport Marketing

1 Marketing is a complex function that is extremely important to the overall success of sport organizations. You probably have heard the term sport marketing in many contexts, and you might be wondering exactly what it means. That's a good question because sport marketing is composed of several elements, and the term sport marketing frequently is used incorrectly. People tend to define marketing in terms of their experiences, instead of recognizing one of the most important roles of marketing—carrying out the mission of an organization.

2 Some corporate executives might describe sport marketing as selling goods and services to generate a profit. But sport marketing is more than selling. People who work in advertising and public relations might consider sport marketing as obtaining Super Bowl tickets for clients or entertaining a corporate sponsor at the US Open Golf Tournament. But sport marketing is more than

advertising and public relations. Those who provide services for professional athletes might view sport marketing as arranging for athletes to attend the grand opening of a shopping mall or arranging to have corporate executives play tennis with Lleyton Hewitt or Lindsay Davenport. But sport marketing is more than community relations.

3 Sport marketing is defined as "the process of designing and implementing activities for the production, pricing, promotion and distribution of a sport product or sport business product to satisfy the needs or desires of consumers and to achieve the company's objectives". Balancing a company's business objectives with consumer wants and needs is a challenge in any industry, but sport marketing is even more complex because sport has certain characteristics that make it unique. A brief examination of sport's unique combination of characteristics will show how sport differs from other products, goods, and services and therefore why the approach to marketing sport is unique.

4 First, aspects of sport are intangible. For example, you cannot touch the actual competition that takes place between two football teams. You can, however, touch products associated with the experience such as equipment, the seats in the stadium, hats, T-shirts, videos, and so on. In addition, it has been pointed out that sport has an intangible dimension that is internally generated and represented by the emotions and experiences of sport participants and spectators. Examples include the following:

- the emotional high that sport participants experience when running their personal best time
- the thrill that sport spectators experience when watching a spectacular play in sport such as a slam dunk in basketball
- the satisfaction that athletes derive when overcoming challenges posed by competitors or the sport environment
- the agony that sport spectators feel when their favorite team or athlete loses a competition

5 Second, sport is subjective and heterogeneous because the impressions, experiences, and interpretations about the sport experience may vary from person to person. Two people who attend the same field hockey game might have markedly different experiences. One might view the game as low scoring and unexciting, whereas the other might appreciate the strategy involved in the game and consider it interesting. Because sport marketers cannot easily predict the impressions, experiences, and interpretations that consumers will have about the sport consumption experience, they will find it difficult to ensure that consumers will have satisfying sport experiences.

6 Third, sports are inconsistent and unpredictable for a variety of reasons. A few of the many factors that influence the sport experience include injuries to players, the emotional state of players, the momentum of teams, and the weather. Sport marketers have little if any control over these factors. On the other hand, although the uncertainty and unpredictability of sport events prevent sport marketers from offering consumers any guarantees, the uncertainty adds an extra appeal and excitement that sport spectators (and sport marketers) enjoy.

7 Fourth, sport is perishable because the sport experience is simultaneously produced and consumed. For example, as the athletes are competing (i.e., producing the action and experience), the spectators are watching the competition (i.e., consuming the action and experience). Few people are interested in seeing yesterday's soccer match or field hockey game. Consequently, marketers must focus on generating pre-event excitement to promote advance ticket sales. Based on the perishability of sport competitions, sport marketers often offer tangible items (such as T-shirts, souvenirs, and other merchandise) that serve as lasting reminders of the perishable sport experience.

8 Fifth, as alluded to in the discussion of the intangible aspects of sports, sport involves emotions. Some spectators become emotionally attached to their teams and are referred to as fanatics or fans. Other consumers might buy licensed products with team logos and uniform replicas as a way of identifying with their teams. Consumers do not often display such heightened emotions or psychological attachment to other goods or products, such as vacuum cleaners.

Evolution of Sport Marketing in America

9 The history of American sport marketing can be devided into three periods: (1) the Era of Origins, 1820-1880; (2) the Era of Institutional Development, 1880-1920; and (3) the Era of Refinement and Formulation, 1920-1990.

10 During the Era of Origins, micromarketing decisions emerged in response to the growth and greater effect of external forces. The tactics of William Fuller, a boxing promoter in South Carolina, have been examined. In 1824 Fuller enticed paying customers to his "Extravaganza of Fun, Frolic, Fashion, and Flash" through newspaper advertisements and handbills that announced theater plays, boxing, and fireworks. Boxing was thus only one aspect of his complete product. Unlike today's high-powered marketing strategies, Fuller's effort did not include an announcement of the price and the location if the event was hard to reach. Moreover, although the promotions included

newspapers and handbills, they still relied heavily on word of mouth among a small sporting fraternity.

11 During the 1850s and 1860s, Michael Phelan's promotion of billiards and billiard tables marked a significant advance over the earlier boxing promotions. As a means to market billiards and billiard tables, Phelan identified a growing sporting fraternity of white males age 18 to 35 and the proprietors of poolrooms and taverns who catered to this fraternity. Phelan also recognized that the billiard market extended beyond a local market to other cities. By organizing national billiard tournaments, publishing the *Billiard Cue*, and holding a leadership position in the American Billiard Players Association, he was able to achieve brand-name recognition and promote his products as the best billiard events and equipment. As a result, Phelan was able to compete successfully with a growing number of firms, and his control over technological developments in billiard equipment and standardized rules of the game allowed him to influence buyer preferences for different kinds of billiard products. Phelan's marketing tactics were a prelude to more thorough development of micromarketing techniques during the 1865 to 1870 baseball fad, which included charging admission fees for a sport entertainment product; promoting sports rivalries; promoting games, tours, tournaments, all-star games, and championship games through newspapers, weekly journals, and special baseball publications; publishing statistical reviews of games and seasons; and promoting baseball as America's national pastime. Early baseball promoters made decisions about price, promotion, and place based on market size and growth, and they took advantage of the increase in per capita income and discretionary time.

12 The micro and macro concepts associated with modern sport marketing evolved during the Era of Institutionalized Development (1880-1920): product planning, product management, distribution, pricing, and promotion. During this period, sport products were branded, trademarked, and packaged to enhance their appeal to consumers. Market analysis to determine customer needs, estimate market potential, and study competition began at the turn of the century. Before 1880 price was a matter of guesswork. After 1880 the pricing decision became an important part of the marketing strategy. Promotional activities expanded in volume and intensity, building on the tactics used by baseball promoters.

13 Population expansion and concentration were accompanied by a significant increase in discretionary money. Sport benefited from these developments because consumers demanded more sport products and more forms of sport entertainment. Technological changes influenced the distri-

bution and production of sporting goods. The railroad and an overland truck line transport system allowed wide distribution of products to cities, towns, and hamlets. The emergence of the telegraph and telephone provided improved and broadened means of communications that could be used as a business and marketing tool. During this era, sporting goods manufacturers and promoters of sports developed and refined micromarketing tactics in response to new and powerful external forces.

14 During the Era of Refinement and Formulation (1920-1990), sport marketing continued to develop along the lines established during the Era of Institutionalized Development. And new external forces played an important role in this development. These forces included increased popularity and diversification of sport interests; developing sport fads that periodically increased market growth rates; government policies (National Industrial Recovery Act, 1933; Title IX, 1972; Consumer Pricing Act, 1975; the Brady Bill 1994); technological advancements (new materials such as plastics, fiberglass, alloys, and so on; computers; and the Internet); and the emergence of specialized sports trade journals, sports radio, and sports television programs. In the 21st century, we can expect that new emerging external forces, especially new technological advancements, will influence sport marketing developments.

Total words: 1552
Total reading time: __________minutes________seconds

** The text is based on Marketing is a complex function that is extremely important to the overall success of sport organizations by Paul Mark Pedersen, Janet Parks, Jerome Quarterman and Lucie Thibault*

Vocabulary and Expressions

heterogeneous /ˌhetərə'dʒiːnɪəs/ *adj.* consisting of parts or things that are very different from each other

momentum /mə'mentəm/ *n.* the force that keeps an object moving or keeps an event developing after it has started

souvenir /ˌsuːvə'nɪə/ *n.* something you buy or keep to help you remember a holiday or special event

fanatic /fə'nætɪk/ *n.* a person whose strong admiration for something is considered to be extreme or unreasonable

replica /'replɪkə/ *n.* an exact copy of an object

entice /ɪn'taɪs/ *vt.* to persuade someone to do something by offering them something pleasant

frolic /'frɒlɪk/ *n.* a playful and lively movement or activity

billiards /'bɪljədz/ *n.* a game played by two people on a table covered in green cloth in which a cue (= a long pole) is used to hit balls against each other and into pockets around the table

proprietor /prə'praɪətə/ *n.* a person who owns a particular type of business, especially a hotel, a shop or a company that makes newspapers

poolroom /'puːlruːm/ *n.* a hall or establishment where pool, billiards, etc. are played

tavern /'tævən/ *n.* a place where alcohol is sold and drunk

discretionary /dɪ'skreʃənərɪ/ *adj.* having or using the ability to act or decide according to your own discretion or judgment

alloy /'ælɒɪ/ *n.* a metal that is made by mixing two or more metals, or a metal and another substance

Comprehension Check

1. What makes sport marketing different from other business marketing?
2. Is there anything wrong with sport being subjective and heterogeneous?
3. What does it mean when it says, "sport is perishable" (in paragraph 7)?
4. In paragraph 10, the article mentions "micromarketing" decisions. Based on the example given, what do you think micromarketing means?
5. Why is discretionary money important in the development of sport marketing?

Critical Thinking Starters

1. Analyze a sport advertisement comparing the techniques used in the ad to the five aspects that make sports unique. Show which aspect or aspects are obviously affecting the ad.
2. According to the passage, sports are inconsistent and unpredictable for a variety of reasons. What are those factors that may influence the sport experience? Illustrate your point of view with practical sport experience.
3. In the 21st century, new technological advancements will influence sport marketing developments. Based on what you have learned from the passage, can you predict or imagine how such new emerging external forces like *digital media, smart phone, big data, cloud storage, etc.* may affect sport marketing developments?

More to Know

Ever since the first modern Games were staged in Athens in 1896, the Olympic Movement has received contributions from commercial entities in order to support the staging of the Games. Nowadays, the International Olympic Committee operates a multi-faceted Olympic marketing programme built on the unique global marketing platform created by the Olympic brand and the Olympic Games. Long-term marketing initiatives play a key role in the promotion of the Games and the Olympic values, while also generating revenue in order to ensure the future financial security and stability of the Olympic Movement as a whole. Through the sale of Olympic broadcast rights, for instance, the IOC is able to guarantee that the Games can be experienced by the maximum number of people around the world, while the efforts of the IOC's Olympic marketing partners also ensure the global promotion of Olympism and support sports development activities around the world.

The Olympic Partners (TOP) programme is the worldwide sponsorship programme managed by the IOC. The IOC created the TOP programme in 1985 in order to develop a diversified revenue base for the Olympic Games and to establish long-term corporate partnerships that would benefit the Olympic Movement as a whole. The TOP programme operated on a four-year term — the Olympic quadrennium. It generates support for the Organising Committees of the Olympic Games and Olympic Winter Games, the NOCs and the IOC.

The TOP programme provides each Worldwide Olympic Partner with exclusive global marketing rights and opportunities within a designated product or service category. The global marketing rights include partnerships with the IOC, all active NOCs and their Olympic teams, and the two OCOGs and the Games of each quadrennium. The TOP Partners may exercise these rights worldwide and may activate marketing initiatives with all the members of the Olympic Movement that participate in the TOP programme.

Eleven corporations currently participate in the eighth generation of the TOP programme, known as TOP VIII. During the 2013-2016 Olympic quadrennium, TOP VIII Partners provide support for the 2014 Olympic Winter Games in Sochi and the 2016 Olympic Games in Rio. The TOP VIII Partners are Coca-Cola, Atos Origin, Dow, GE, McDonald's, Omega, Panasonic, Procter & Gamble, Samsung, and Visa.

Expert's View

In the brief, *The Future of Sports Marketing: Play Locally, Think Globally, Drive Loyalty*, co-authored by Mark Lehaw, global head of SAP's Sports & Entertainment industry and Rob O'Regan, founder and principal of 822 Media, they identify and outline how mining customer insights will influence the future of sports marketing, which will have organizations thinking outside the stadium and beyond the field to go global and drive loyalty.

They discuss the four key channels where leagues and teams are investing more resources to mine consumer insights, which includes:

Fantasy sports — Fantasy sports is a huge industry and a big opportunity to collect data. With the huge reach and loyal fan following, the engagement and activity within these networks can reveal a lot about fan behavior and interests.

Web and mobile content — With sports being more than just an "at the game" experience, leagues and teams are making sure their web content has all the stats, facts, and interactivity that fans want. They are also making mobile content, such as apps, a part of the full experience by supplementing what fans are seeing at/during the game.

Social media — Networks such as Twitter can provide a wealth of information, especially when it comes to fan sentiment. Leagues and teams are looking to social networks for engagement, interaction, and to keep a pulse on fan feedback that cannot be found elsewhere.

Loyalty programs — With a push toward personalization and customization, leagues and teams are thinking like your local grocery store and investing in ways to track individuals to provide a more individualized and engaging experience.

These channels are all opportunities for teams and leagues to extend their current practices and work to win fans, even when they're not in the stadium or at the field.

Activity Time-Out

The last 5 years has seen the most significant developments in digital media we have ever seen, which when combined, will see the biggest change in spectating habits. Think about it — in 2008 there were no iPad; no 3D or smart TVs; and smart phones were still in their infancy. Twitter hadn't broken the mainstream, and Facebook, although growing rapidly, wasn't ingrained in daily life as it is today. In fact arguably, 2008 was the year that social media exploded — but the Beijing games were just too early to catch the wave. Now Beijing Now the 2022 Winter Olympic is awarded to Beijing. With digital coverage of the coming age, how can we promote those winter Olympic sports events to local Chinese, stimulate their interests and increase their knowledge about Winter Games. Work in groups to make your winter sports events marketing plan and if it is possible, produce a short video to introduce your ideas, or make an advertisement for a certain winter event.

Sports in Focus

Billiards or cue sports（台球）are games played with a cue stick（球杆）, which is used to strike hard balls on a rectangular, cloth-covered（台呢）table. The table has a slate base（石板台面）and is bounded by rubber cushions（橡胶台岸）.

The history of billiards is long and very rich. The game has been played by kings and commoners, presidents, mental patients, ladies, gentlemen, and hustlers alike. It evolved from a lawn game similar to the croquet（槌球）played some-time during the 15th century in Northern Europe and probably in France. Play moved indoors to a wooden table with green cloth to simulate grass, and a simple border was placed around the edges. The balls were shoved, rather than struck, with wooden sticks called "maces（球杖）". The term "billiard" is derived from French, either from the word "billart", one of the wooden sticks, or "bille", a ball. Since early billiards comes from accounts of playing by royalty and other nobles, it has been known as the "Noble Game of Billiards" since the early 1800's.

Billiard equipment improved rapidly in England after 1800, largely because of the Industrial Revolution. Chalk（巧克/壳粉）was used to increase friction between the ball and the cue stick even before cues had tips（杆头）. The leather cue tip, with which a player can apply side-spin（偏杆）to the ball, was perfected by 1823. Slate became popular as a material for table beds around 1835. Goodyear discovered vulcanization of rubber（橡胶的硫化）in 1839 and by 1845 it was used to make billiard cushions. A two-to-one ratio of length to width became standard in the 18th century. Before then, there were no fixed table dimensions. By 1850, the billiard table had essentially evolved into its current form.

There are three main types of billiards: carom billiards（开伦台球）, pocket billiards （落袋台球）(also known as pool（美式普尔）), and snooker（斯诺克台球）. Carom billiards is played with three balls, a cue ball（主球/母球）and two object balls（目标球）, on a pocket-less table（无袋球桌）; scoring is by caroms （连撞两球, 连击）only, i.e., by causing the cue ball to strike the object balls in specified ways. Pocket billiards is played with 15 object balls and a cue ball on a table with six pockets（球袋）; the essential object of the game is to cause the object balls to enter the pockets. Snooker, a complex and colorful game combining offensive and defensive aspects, is similar to pocket billiards, except that it uses 21 object balls (15 red balls and six balls of other colours) and smaller pockets. The British appetite for snooker is approached only by the American passion for baseball; it is possible to see a snooker competition every day in Britain. Historically, snooker balls were made exclusively from heavy ivory. Thankfully, these quickly became a thing of the past and were replaced before the Second World War by lighter Crystallite balls（微晶球）made from the crushed shin bones of cows. Today, snooker balls are entirely made from synthetic materials. In much the same way as golf, snooker demands high standards of etiquette and behavior from all players, at all levels, at all times. This applies in the same way to a local league match as it does to a big game in a professional tournament.

There are many additional variations of the basic games like eight-ball（八球）, straight pool（14-1连续击球比赛）, nine-ball（九球）, etc., depending on the number of balls used, the positioning of the balls, the boundaries on the table, and the scoring. Billiard sports require great touch, feel and excellent hand to eye co-ordination.

Relevant Words and Phrases

rack	extension	bridge
English	snookered	cannon

Text B

Sports Agents

1 Sports agents act, first and foremost, as intermediaries between sportspersons and sport clubs/organizers of sport events with a view to hiring an athlete or sportsperson. They bring together the parties interested in concluding an agreement. Finding a job for a sportsperson is the main role of sports agents. Sports agents may however engage in a broader range of activities, including the arrangement of contracts on behalf of the sportsperson such as image rights contracts, sponsoring contracts, and advertising contracts, or the managing of assets of the sportsperson. Sports agents have thus become essential partners of sportspersons and organizers of sport events, acting as a go-between and advisor for either side. Agents facilitate transactions between sport clubs or organizers of sport events and sportspersons. They are an integral part of the market.

2 Sports agents today have a variety of different social and professional profiles and offer a wide range of services. Thus, the definition of sports agent is fairly broad. Furthermore, because of the internationalization of sports, Sports agents' activities are often transnational in nature.

Sports in the United States and the Influence of Sports Agents

3 The presence of sports agents is closely linked to the progressive professionalization of sport. At a time when Europe was still advocating sporting amateurism[1], professional sports were becoming increasingly more important in the United States. The reason sports agents played a bigger role in American sports is basically because in the United States the growth of professional sports took place mostly independently of government.

[1]amateurism /'æmətərɪzəm / *n.* the conviction that people should participate in sports as a hobby (for the fun of it) rather than as a job for money

4 As the various sport activities gradually became organized, the U.S. government chose not to regard sport as a State matter. Sport therefore was largely structured by the private sector. This situation gave the promoters and organizers of sport a great deal of independence. As a result, many individuals had the opportunity to introduce to sport what, for the times, were remarkable innovations. Albert G. Spalding was one such person. A former baseball player turned promoter and then baseball agent, he organized, in 1888, the first world tour of an American all-stars baseball team. Thus, Spalding undoubtedly played a key role in the professionalization of baseball. He convinced promising players to follow him around the world for a wage of 50 dollars a week (which was good money for amateur players who usually had to work for a living outside the baseball season).

5 Spalding also contributed to promoting baseball as a founding member of the National Baseball League. He helped to draw up the rules of the game. At the time, the participation of intermediaries[2] in organizing and managing sport competitions was not seen as a problem. Instead in the United States, the payment and professionalization of players was considered an effective tool to develop sports. In that period, sports agents did not fight for higher wages and benefits so much, but rather fought for the recognition of sport as a form of work. It was not until the 1920s that agents started securing high revenues for their clients.

6 Gradually, the budding sport industry attracted all kinds of entrepreneurs who introduced in the sport sector negotiation strategies from the business sector. The increase in the financial inflows as a result of sponsorship and increased media coverage of sport partly explains the increase in the number of sports agents. As athletics became recognized as a legitimate career and regulations increased, these then attracted different kinds of intermediaries to the sport sector.

7 Nevertheless, the sporting community did not welcome the growing influence of sports agents. Both sport authorities and politicians were opposed to the role of sports agents. Not only were the roles sports agents played unclear, they also stood in opposition to the interests of the organizers. Sport authorities regarded the autonomy[3] and the business dynamics enjoyed by agents

---

[2]intermediary /ˌɪntə'miːdɪərɪ/ *n.* someone who carries messages between people who are unwilling or unable to meet

[3]autonomy /ɔː'tɒnəmɪ/ *n.* the right of a group of people to govern itself, or to organize its own activities

as a threat to their own interests. These conflicts were not only financial but very soon also became ethical in nature, foreshadowing the typical tug-of-war[4] between club managers and agents we see today.

8 Laws designed to regulate the sports agent's profession were first introduced in the 1990s. Focusing mainly on protecting university athletes, these regulations generally established that agents must be registered with a competent authority and be issued a licence. At the beginning of 2000, fewer than 30 American States had introduced legislation regulating the activities of sports agents, but by August of that year the Uniform Athlete Agents Act —applicable to all the States of the Union— had been passed. The main aim of this law was to harmonize[5] the regulations in force in different States in order to significantly limit abuses in this area.

9 European agents have tried to import into their sport markets the strategies, tactics and techniques successfully applied in the United States. This is particularly true in the case of certain professional sports, including tennis, football and basketball.

Different Types of Sports Agents

10 Based on their background and careers, we may distinguish five categories of sports agents.

Agents who are former athletes or players

11 The network of relations—as well as the experience and knowledge of the sport environment—which top sportspersons acquire by the end of their sporting career, are invaluable assets facilitating their transition to a new career as sports agents. Research shows that the decision to become a sports agent is often linked to the end of someone's sporting career. Between the end of their sporting career and the beginning of a new job, sportspersons go through a transitional period during which they are particularly attentive[6] to any employment opportunities that might arise, particularly through the network of connections they have built in the course of their career.

Agents who are influential and well-connected in the sports market

12 Agents who are influential in the sports field usually hold a more or less substantial

[4]tug-of-war /ˌtʌgəv'wɔ:/ *n.* any hard struggle between equally matched groups
[5]harmonize /'hɑ:mənaɪz/ *vt.* people agree in a friendly way to make laws, systems, or regulations the same or similar
[6]attentive /ə'tentɪv/ *adj.* (often followed by "to") giving care or attention

financial share in the sport market. Because of their knowledge of the sport environment and their links with decision-makers in that environment, they are often essential participants in negotiations which might be difficult and which they can influence positively. Such sports agents are present in sports where the financial stakes are high and there are many challenges that need to be overcome, notably in tennis, football, boxing and motor sport. They rarely have a licence and they willingly describe themselves as "advisers" or "go-betweens", in that their main role consists in putting in touch people who do not know each other personally but who may wish to work together. In general, because they own a share in a segment of the sport market this strengthens the legitimacy[7] of their role, both in personal and professional terms. The data show that this type of agent deals mainly with sponsorship or image-rights contracts and does not always receive payment for the services rendered[8].

Casual agents

13 The concept of "casual agent" refers to individuals who, without wishing to have a career as a sports agent, are occasionally led to play the role of an agent and are paid for this role. Casual agents seem to be present in most professional sports.

Agents who are coaches

14 The "coach/agent" is a little-known category of agents. However, the research shows that, across all sports, there are many coaches who have played the role of a sports agent at one point or another, and some have been paid for fulfilling this role. This type of sports agent is mainly present in football, boxing, athletics and so-called amateur Olympic sports, such as gymnastics and combat sports.

Agents who are relatives

15 Most sport organizations have allowed for sportspersons to use a member of their family to represent their interests. While it is true that this kind of agent was very widespread in professional sports in the past, today very few sportspersons choose to be represented by a family member.

16 Not all "professional" agents necessarily fall into one of the five categories described above. There are in fact individuals whose employment as sports agents is their only source of income and who are not former sportspersons or coaches. Others have chosen the profession as

[7]legitimacy /lɪ'dʒɪtɪməsɪ/ *n.* the quality of being legal or acceptable
[8]render /'rendə/ *vt.* give or supply

their sole livelihood without even setting up a network beforehand.

Services Provided by Sports Agents

17 Individual sports agents may fulfill a range of tasks and are in fact increasingly led to provide different kinds of services, so though it is difficult to provide a complete list of activities, the following are some typical services provided by sports agents.

Providing advice

18 All sports seem to have agents who are advisors or consultants. Their main role is to guide the sportsperson in making the best choices at different stages in his/her career. Whether licensed or unlicensed this agent is knowledgeable about the world of sport and so is seen as a valuable adviser in the eyes of the sportsperson. They mainly give advice that is required before signing a contract, when a sportsperson may have doubts about this or that aspect of the deal. Thus, many football players report that they rely on an adviser to "make the right decision". This kind of agent is also present in "tour-based" sports such as athletics, boxing, golf and tennis. An advisory agent may also act on behalf of a club, for example to ensure that the lowest possible price is paid for a player.

Brokering

19 The concept of the agent as broker or go-between —i.e. the most frequent type of agent in professional sports— refers to the agent's role in negotiations between three parties, the sportsperson, the agent and the club or organizer of a sport event. In this capacity, the agent acts as an intermediary between at least two parties and represents the interests of one of them. The contract between the parties may be in writing, in the form of an agency contract, or by spoken communication.

Organizing and promoting sport competitions

20 The "organizing agent" is involved in the organization of sport events or competitions. The sports agent is asked to take part in the organization of a sport event particularly when the agent in question has a wide network of connections. Some agents specialize in organizing athletics meetings. Their privileged relations with top athletes enable them to set up major events. In boxing, the organizing agent is not really responsible for the details of the matches. Rather, his role is to promote the event and ensure the boxers will be able to fight in the best possible conditions.

Managing the player's image and communication

21 Agents acting as spokespersons for a player are similar to press officers. They basically manage the sportsperson's image. In sports where no transfers take place, sports agents spend most of their time managing the sportsperson's image. This role is also very common in sports in which transfers are more or less frequent.

Managing the player's assets

22 In addition to helping to manage the career of the sportsperson concerned, a sports agent sometimes manages the athlete's financial assets. Trust is an essential basis for this kind of relationship between the sportsperson and the agent. In general terms, the sportsperson asks the agent to assist him in preparing for his retirement from sport and investing his assets wisely. Some sportspersons do not hesitate to enter into partnerships with their agents and to invest in deals suggested by the agent.

23 In summary, as previously mentioned, it is difficult to define sports agents' activities since sports agents play various roles and provide different services, some to the athletes and some to the sport association. Taking the above into considerations, a sports agent may be defined as any natural or legal person occasionally or regularly engaging in one or more of the following activities in return for payment:

— negotiating a contract between two parties related to a sporting activity for pay

— negotiating different kinds of contracts for a professional sportsperson, such as image rights contract, sponsoring contract, advertising contract

— managing the assets of a professional sportsperson

— acting as an intermediary to help conclude a contract is the most typical role of a sports agent.

Total words: 2014

Total reading time: __________minutes________seconds

* *The text is based on KEA-CDES-EOSE: Study on Sports Agents in the European Union by the European Commission.*

Comprehension Check

1. How do you understand the statement "Sports agents today have a variety of different social and professional profiles" in paragraph 2?
2. What do "the autonomy and the business dynamics" in paragraph 7 mean? Explain it in your own words.
3. What were the factors that allowed the sports agent business to grow in North America?
4. What are the major types of sports agents? And what is the expertise for each type?
5. Based on the description of sports agents' duties, what are the characteristics a sports agent must have to excel in this career?

Pop Culture

Agents ... they are some of the most hated people in professional sports. Long thought to be nothing but greedy and ruthless hustlers, agents are the ultimate backroom operators. When there is some high-stakes contract negotiation between millionaire players and billionaire owners, you can bet in the center of it, is an agent. But what do we really know about them?

With "The Dotted Line," acclaimed director Morgan Spurlock pulls back the curtain on the ultra-secretive sports agent industry to expose what these guys really do in the trenches. Top agents in the NFL, the NBA, and MLB are followed to explore the turbulent and emotional ups and downs of recruiting, marketing and negotiating record-breaking contracts for their top-tier clients. The film also explores recent NCAA agent scandals and the complex issues that can arise when college athletes turn pro.

Are these guys really the sleazeballs people think they are? Or are they just skilled businessmen, simply acting in the best interests of their clients? "The Dotted Line" paints a well-rounded portrait of a fascinating and complex industry.

Vocabulary Building

Look up the following words and expressions in reference books and on the Internet.

Words and Expressions	Meaning
market segment	
gross impression	
niche marketing	
turnkey operation	

13

UNIT

Gender Issues

All my life, I believed that I couldn't show weakness, I couldn't pull myself out if I was hurt, I couldn't let people say, "She's just a girl." ... I had to be tougher [than men], because only then did you get respect.

—Lauren Arase, goalie for NCAA soccer champions

Pre-reading Thoughts

1. What are considered the norms in society for men and women? In other words, what makes a woman feminine and a man masculine?

2. Which do you prefer to watch, women's sports or men's sports? Are athletics making girls masculine?

3. Do you think women are treated fairly in the world of sports? In which sports do women attract a lot of media attention?

Text A

Gender Differences: Sports Sexualizing Women

1 In our society we have many different ideologies and standards that put pressure on the way that we present ourselves. One of the main struggles is deciphering what it means to be male or female. This is a struggle between masculinity and femininity. Many social institutions add to this struggle and stress the differences beyond their already taxing nature. Professional sports specifically strains gender differences. These differences present an overwhelming challenge for women to be accepted in a male dominated and masculine institution. Sports encourage and in many cases force women to sexualize themselves either by choice or by the media. It is in our society's makeup to underappreciate female athletes and their sports.

2 To understand the pressures of athletics on women, there must be an understanding of gender. According to colleagues Candace West and Don H. Zimmerman, gender is a socially con-

structed idea that people then strive to achieve. They said that gender was "an achieved status: that which is constructed through psychological, cultural, and social means". This idea tells us that each individual continually attempts to achieve a higher status of his or her gender. Society focuses on traditional gender roles where men are considered masculine, big, strong, competitive, determined and hard headed. Women are traditionally feminine, soft, gentle, petite and kind. These roles are continually reshaped but for the most part the societal views have, generally speaking, stayed the same. These gender roles and other aspects of gender differences have fueled the construction of sports today.

3 Sports have been around for over 3,000 years and since ancient Greece introduced formal sports, it was presented as a masculine thing to do. The first Olympics included events such as human and chariot races, wrestling, jumping and javelin-throwing. Men would compete for large crowds of people cheering and chanting. Women were excluded from these games and were forced to develop their own way of competing called the Games of Hera. Since then, there has been a separation and a clear dominance of male sports. Even though women have many of their own professional sports and even compete in the Olympics, the gap is still there. For the massed majority, women do not compete in sports with men. This is because it is believed that women are naturally less athletic, not as strong and not as skilled. M.D. Dudley A. Sargent, in his article *Are Athletics Making Girls Masculine?*, discusses the idea that sports should be adapted to women. After talking about men's sports being masculine he states that it is less dangerous, "if the sports are modified so as to meet their peculiar qualifications as to strength, height, weight, etc. inasmuch as the average woman is inferior to the average man in nearly every physical qualification". He goes on to talk about women's disadvantages in strength, height and endurance. The nature of sports today reflects this view and sports are for the most part separated and made to reflect the fact that women are supposedly physically inferior to men in sports. Women's sports are adapted to reflect such views. Let's take a look at two such examples. A woman's basketball is sized one inch smaller than that of the men's basketball. Women play softball or fast pitch instead of baseball. They have a shorter fence, use bats with more power and pitch underhand instead of overhand. The differences stretch beyond the rules of the sports, television and media coverage is extremely lopsided.

4 From live game coverage to after game highlights and recaps, women's sports have far less coverage than the male sports. In a study done by Margaret Carlisle Duncan, Ph.D. and Michael A. Messner, Ph.D. the discrepancy is consistent across the board. Women's sports took only 6.3% of airtime where men's took up 91.4% with the rest being gender neutral. One possible attribution for

this discrepancy is societies' views of sports being masculine. With traditional gender roles and the history of sports, this theory makes sense. Even though women's sports have come a long way and they continually gain more respect, society still sees women athletes as deviants to the gender roles that so dominate popular views. For men, being an athlete and being on top of your sport is enough because they are achieving that status of being masculine. For women this is not enough because they are not performing their gender role according to traditional views. This discrepancy lays the groundwork for women to have to look towards other places to gain respect, attention and financial gains.

5 Athletic men are looked upon as heroes and role models. If a man is extremely athletic and skilled in his sport then he gains respect and popularity. Because of this popularity he is able to gain many financial benefits. As laid out earlier, the popularity difference is vast. Men's sports have more media coverage, and they have more fans so therefore they are able to make more money. Men in sports are able to make a higher salary because of their popularity and skill. Because more people go to men's sporting events and spend more money on men's teams, men make more money. Women are at an extreme disadvantage when it comes to their salaries paid by their teams. To see this in action, the largest contract signed by a male athlete is a contract with a total value of $275,000,000. This is to be paid over ten years which is $27,500,000 paid each year to Alex Rodriguez from the New York Yankees. 2011's top paid female athlete made $25,000,000 and that is total earnings including any revenue from sponsorships, endorsements and marketing she has done.

6 To add insult to injury, women are at a further disadvantage when it comes to earnings outside of contracts. These include endorsements sponsorship and marketing. For men, once again, it is enough to be a great in your sport. For instance, LeBron James (current NBA star) received a $90,000,000 contract from Nike shoes when he was in high school. Nike's decision seemed to pay off but their reasoning was because of his talent. This would never be the case for a female athlete. To be a star in their sport isn't enough. If you take a look at all the female athletes that are making money out of marketing and endorsements, they are all doing so by sexualizing themselves. Maria Sharapova, Danica Patrick and Venus Williams all add some sexual aspect to themselves to gain marketing opportunities. This ESPN video shows the view of three sports pundits on the topic. (http://espn.go.com/video/clip?id=7558303)

7 In the video they talk about the female athletes sexualizing themselves. They discuss what level of sexuality that women should subject themselves to. They refer to it as finding the balance

of being sexual to create a brand. Why can't a female athlete's brand be pure in her talents and skills of her sport? These three athletes sexualize themselves in different ways. Magazines and media portray female athletes in a sexual manner while men are portrayed as competent in their sport.

8 The issue lies in the fact that they have to be sexual and desirable to gain the same attention as men do. This can be seen in the media as well as in the uniforms that they wear. Women's tennis is arguably the most popular of the women's sports. They wear very short skirts and tight tops that show off their bodies. Venus Williams is one of the pioneers of this. She used her uniform to create her brand. Other sports such as volleyball have women in very tight, short shorts or even bikinis in beach volleyball. The point is that they don't need these types of uniforms to functionally play their sport. This is a choice, a strategic one, to get more attention.

9 Additionally, female athletes struggle with the conflicts of being an athlete and being a female in society. As previously mentioned athletics is predominately seen as a masculine thing. Females in athletics are deemed masculine in society unless they prove otherwise. Because of the nature of sports and the role of gender in our society, women must over sexualize themselves and prove that they are still feminine in spite of the fact that they are athletes.

10 Sports as a social institution emphasize the gap between genders that exists because of societal constructions. Ideally men and women in sports would be considered equal. They would get the same media coverage, they would make a similar pay and sports would not take away from their gender. Unfortunately this is not the case. Because of societal views and the structure of the institution that is professional sports, it is likely that the ideal will not be reached.

Total words: 1462
Total reading time:__________minutes________seconds

* *The text is based on Gender Differences: Sports Sexualizing Women*

Vocabulary and Expressions

decipher /dɪ'saɪfə/ *vt.* to discover the meaning of something written badly or in a difficult or hidden way

strain /streɪn/ *vt.* cause to be tense and uneasy or nervous or anxious

petite /pə'ti:t/ *adj.* (of a woman) attractively small and thin

lopsided /lɒp'saɪdɪd/ *adj.* with one side bigger, higher, etc. than the other; not equally balanced

recap /'ri:kæp/ *n.* a summary at the end that repeats the substance of a longer discussion

discrepancy /dɪs'krepənsɪ/ *n.* a difference between conflicting facts or claims or opinions

pundit /'pʌndɪt/ *n.* a person who knows a lot about a particular subject and is therefore often asked to give an opinion about it

Comprehension Check

1. Paragraph two gives a definition of gender and states, "gender is an achieved status: that which is constructed through psychological, cultural, and social means". Explain in other words what it means. Do you agree? Is there any other explanation for gender?
2. What are some of the modifications made to sports to make it more suitable for women?
3. According to the passage, why do societies' views of sports being masculine make sense? And in what ways do female athletes deviate from societal norms?
4. How might female athletes sexualize themselves? And why?

Critical Thinking Starters

1. What are some of the obvious inequalities that exist for women in sports?
2. Do you think something should be done to change the media's lack of coverage of women's sports, or should it be left alone as just a matter of supply and demand?
3. In China, do women athletes suffer from gender confusion as it's described in this article? Give some examples to support your idea.

More to Know

Policy development at the nexus of sport, gender and development has centered mainly on sport and gender. Increasingly, there is recognition of the need to involve and engage with gender issues through sport in the context of developing countries.

Major highlights in policy development in sport, gender and development:

- 1949 — International Association of Physical Education and Sport for Girls and Women (IAPESGW) is formed.
- 1968 — a female athlete lights the Olympic fire for the first time at the Olympic Games in Mexico city.
- 1975 — UN Women's World Conference in Mexico City leads to the creation of the International Research and Training Institute for the Advancement of Women (INSTRAW) and the United Nations Development Fund for Women (UNIFEM).
- 1979 — UN General Assembly adopts the UN Convention on the Elimination of All Forms of Discrimination Against Women (CEDAW) .
- 1981 — Canadian Association for the Advancement of Women and Sport and Physical Activity (CAAWS) is formed.
- 1981 — two female members are elected to join the International Olympic Committee.
- 1984 — Women's Sports Foundation is founded in Great Britain.
- 1994 — the first World Conference on Women and Sport and the signing of the Brighton Declaration, signals the 'women in sport' movement taking on an international dimension.
- 1995 — the International Working Group on Women and Sport is formed and receives the status of official IOC commission.
- 1995 — the fourth UN Women's World Conference takes place in Beijing, signaling the shift in discourse from 'Women in Development' (WID) to 'Gender and Development' (GAD).
- 1996 — the promotion of female sport is added to the Olympic Charter.
- 1996 — the first IOC World Conference on Women and Sport, Lausanne, Switzerland. A resolution on women and sport is passed.
- 1998 — the second IWG World Conference on Women and Sport, Windhoek, Namibia. The conference produced the 'Windhoek Call for Action' legacy.

- 2002 — the third IWG World Conference on Women and Sport, Montreal, Canada. The conference produced the 'Montreal Toolkit' and 'Montreal Communique' legacies.
- 2004 — the third IOC World Conference on Women and Sport is held in Morocco, entitled: 'Sport as a Vehicle for Social Change'.
- 2006 — the fourth IWG World Conference on Women and Sport, Kumamoto, Japan. The conference produced the 'Kumamoto Commitment to Collaboration' legacy.
- 2008 — the fourth IOC World Conference on Women and Sport, Dead Sea, Jordan.
- 2010 — the fifth IWG World Conference on Women and Sport, Sydney, Australia. The conference produced the 'Sydney Scoreboard' legacy.
- 2012 — the fifth IOC World Conference on Women and Sport, Los Angeles, USA. The conference produced the 'Los Angeles Declaration'.
- 2014 — the sixth IWG World Conference on Women and Sport, Helsinki, Finland. The motto is "Lead the Change, Be the Change".

Expert's View

Sociologists Brett Smith and Andrew Sparkes (2002) point out that people create identities, including feminine and masculine identities, through narratives — that is, stories they tell others about themselves. Their research indicates that playing power and performance sports provides men with a masculinizing narrative — a story in which manhood is constructed through physical accomplishments and dominance over other men. These narratives are the foundation of hegemonic masculinity in many societies. But the identity-creating narratives available to women are unlikely to involve sport participation, because sports don't contain femininity stories.

Sport participation among girls and women will not continue to increase automatically (Cooky and McDonald, 2005). Without efforts to maintain progress toward achieving gender equity, there's tendency in most cultures to give priority to men's sports and male athletes. This is because sport world usually are

1. *male-dominated*, so that power and qualifications are associated with manhood and

men — that is, being qualified in a sport world means possessing characteristics associated with masculinity;

2. *male-identified*, so that a typical sport world is a "man's world" — that is, people assume it involves men and is about men, unless it is identified as "women's sports" — such as "the Women's World Cup" or "the Women's Final Four";

3. *male-centered*, so that men and men's lives are the expected focus of attention when people talk about sport stories, legends, records, events, halls of fame, and media programming.

This framework was developed by Allan Johnson in his chapter on "How systems of privilege work" in *Privilege, Power, and Difference* (McGraw-Hill, 2006).

Activity Time-Out

Task 1

Take a survey of students on campus. Find out if they perceive women athletes as too masculine. Make up a survey of 5 or more questions about women in sports. Ask 20-30 students outside of your class to fill out the survey. You might consider doing one for Chinese students in Chinese, of course, and one for international students in English. Bring the results of the survey to class and be prepared to present your findings to the class.

Task 2

Do a search on-line for more articles related to women and sports. Pick one of the issues written about in the article and search for that issue. For instance, you could search for women athletes and wages, or women athletes and sexualization. Write a summary of the article and prepare to share it with the class.

Sports in Focus

Athletics is the "Mother of Sports". It is an official competition sport both on the 1st Olympic and Asian Games. The modern Olympic motto Citius, Altius, Fortius (faster, higher, stronger) best captures track-and-field (田径) competition. Each event determines who can run the fastest, who can jump the highest or the longest, or who can throw the farthest.

The origins of modern athletics can be traced to the second half of the 19th century. Popular interest in and enthusiasm for all types of physical exercise had caused a boom in participation in sports. Athletics was especially popular and soon became central to the physical exercise elements of national educational systems. Of course, the most important event in the early history of modern athletics was the inaugural edition of the Olympic Games, which took place at Athens, in Greece, in the spring of 1896. Over 100 years has elapsed since then and, thanks to the miracle of television, millions of people around the world are able to follow the world's greatest athletes at the World Championship (世界锦标赛) or the Olympic Games. On July 17, 1912, two days after the last athletics event of the Stockholm Olympic Games, a congress was held to form an umbrella organization for international athletics. At the Congress, the International Amateur Athletic Federation (国际业余田径联合会) or IAAF (国际田联) came into being. Over the years, the IAAF has grown into a vast organization as the world governing body of track and field athletics, road running (公路跑), race walking (竞走) and cross-country(越野跑). In 2001, the IAAF Congress voted unanimously for the organization's name to be changed into the International Association of Athletics Federations.

Generally speaking, athletic events can be split into four parts: track (径赛), field (田赛), road (公路赛), and combined events (全能项目). Track events are running races that take place on a 400m outdoor track in the main stadium. The athletes shall be placed in the order in which any part of their bodies (i.e., torso (躯干), as distinguished from the head, neck, arms, legs, hands or feet) reaches the vertical plane of the nearer edge of the finish line.

Field events are throwing (投掷) and jumping (跳跃) competitions that usually take place inside the track. Except for the fouls (犯规), the performance of each trial (试跳) will be regarded as the valid (有效) jump in all horizontal jumping field events (跳远比赛). Except for the fouls, the height the athletes have jumped over in each trial will be regarded as valid in the high jump (跳高) and pole vault (撑杆跳高). In all throwing events (投掷项目), if the apparatuses (器械) fall into the landing area completely (not including the sideline of the landing area), it will be regarded as valid throwing.

Road events (公路赛项目) are long running (长跑) and walking races (竞走比赛) that take place on public roads, while they often finish on the track inside the stadium.

Combined events feature a selection of track and field events that take place over two days and are designed to find the best all-round athlete, such as the decathlon (十项全能运动) and the heptathlon (七项全能运动). In the combined events competition, the winner shall be the athlete who has obtained the highest total points.

Relevant Words and Phrases

runway	hop	shot put
discus	hammer throw	stride

Text B

Caster Semenya and the IOC's Olympics Gender Bender

1 The person carrying the flag for South Africa at Friday's opening ceremonies might be one of the most-famous athletes on the planet. But her notoriety has little to do with her talent on the track; nor does it stem from her hardscrabble personal story. Instead, this girl—who went from a village where few have running water to reigning world champion—is best known for the fact that three years ago, the whole world was openly speculating about what, exactly, was going on under her running shorts.

2 Though she has since been cleared for competition, the subject of Caster Se-

menya's gender is still pretty much all anyone talks about when they talk about the powerhouse runner. In 2009, after shaving eight seconds off of her personal best during the run-up to the World Athletic Championships in Berlin, the rumors that had long swirled around the now 21-year old athlete reached a fever pitch. In the weeks that followed, Semenya made headlines around the world—under some of the most unenviable circumstances imaginable. As one of her competitors put it bluntly: "For me, she's not a woman. She is a man."

3 On the day before the Berlin event, the International Association of Athletics Federations announced that Semenya was undergoing gender-verification testing, a weeks-long process that had started in South Africa and would continue in Berlin. Semenya, it was later reported, had been told she was being tested for doping. But in spite of the humiliating public reveal, her victory the following day was as definite as it was defiant. Her nearest competition crossed the finish line a full bus-length behind her. She won gold, beat her own personal best, and became the world champion in the 800 meters. It should have been the best day of her life. Instead, after the race, she retreated from cameras and microphones, avoided all interviews, and, ultimately, disappeared for eleven months. Banned from competition by the IAAF, Semenya underwent a slew[1] of further tests before being cleared for competition as a woman.

4 Semenya, of course, is far from the first competitor to face this kind of scrutiny[2]. Female athletes, especially the talented ones, have been accused of not really being female for almost as long as they've been allowed to compete. Early in her career, Serena Williams—who just won her fifth Wimbledon and who will be trying for her third Olympic gold in London—was called a "she-male" and a transsexual. Brittney Griner, who this year led Baylor University's women's basketball team to an undefeated season and an NCAA championship and earlier this month was named athlete of the year at the ESPN ESPY Awards, has been so dogged by rumors that she's actually a man that her coach once publicly pleaded for the speculation to cease.

5 Such accusations go back at least half a century. The IOC adopted its first set of gender tests in the 1960s, with "nude parades" that were exactly what they sound like: female competitors made to walk naked before a panel of judges. But as the IOC later realized, what's on the outside doesn't

[1]slew /sluː/ *n.* a slew of things is a large number of them

[2]scrutiny /ˈskruːtɪnɪ/ *n.* the careful and detailed examination of something in order to get information about it

always match what's on the inside, so the committee moved on to chromosome[3] testing. Once it was shown that women can have a single X chromosome (just as men can have two of them) that was abandoned as well. Then came SRY gene detection (the gene that triggers male sex determination), but after the Atlanta games, in which 8 women tested positive for it, and all were cleared for competition, this method, too, was deemed insufficient. A decade ago, the committee decided to chuck[4] the testing altogether. But in the wake of Semenya's case, and the international scrutiny it prompted, the IOC announced that it would try, once again, to devise a way to decisively determine what makes a woman a woman.

6 The committee's medical commission assembled a group of two-dozen experts to debate the various aspects of sex characteristics and the merits of various methods of testing. The result of those meetings concluded that the determining factor making men men and women women—and the source of what was deemed an unfair competitive edge—lies in naturally-occurring levels of testosterone[5]. The testing, which will be administered on a case-by-case basis rather than across the board, will result in the ban of any female athlete deemed to have an unfair advantage because of high testosterone levels. Unlike the IAAF, it doesn't elaborate on interventions or treatments. But for female athletes who want to compete, the option is not off the table. This could mean anything from surgical interventions (removing internal, essentially dormant testes) to pharmaceutical ones (hormone replacement therapies).

7 Semenya, her coach, and sports officials have been cryptic [6] about the results of her tests and the treatments she might be undergoing—but details of the exams have leaked out nonetheless. According to a story published in Australia's *Daily Telegraph*, Semenya's body has both male and female characteristics—she's externally female, and internally male, essentially— and produces far more testosterone than the average woman. The track and field manager at the University of Pretoria's High Performance Centre, recently confirmed that Semenya has submitted to an unspecified treatment in order to compete in the London games. According to critics of testosterone testing, there's been little research done on how the hormone actually affects female athletes.

---

[3]chromosome /'krəʊməsəʊm/ *n.* the rod-like structure found in all living cells, containing the chemical patterns which control what an animal or plant is like

[4]chuck /tʃʌk/ *vt.* stop doing something

[5]testosterone /te'stɒstərəʊn/ *n.* a male hormone that causes a stage of growth in older boys and change in their reproductive organs

[6]cryptic /'krɪptɪk/ *adj.* having a meaning that is mysterious or obscure

8 What most troubles the researchers is the fact that female athletes found to have excessive levels of testosterone might have to submit to medical intervention to lower those levels if they want to compete—even when medical intervention might otherwise be unnecessary. Even though they are among the healthiest people on the planet, the treatment is risky since the drugs are not benign.[7] According to studies, patients treated via hormone replacement therapy are more likely to develop breast cancer, ovarian[8] cancer, strokes, and heart attacks. To be clear, what the IOC committee is looking for is levels of naturally-occurring testosterone that the body produces on its own, without help from injected hormones. It's simple to test for synthetic versions of testosterone, and not even the IOC claims this is analogous to testing for doping. Having abnormally high levels of natural testosterone, critics say, is more akin to having an oversized heart, like Lance Armstrong, or double-jointed ankles, like Michael Phelps. It's genetic, biological, and it may or may not confer an advantage. Even supporters of the new policy acknowledge that it is far from perfect. "It is a social-imposed categorization which sports authorities have always struggled to comply with," says Dr. Eric Vilain, a professor of human genetics at UCLA. The reason so many methods have been adopted and then abandoned is because there is no single indicator that can be used to definitively distinguishes between the sexes—not chromosomes, nor hormones, nor secondary characteristics, nor external appearance. "The reality is it's absolutely never going to be perfect."

9 What the IOC has struggled with all these years exposes something that many of us might find difficult to process: between M and F exists a tremendous swath of gray. Exact numbers are hard to pin down, but by some estimates, at least one in every 2,000 babies is born intersex, and still more are diagnosed as teenagers or adults. In recent years, public attitudes towards gender roles and identity have begun to loosen considerably. A Denver father of six recently made international headlines after he somewhat cheerfully told a local paper that doctors had discovered ovaries in the place of testes during a routine treatment for kidney stones. Four countries have third-gender options on their passport forms. And this spring, Sweden introduced a gender-neutral pronoun.

10 When it comes to the transgendered, the IOC saw the writing on the wall almost a decade ago. In 2004, it issued a set of guidelines called the Stockholm Consensus, which stipulates that trans athletes may compete as long as surgeries and hormone treatments have been completed and the individual's new sex is legally recognized. But in the upper echelons[9] of professional sports,

[7]benign /bɪˈnaɪn/ *adj.* describes a growth that is not likely to cause death or serious harm
[8]ovarian /əʊˈveərɪən/ *adj.* of or relating to the ovaries or an ovary
[9]echelon /ˈeʃəlɒn/ *n.* a particular level or group of people within an organization

the idea that there might be something other than male or female isn't so easy to accommodate.

11 "In what other institutional setting in society could ever you have a sex test and not only legitimize it but present it as if it was a necessary policy?" asks Ian Richie, a professor of Health Sciences at Canada's Brock University. "To test somebody's sex, to have them prove that they are what they are in terms of their sex, is in many countries completely unethical, contrary to human rights, in some cases unconstitutional. But in the context of sport it's seen as an inevitable thing we have to do. Sport is the only place that could happen, because sport is based on the idea that men are men and women are women and that's it."

12 Semenya may be carrying her country's flag in London, but there's no denying that her journey to the world's stage was at times an agonizing one. In a 2011 British television documentary called Too Fast to Be a Woman, Semenya spoke of sinking into a deep depression after being subjected to the tests, and even considered quitting athletics altogether.

13 It all highlights a cruel injustice: the policy—and the testing, treatment, and humiliation that can come with it—only applies to female athletes. Men who excel at, say, ice dancing or synchronized swimming, where success has more to do with grace and rhythm than brute strength or speed, simply aren't questioned in the same way women are. In 2010, after two French-Canadian sports commentators snickered over the flamboyant[10] skating champion Johnny Weir and suggested that he should compete with the women, they were immediately and vociferously condemned for what was widely perceived as homophobic, despicable language. Similarly, there is no upper—or lower, for that matter—limit to the amount of testosterone their bodies naturally produce.

14 This past winter, Bruce Kidd, a Canadian professor of physical education and health, called on IOC to abandon not just gender testing, but segregation too. Similar changes have been called, noting that size and strength could, in the future, provide a better basis for groupings than sex alone. Already, male and female athletes compete against one another in all equestrian and sailing events, and in some of the luge, badminton, and tennis ones.

15 But eliminating gender segregation altogether could, in practical terms, lead to something that looks nothing like equality. It's been mere weeks since the fortieth anniversary of Title IX,

[10]flamboyant/flæm'bɒɪənt/ *adj.* very confident in behavior, or intended to be noticed, especially by being brightly colored

which ensured that girls had the same access to athletics that their male classmates did. Isn't there something counter-intuitive about the notion of dismantling[11] women-specific sports in the name of gender equity? Wouldn't such a move just eliminate women from the competition altogether?

16 Maybe not. A recent ESPN feature on the future of women in sports called, "You Ain't Seen Nothing Yet," argued that "women are not necessarily just getting bigger, they're also getting better." Sport is, essentially, a numbers game, and in the United States 4.5 million high school boys are on athletic teams, versus just 3.2 million girls. "Women are already as good, or better, than men."

17 If true, the need for gender testing may be moot[12] soon enough. But that's probably little consolation for today's athletes. "The way you were born is the way you were born," Semenya says in the British documentary. "Nothing can change it. I've got a deep voice. I know. I might look tough but what are you going to do? Do you think you can change it? No. If someone was born the way she was born, are you going to blame him or are you going to blame God? Whose fault is that? Nobody's."

Total words: 2171
Total reading time:__________minutes_________seconds

* *The text is based on Caster Semenya and the IOC's Olympics Gender Bender by Jesse Ellison.*

Comprehension Check

1. What is Semenya famous for? Retell the story in your own words.
2. In paragraph 5, the writer states, "But as the IOC later realized, what's on the outside doesn't always match what's on the inside," What do they mean by this?
3. According to the passage, is the testing for synthetic testosterone similar to the testing for doping?
4. What are some of the problems the IOC has had in determining whether a female athlete is really female or not? Which test is the most reliable so far?

[11]dismantle /dɪsˈmæntl/ *vt.* to get rid of a system or organization, usually over a period of time
[12]moot /muːt/ *adj.* of no legal significance (as having been previously decided)

Pop Culture

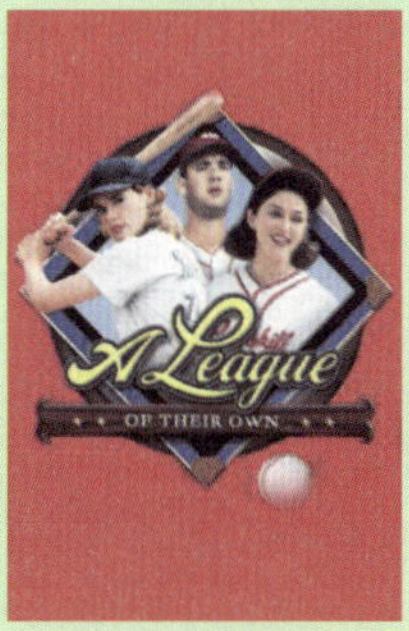

In 1992, Columbia Pictures released **A League of Their Own**, a fictionalized account of the All-American Girl's Professional Baseball League. The league was founded in 1943, when most of the men of baseball-playing age were far away in Europe and Asia fighting World War II. In the absence of male players, women were propelled to the forefront of baseball. Funny, charming and surprisingly moving, the movie depicts with respectful historical detail the long neglected beginnings of the Women's Baseball League. It may lapse into sentimentality from time to time, but despite this Penny Marshall directs this heartfelt story of some groundbreaking women.

Vocabulary Building

Look up the following words and expressions in reference books and on the Internet.

Words and Expressions	Meaning
homophobia	
feminist	
sissies	
underrepresentation	

14

UNIT

Sports Medicine

The good physician treats the disease; the great physician treats the patient who has the disease.

— William Osler

Pre-reading Thoughts

1. How is "sports medicine" translated into Chinese? What does this subject focus on?

2. If you get hurt when doing sports, will you go to hospital? Will you go to a general hospital or a hospital specialized in sports-related injuries?

3. What professions are related with sports medicine?

Text A

Nature and Scope of Sports Medicine

1 Sports medicine is a term that includes a broad range of clinical and scientific aspects of sport and exercise. For example, exercise therapies, such as ultrasound or electrical stimulation, are considered forms of sports medicine. Exercise prescriptions, such as weight training, and endurance (aerobic) running, jogging, and walking are also forms of sports medicine. Likewise, the exercise sciences, athletic training, and nutrition are part of the larger concept known as sports medicine.

2 Sometimes people are confused about the meaning of sports medicine because terms associated with it are often used interchangeably. Therefore, the Sports Medicine Umbrella was created to clarify sports medicine and its terminology.

3 The cover, or canopy, of the umbrella shows that disciplines such as physiology, biology, and kinesiology provide the overarching knowledge base for sports medicine. A strong disciplinary background is essential for prospective sports medicine professionals. These individuals must make knowledgeable decisions based on theory and scientific research that is a fundamental part of each discipline. They can not engage in trial and error practice on clients. Each client's situation is unique, and the competent sports medicine professional blends theory with application to help the client.

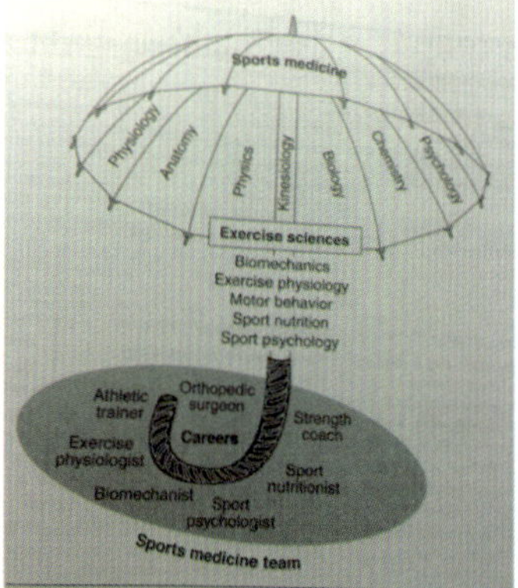

Figure 14.1 Sports medicine umbrella.

4 In the shaft of the umbrella, you see the exercise sciences (e.g., biomechanics, exercise physiology). Sometimes called subdisciplines, these fields of study use theories and knowledge from the disciplines as they specifically relate to sport and physical activity. These disciplines and subdisciplines provide the specialized scientific information that sports medicine professionals need to provide quality service to their clients.

5 Around the handle of the umbrella, several sports medicine professions are shown. These are examples of careers in which people could apply the knowledge gained through studying the disciplines, subdisciplines, and exercise sciences of sports medicine. For example, the athletic trainer and the strength coach are practitioners who provide unique services in sport and activity settings. Athletic trainers frequently prescribe range of motion exercise in the whirlpool, and strength coaches will provide instruction on proper body positions for weight lifting. To be effective, the athletic trainer must understand the effect of heat and movement during whirlpool therapy (exercise physiology), and the strength coach must understand the angle of pull and force generated by muscles during a lift (biomechanics). Therefore, both professionals rely on knowledge from the exercise sciences to perform their duties.

6 When several sports medicine professionals work together and a medical doctor (e.g., orthopedic surgeon or athletic team physician) is part of the group, the unit is known as a sports medicine team (note the shaded area under and encompassed by the sports medicine umbrella). You are probably familiar with this concept as it is used in association with sports medicine clinics, a relatively new concept that has captured the imagination of health care professionals during the past decade. Sports medicine clinics may be associated with hospitals or be managed privately by

a sports medicine team. These clinics have emerged because of the wants and needs of a diverse group of participants in sport and physical activity who seek the varied sports medicine information and services.

History of Sports Medicine

Ancient History

7 In ancient Greece and Rome, athletic contests were the way of everyday life. Physical education and training were a necessity, and medical specialists evolved for the care of the athletes. In fact, the first use of therapeutic exercise is credited to Herodicus, a fifth-century BCE physician whose theories are considered the foundation of sports medicine and who is considered the teacher of Hippocrates, the Father of Medicine.

8 Other important sports medicine figures during this time include Iccus of Tarentum (about 444 BCE), who wrote the first textbook on athletic training, and Milo of Croton, who was a heroic athlete and winner of five consecutive Olympic championships. Milo encouraged athletes to gain strength by lifting a bull every day, starting from the day of the bull's birth. By doing this, the athlete would be able to lift the animal when it was full-grown. Some scholars consider this the first record of progressive resistance training.

9 The first documented team physician arrived much later, during the second century CE. Appointed to treat the intrepid gladiators, Galen performed copious amounts of research in anatomy and physiology. Galen's works became the dogma of the medical knowledge of the Western world.

Jump to the 1900s

10 The term sports medicine was coined at the 1928 Olympics in St. Moritz, Switzerland, when the Association International Medico-Sportive(AIMS) committee met to plan the First International Congress of Sports Medicine, which was being held that year during the ninth Summer Olympic Games in Amsterdam. At least 280 sports physicians from twenty countries attended.

11 In 1968, while attending the Summer Olympics in Mexico City, Canadian doctor J. C. Kennedy concluded that well-organized and qualified medical care should accompany competing athletic teams. He became instrumental in the founding of the Canadian Academy of Sport Medicine (CASM) in 1970. Soon after, Dr. Kennedy was appointed Chief Medical Officer of the first true

medical team at the 1972 Summer Olympics in Munich, Germany. The United States has followed the lead of other countries in the development of sports medicine.

12 The American College of Sports Medicine (ACSM) was founded in 1954, and today it is the largest sports medicine and exercise science organization in the world, encompassing more than 20,000 international, national, and regional chapter members.

13 In addition, the *American Journal of Sports Medicine*, first published in 1974, is a leading peer-reviewed scientific journal of the American Orthopaedic Society for Sports Medicine (AOSSM). Interestingly, though, it was not until 1989 that the American Board of Medical Specialties recognized sports medicine as a legitimate subspecialty.

The Advent of Sports Medicine

14 The true advent of sports medicine in the United States arrived with the development of specialized physicians and clinics, such as Drs. Augustus Thorndike of Harvard and Edward Hitchcock of Amherst College, Drs. Robert Kerlan and Frank Jobe of the Kerlan-Jobe Orthopedics Clinic, and Dr. Jack C. Hughston of the Hughston Clinic.

15 Augustus Thorndike, MD, published his textbook *Athletic Injuries, Prevention, Diagnosis, and Treatment* in 1938. This book was the first general American text of sports medicine, and it still serves as the model text.

16 Edward Hitchcock, MD, was appointed as the first instructor of physical education and hygiene at Amherst College in 1954. Not only is he known as the father of physical education in America, but he is also regarded as the first sports medicine physician and the first team physician in America.

17 Robert Kerlan, MD, was the Los Angeles Dodgers' first team doctor in 1958. He was responsible for diagnosing Dodgers' pitcher, Sandy Koufax, with traumatic arthritis in her left elbow. As Kerlan's popularity grew, his personal practice flourished. He began work as an orthopedic consultant to several other professional teams in a variety of sports, including hockey, basketball, football, and horse racing. Together, Kerlan and his friend and colleague, Frank Jobe, MD, founded the Southwestern Orthopedic Medical Group in 1965. The name was changed in 1985 to the Kerlan-Jobe Orthopedic Clinic. This sports medicine clinic is regarded as one of the top centers.

18 Jack C. Hughston, MD, is another visionary in the field of sports medicine. He was one of the founders of the American Orthopedic Society for Sports Medicine. In 1949, he established the Hughston Sports Medicine Hospital, the first hospital of its kind, and the manifestation of his vision of a clinic that focused on the total health of an athlete. Originally, the institution was known as the Hughston Orthopedic Clinic, but after a broader range of services was introduced, the name was changed to the Hughston Clinic in acknowledgement of its wider scope.

Scientific Advancements

19 Without science, sports wouldn't be what it is today. Injury is inevitable, and prevention is the key. Today's scientists are redefining old sports equipment and developing new equipment to aid in the prevention of sports-related injuries. In addition, they are unveiling innovative gear designed to enable disabled athletes to safely join the ranks.

20 Science and technology also play a role in accurate and rapid diagnosis of a sports injury, which increases the chances of a complete recovery. New diagnostic techniques, such as various imaging modalities, permit physicians to peer into the body without breaking the skin. Injuries of bones, ligaments, and muscles are readily discernible when visualized in a digital 3-D reconstruction.

21 Science also breeds specialized care and new therapies. Studies are evaluating the advantages of certain therapies as compared with wait-and-watch approaches. New surgical techniques are more discriminate and less intrusive, thus promoting faster and more complete healing. Science also has opened nutritional understanding of the athlete and how diets, supplements, foods, and drinks affect athletic performance.

22 Sports science does not concentrate on injuries alone. In fact, most sports research targets game engineering. Scientists and athletes are always looking for cutting-edge equipment to enhance athletic performance. Such innovations include lighter shoes with bigger bounce; faster and more aerodynamic skates, skis, and wheelchairs; and tougher and stronger bats and rackets.

23 Other research targets body engineering. Scientists search for physiological and chemical pathways in the body that can be manipulated to produce better athletes; the study of endorphins

and their actions in the body is an example. They explore various doping strategies—some to formulate agents not detectable on health screens and others to look for better detection methods of such agents. Doping in sports is even taken one step further to gene doping, which is on the rise. From this process, some scientists are producing genetically modified athletes who are physically superior to their counterparts.

Total words: 1582
Total reading time: __________minutes_________seconds

* *The text is based on Sports Medicine by Jennifer L. Minigh*

Vocabulary and Expressions

canopy /'kænəpɪ/ *n.* a covering (usually of cloth) that serves as a roof to shelter an area from the weather

overarching /ˌəuvə'ɑːtʃɪŋ/ *adj.* most important, because of including or affecting all other areas

shaft / ʃɑːft / *n.* a pole or rod that forms the handle of a tool or weapon

orthopedic /ˌɔːθə'piːdɪk/ *adj.* relating to problems affecting people's joints and spines

BCE (before common era) Non-Christians often use BCE instead of BC in dates. BCE indicates a number of years or centuries before the year in which Jesus Christ is believed to have been born.

intrepid /ɪn'trepɪd/ *adj.* extremely brave and showing no fear of dangerous situations

copious /'kəupɪəs/ *adj.* in large amounts; more than enough

dogma /'dɒgmə/ *n.* a fixed, especially religious, belief or set of beliefs that people are expected to accept without any doubts

peer-review /ˌpɪərɪ'vjuː/ *vt.* to read, check, and give your opinion about something that has been written by another scientist or expert working in the same subject area as you

traumatic / /trɔː'mætɪk / *adj.* causing severe emotional shock and upset

discernible / dɪ'sɜːnɪbl̩ / *adj.* able to be seen or understood

endorphin /en'dɔːfɪn/ *n.* a chemical naturally released in the brain to reduce pain, and which in large amounts can make you feel relaxed and/or energetic

Comprehension Check

1. The author does not give a definition of sports medicine in the passage. But according to the description of it, can you give a definition of sports medicine?
2. How is a sports medicine team formed? What services can it provide?
3. Can you use another diagram to illustrate the sports medicine umbrella? What should be the core part of your diagram?
4. In the second subtitle of the part "History of Sports Medicine", the author uses the word "jump". Why do you think "jump" is used here?
5. There are several roles of science and technology in sports mentioned in the passage. Among these roles, which ones are related with sports medicine? Why does not the author just focus on the roles related with sports medicine in the passage?

Critical Thinking Starters

1. Informed consent is a fundamental principle of medical ethics. The team physician must have an athlete's informed consent before providing any medical treatment. This requirement is based on the principle of individual autonomy, the idea that a competent adult has the legal right to determine what to do with her or his body. This means she or he can accept or refuse medical treatment at any time. Some argue that a blanket informed consent should be obtained at the beginning of a sports season. This arrangement would curb the discussion of risks and benefits with an injured athlete and possibly curtail the overwhelming desire to return to play despite the consequences. Furthermore, treatment could be hastened. However, others believe that each treatment deserves a separate informed consent because every injury is different. With each new injury comes a choice of treatments and a different assumption of risk. Separate informed consents would permit the injured athlete an opportunity to weigh each decision independently of the others. What would you do as an athlete?

More to Know

Exercise Is Medicine—A Global Health Initiative

In 2007, the American Medical Association (AMA) and the American College of Sports Medicine (ACSM) co-launched Exercise is Medicine (EIM) —a United States-based health initiative that has since been coordinated by ACSM. The initial purpose of EIM was to make the scientifically proven benefits of physical activity the standard in the U.S. healthcare system. Within two years of its launch, representatives from international public health, medical and scientific associations asked ACSM to expand its initial scope beyond the United States and begin a multinational collaboration to make EIM a global effort, launching the EIM Global headquarters in Indianapolis, IN. Currently there are seven regional centers and 43 national centers across the globe.

The vision of EIM is to:

* have healthcare providers assess every patient's level of physical activity at every clinic visit
* determine if the patient is meeting the U.S. National Physical Activity Guidelines
* provide patients with brief counseling to help him/her meet the guidelines and/or refer the patient to either healthcare or community-based resources for further physical activity (PA) counseling.

Activity Time-Out

According to Text A, there are many professions associated with sports medicine. To learn more about them, each group will choose one career, create a poster for the career and present it to the class.

Sports in Focus

Competitive **diving**, which developed from gymnastics, started in Sweden and Germany in the 18th century. In the late 19th century a group of Swedish divers visited Great Britain. They put on diving displays that proved hugely popular and led to the formation of the first diving organisation, the Amateur Diving Association, in 1901.

Diving was included in the Olympic Games for the first time at the 1904 Games in St Louis. The springboard and platform events have been included since the 1908 Olympic Games in London. Since the Stockholm Games in 1912, women have taken part in the diving events. The diving programme has been relatively stable since the 1928 Games in Amsterdam: men and women take part in 10-metre high-dive and 3-metre springboard events. In 2000, the Sydney Games witnessed the entrance of synchronised diving（双人跳水） on both the springboard and the platform.

In competitions, divers are awarded points up to 10 by each of a panel of judges. In international competition, there are seven judges. Each member of the panel scores a dive based on elements such as approach（走板，跑台）, take-off（起跳）, execution（完成） and entry into the water（入水）. Nine judges assess synchronised diving. Four judge the execution of individual dives, and five assess synchronization——how the pairs mirror timing, height, distance, speed of rotation and entry into the water.

The highest and lowest marks awarded are disregarded, and the scores from the remaining judges are added together. This score is then multiplied by the degree of difficulty (or "tariff") of the dive, which is based on the number and types of manoeuvres attempted, such as somersaults（空翻）, pikes（屈体）, tucks（抱膝） and twists（旋转）.

Relevant Words and Phrases

arm stand dive	back dive	forward dive
inward dive	standing dive	running dive

Text B

Medical Considerations for Children in Sports

1 Children are not "little adults". They are different structurally, physiologically, neurologically and psychologically. Furthermore, these developmental characteristics will vary tremendously between children who are the same age. For example, there may be as much as six years' body size (height and mass) difference between children at the chronological age of 13 years.

Medical Considerations

2 A number of general medical considerations for active children warrant discussion. Too little or too much sport and exercise can have multiple deleterious[1] adverse health effects.

Personal Development and Mental Health

3 The definition of "too much" sport and exercise will vary enormously depending on the individual child. A certain amount or "dose" of activity for one child may be adverse to their health (i.e. cause physical and/or emotional distress) whereas for another child, that same level will not be enough to cause them harm and they may wish to do more activities to keep them happy. As a rule of thumb, if the child is not happy and/or suffering recurrent musculoskeletal[2] injury and/or medical illness (including excessive fatigue), then the present level of activity is too much. For the younger child, the responsibility to recognise and monitor this rests with the parents and/or coach, and on occasion the clinician.

4 The "ugly parent" syndrome[3] is a well-recognised phenomenon where a parent or parents are over-invested in the sporting participation of their child to the point where the child suffers emotional distress and often musculoskeletal overuse injury or illness.

Nutrition

5 Active children need enough calories to not only fuel their activities but also to grow nor-

[1]deleterious /ˌdelɪ'tɪərɪəs/ *adj.* harmful
[2]musculoskeletal / ˌmʌskjʊləʊ'skelɪtl/ *adj.* related to muscles and skeleton
[3]ugly parent syndrome: a syndrome where spectating adults, and in particular, parents, become "ugly", and verbally or physically abuse children, other spectators, coaches or refs, which particularly prevalent in junior sports

mally. This means that for these children, they not only require a healthy, balanced diet but also require numerous snacks to supplement their three meals a day. Unfortunately in some sports, such as ballet, gymnastics and track and field where a lean body mass offers a perceived performance and/or aesthetic advantage, restriction of calories from disordered eating behavior is prevalent. This is particularly concerning as the adolescent growth spurt[4] is when 15% of adult height, 48% of adult skeletal mass and the majority of adult skeletal bone mineral density is accrued. Disordered eating during childhood and adolescence in mild to moderate cases can cause excessive fatigue and reversible growth retardation, but in severe cases can result in growth retardation and osteopenia[5] that in some circumstances can never be reversed. Parents and coaches need to be vigilant and intervene early and carefully for the best treatment outcomes.

Environmental Illness

6 Children are more susceptible to both heat and cold illness secondary to their relatively immature physiological thermoregulatory[6] mechanisms. For this reason, parents and coaches need to protect children from both heat and cold stress and to have a number of preventative strategies in place. Furthermore, care needs to be taken for the child with asthma when they exercise in the cold or in air with various pollutants and allergens. The child athlete should consult their general practitioner regarding certain prophylactic[7] medications and measures to optimise the child's lung function.

Immunity and Infectious Disease

7 The immune system responds to exercise in children in a similar fashion to adults, with an <u>inverted bell-shaped response</u>. A healthy dose of exercise will strengthen immunity and excessive exercise will lead to an exponential[8] decrease in immunity. Mucosal immunity is often first affected and the child may suffer more upper respiratory tract infections. If this becomes a recurrent problem, simply reducing the level of activity often will promptly reverse the problem.

---

[4]spurt /spɜːt/ *n.* a sudden, brief period of intense activity, effort, or emotion
[5]osteopenia /ˌɒstɪəʊ'piːnɪə/ *n.* loss of bony tissue which makes bones more likely to break
[6]thermoregulatory /ˌθəːməu'regjulətərɪ/ *adj.* of regulating one's temperature
[7]prophylactic / ˌprɒfɪ'læktɪk/ *adj.* preventing or contributing to the prevention of disease
[8]exponential /ˌekspə'nenʃl/ *adj.* growing or increasing very rapidly

Head Injury

8 Concussion[9] is defined as a transient[10] disturbance of neurological functioning for a variable period of time with no long-term neurological harm. However, there are some scientists who do believe there may be subtle long-term neurological consequences from one or more concussive injuries, but that these effects are very hard to study and measure as there are numerous confounders[11] for this research, and also such a study would require large numbers and would need to be done over a long period.

9 In general, concussion should be taken seriously in both adults and children, but even more so in children as their neurological development is incomplete. The child who is concussed should be immediately removed from the field of play and not be allowed to return to play that day. Any "red flag" symptoms or signs, including worsening headache, nausea/vomiting, decreased level of consciousness, requires urgent transfer to hospital.

10 The child may take days and sometimes many weeks to recover. Children (aged less than 16 years) should not be returned to play following a concussive injury without medical clearance. As a general rule, the doctor needs to be more conservative in returning children to play after concussion compared to adults, as there are data to suggest children take longer to recover than adults. Recovery is when there is no headache, normal concentration and no fatigue. The child can then return to aerobic exercise with no contact. If symptoms recur, they should be rested longer and then try again. To simplify matters, in schoolboy football a mandatory three-week exclusion rule exists where the footballer cannot return to play. This is enough time for the vast majority of concussions to improve. However, three weeks may not be enough time for some to recover and this is why medical consultation is recommended prior to returning to play. If symptoms do persist or any "red flag" features occur during the recovery period, the child requires prompt investigation, usually involving an MRI(magnetic resonance imaging) of the brain.

11 There are certain children and adults who do suffer concussive injury more easily than others and often suffer numerous concussions. This often relates to the intrinsic vulnerability of their brain to deceleration/acceleration forces and occasionally is also related to the style of play of the

[9]concussion /kən'kʌʃn/ *n.* injury to the brain caused by a blow; usually resulting in loss of consciousness

[10]transient / 'trænzɪənt/ *adj.* lasting a very short time

[11]confounder /kən'faundə/ *n.* factors that make things confusing

athlete. Such athletes should be identified, monitored closely and on occasion advised to change sports. Concussion is a significant sports medicine problem and for this reason an international collaborative society exists.

Diagnostic Radiation Exposure

12 Talented active children may suffer numerous injuries during their childhood, and then into their adult years. Therefore, they may require numerous X-rays, CT scans and bone scans to diagnose their injuries. These tests all involve diagnostic radiation. The radiation dose and, in turn, the health risks incurred from these numerous investigations is cumulative. A critically important consideration is that children not only have more "radio-sensitive" tissue than adults do, but also because of their younger age they will carry the health risk of that radiation exposure for longer. It is therefore incumbent[12] on the doctors and parents to limit and monitor the number of these tests. The diagnostic test should only be performed if it is truly indicated and another test that does not involve diagnostic radiation (ultrasound or MRI) cannot be used.

"Red Flag" Conditions

13 The aphorism "not everything that presents as a sports medicine/musculoskeletal problem should be strictly regarded as a sports injury" is true both in adults and in children.

Tumours

14 Unfortunately benign and malignant tumours do occur in children. Local trauma often focuses attention on an area in which a tumour is subsequently diagnosed. Tumours can present with pain, swelling or pathological[13] fracture, and one should always bear this diagnosis in mind when the symptoms and signs are atypical. For example, rest pain and night pain are absolute "red flag" symptoms that require thorough investigation.

Infection

15 The most common organisms responsible for osteomyelitis[14] are staphylococcus aureus[15],

---

[12]incumbent /ɪn'kʌmbənt/ *adj.* If it is incumbent on or upon you to do something, it is your duty or responsibility to do it.

[13]pathological / pæθə'lɒdʒɪkl/ *adj.* relating to illness

[14]osteomyelitis /ˌɒstɪəʊmaɪɪ'laɪtɪs/ *n.* inflammation of bone marrow, caused by infection

[15]staphylococcus aureus /ˌstæfɪlə'kɒkəs'ɔːrɪəs/ *n.* 金黄色酿脓葡萄球菌

streptococci[16], e. coli[17], proteus[18] and pseudomonas[19]. Often no primary infective site is found and the theory is that the microorganism becomes seeded to the bone or joint by haematogenous[20] spread via the oropharynx[21]. On other occasions the microorganism may spread by direct extension from a wound. The most common presentation is pain (once again rest pain and night pain are "red flags"), warmth and tenderness over the affected part, and an unwillingness to move the adjacent joint. All these children should be checked for diabetes or impaired immune function.

Inflammatory conditions

16 Autoimmune conditions occur in children and inflammatory arthritis should also be part of one's differential diagnosis, particularly when assessing an atraumatic[22] swollen painful joint(s).

Hip pathology masquerading as knee pain

17 Just like in adult patients, the clinician should always examine the hip joint first in any child presenting with "knee pain". Serious hip pathologies may present with knee pain only.

18 The management of medical conditions in children requires both an understanding of the biological differences between children and adults, and moreover the age-specific injuries and illnesses children are at risk of sustaining. Armed with this knowledge, the clinician will gain great satisfaction out of caring for these patients and their families.

General Guidelines for Training the Younger Athletes

- Children are not "little adults". They have a unique biology that needs to be considered.
- Specialisation of sporting activity is discouraged before age 10. Young children are encouraged to participate in a wide variety of sports/activities with the emphasis on enjoyment, and delay specialisation for as long as possible. Unfortunately in many sports (tennis, gymnastics, ballet etc.), the child's competitors are specialising at younger ages and this accounts for this trend.
- The coaching and degree of participation of children should be individualised to a certain

[16]streptococci /ˌstreptə'kɒkəs/ *n.* 链球菌
[17]e. coli /ˌiː'kəʊlaɪ/ *n.* 大肠杆菌
[18]proteus /'prəʊtɪəs/ *n.* 变形杆菌
[19]pseudomonas /sjuː'dɒmənəs/ *n.* 假单胞菌
[20]haematogenous / hi:mə'tɔdʒɪnəs/ *adj.* producing blood
[21]oropharynx /ˌɔrəu'færɪŋks/ *n.* 口咽
[22]atraumatic / ˌeɪtrɔː'mætɪk/ *adj.* without physical injury or wound to the body

degree to consider differences in age, biological development, skill level, psychosocial maturation, and enthusiasm.

• How much activity for a child is too much? Some children can train and play for their school, club and representative team without injury or illness with great enjoyment. This level of activity needs to be closely monitored by responsible parents and coaches. If a child is no longer enjoying their sport and exercise, are being injured recurrently or getting fatigued and sick often, the level of activity for that child is too much. For contact sports, particularly the football codes, some children play three games in a given weekend. It is strongly recommended that this be discontinued after year 6 or rather the age of 11–12 years. The risk of injury increases thereafter as the children grow taller and heavier and can therefore generate more force. Moreover, the ability to recover for the next game, sometimes within a 24-hour period, is not possible and this significantly increases the risk of injury. Also the mismatch in sizes of the players is much more marked in the high school years. Furthermore, the child's academic and general curriculum is busier in high school and this creates time pressure.

• Numerous sports have specific guidelines for training and competition volumes to protect children and adolescents from well-recognised sport-specific overuse injuries. For example, in baseball and cricket the number of "pitches" thrown or "overs" bowled respectively is monitored. Injuries to the elbow and shoulder in baseball and injuries to the lumbar[23] spine in cricket are in turn minimised.

• Never ridicule children for mistakes. Constructive comments/coaching and enjoyment is essential. A negative experience for a child may turn them off sport and exercise for life.

• Be aware of the "ugly parent syndrome". This is a very delicate situation for a clinician and all concerned. Intervention is warranted if the child's health is affected/at risk. An opportune time to confront this issue is at the time of consultation for an injury. Consult the parent individually away from the child.

• Create a safe sporting environment for children. Organised sports and activities require responsible adult supervision; for example, protection from dehydration, sunlight, children being mismatched by physical size and identification of dangerous sporting grounds/equipment. General first aid provisions (ice, bandages etc.) should be made available at sporting venues.

• Some active children do not eat enough calories for the requirements to both train and to grow and develop normally. Significant prolonged poor nutrition (chronic negative energy balance)

[23]lumbar /ˈlʌmbə/ *n.* of or relating to or near the part of the back between the ribs and the hipbones

during childhood and adolescence may result in pubertal[24] delay, growth retardation, chronic disordered eating, poor bone health, excessive fatigue and increase risk of injury.

• Children are more at risk of heat/cold illness than adults. They are less efficient at thermoregulation and therefore hydration and clothing are very important considerations.

• Strength training is safe but should only be undertaken with lightweights (e.g. the child can lift that weight more than 12 times) and under responsible adult supervision. Ideally resistance training that utilises the child's own body weight (e.g. push ups) is recommended. In general, this will not arrest growth and therefore will not affect the genotypically determined maximal height for that child.

Total words: 2048
Total reading time:__________minutes________seconds

* *The text is based on Medical Consideration for Children in Sport by Tom Cross*

Comprehension Check

1. According to the passage, is it necessary for parents or coaches to know the medical considerations for children in sports? Why?
2. How do you understand the underlined sentence in paragraph 4? Translate it into Chinese.
3. What does environmental illness refer to according to the passage?
4. How does the author explain "inverted bell-shape response" in paragraph 7?
5. Comparatively speaking, the author uses many more words describing head injury. Why?
6. How can the general guidelines for training the younger athletes be categorized?

Hot Debate

"Little Hercules," ten-year-old Richard Sandrak, is one of the strongest humans in the world pound-for-pound. He began training at three years old. By the age of eight years, he was able to

[24]pubertal /'pju:bətl/ *adj.* relating to the stage in someone's life when their body starts to become physically mature

bench press 210 pounds, while only weighing seventy pounds himself. Sandrak's father allowed him to eat only according to a strict diet consisting of liquid nutrients and vegetables.

Some folks may consider Sandrak an example of too much, too soon. However, others recognize the efforts made to teach youngsters how to take proper care of their bodies and health, and they advocate Sandrak's vigilance.

What is your opinion? Hold a debate with classmates on this issue. Each side should present compelling reasons and specific evidence.

Pop Culture

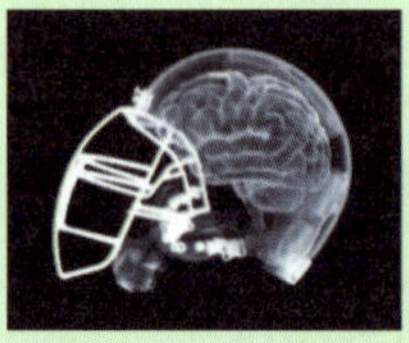

"**Big Hits, Broken Dreams**" Examines Concussion Hazards in Youth Football

Football is a cornerstone of family life in Greenville, NC, and four-time statewide football champion JH Rose High School is one reason why. But the costs for all of that football glory can be very high. The hard hits can mean concussion injuries and the community has borne terrible consequences.

In this one-hour documentary, CNN chief medical correspondent and practicing neurosurgeon Dr. Sanjay Gupta had exclusive access to follow the JH Rose team for their full 2011 season, exploring concussion in high school football – what happens to the brain under concussive brain injury, and what parents, coaches, and athletes need to be aware of to try to protect themselves

Vocabulary Building

Look up the following words and expressions in reference books and on the Internet.

Words and Expressions	Meaning
golfer's elbow	
skier's thumb	
tennis elbow	
turf toe	

15

UNIT

Future Trends of Sports

The world someone is born into is not the same as the one they leave, with many leaps forward contributing to a brighter and better future.

——Andy Reed, Chair of Sport and Recreation Alliance

Pre-reading Thoughts

1. What change that has happened in international sports is most impressive for you? Why?

2. As a spectator, what changes do you expect to see in sports? Are these changes easy or difficult to realize?

3. Sport is a mirror of society. What social changes have been reflected in sports in China in the past 10 years?

Text A

Social Trends' Effects on Sports

1 Social trends are difficult to predict since there is no way of knowing how outside influences in society are likely to affect people's state of mind, economy, or values. Certain worldwide trends such as the rise in terrorism may drastically affect people's lives in ways that are difficult to predict. Likewise, the shrinking of the world into a global economy of interdependence has the potential to either bring the world closer together in cooperation or split people wider apart in conflict.

2 Within the American society, certain social trends seem clear. First, its population is rapidly aging and the proportion of the populace that is older than 50 years will continue to skyrocket in the immediate future. Concerns for quality of life, health care, and productive use of leisure time after retirement will command the attention of a large proportion of the population as they age. In addition to an aging population, the United States are also a declining population. Forecasts for the next 50 years show that Europe will continue to have a declining population. The United States will maintain its low birth rate, but that will be offset by a continued influx of immigrants, most of whom will be of Hispanic descent.

3 Second, the rights of all people regardless of age, race, gender, sexual preference, or disabilities will continue to be protected and discrimination laws are likely to be strengthened in the United States. The stage is set to not only protect the rights of every citizen, but also to enhance their quality of life by opening up avenues for new experiences and adventures.

4 Third, those who have benefited most from supporting performance sport will fight to protect their investment in sport. Rather than just protecting the status quo, they will bring ingenuity to strategies to expand the influence of performance sport. This group will continue to strengthen the bond between big-time collegiate sport, professional sport, and the Olympic Games.

5 The field of sport management is growing rapidly and will continue to expand as sport organizations search for ways to enhance their bottom line by enticing and serving consumers. Education on sport management is available in many universities and includes training in sport-related event management, finance, human resources, law, marketing, public relations, and program management. People training in sport management are playing an increasingly critical role in professional sport, amateur sport, nonprofit organizations such as the YMCA(the Young Men's Christian Association) or YWCA(the Young Women's Christian Association), sporting goods manufacturers, sporting events, and sport facilities.

6 Fourth, the natural human tendency to push against barriers will result in development of new materials and processes to produce better sport equipment, facilities, and training regimens so that elite athletes can challenge the frontier of athletic achievements. Records will continue to be broken as athletes benefit from scientific advances. Another key area of research will be the effort to rid sport of performance-enhancing substances that provide an unfair advantage to some athletes, create mistrust by fans and the media of great performances, and threaten the integrity of athletic competition at every level.

7 Fifth, coaches will adapt to their athletes by increasing their coaching competency and adjusting their coaching philosophy toward meeting the needs of their athletes. At the same time, athletes will pressure coaches to endorse a certification process that indicates coaching knowledge, skill, and competency at various levels of coaching.

Effects of Social Changes

8 Significant social changes in the last 50 years have affected sport and will continue to do so.

The civil rights movement of the 1960s opened up sport to minorities. African Americans have become dominant in football and basketball, and Latinos account for one-third of the players in MLB. As more minorities move into the middle class, their children will begin to explore other sports such as tennis, swimming, golf, or volleyball—all sports that were once the exclusive provenance of affluent Whites. As these sports become more inclusive, positions of influence such as those held by coaches, organizers, and members of governing boards will include members of minority groups.

9 The women's movement that ushered in Title IX in 1972 changed sport dramatically. The explosion in female participants has changed sport forever, but equity with male participants is still an elusive goal. Steady pressure to conform to the law will be required by women's rights advocates and female athletes must continue to be assertive.

10 Girls face some unique issues in sport. Puberty arrives an average of two years earlier in girls, affecting their physical capacity and sometimes their interest in sport. Teenage girls drop out of sport just when many boys, fueled by new levels of testosterone, are consumed by competitive sport. A clear transition from performance sport to participation sport needs to be available for girls at a younger age before they drop out for good.

11 Older women, too, will continue to have a significant effect on sport. Those who loved performance sport will prolong their careers with expanded professional, semiprofessional, and community leagues that offer strong competition. By far, though, most women who don sneakers and activewear are looking for healthy workouts to maintain physical appearance, control body weight, socialize, have fun, and increase their energy for the demands of daily living. New sports or variations on traditional sports must be ready for an influx of females to recreational participation sport. The recent surge of female participation in yoga, tai chi, strength training, and similar physical disciplines is an example of the new trends.

12 As mentioned previously, the aging of the American society may be the most influential trend of all in sports. Age group competition for older adults will continue to grow as seniors seek the thrills of competitive sport and the challenge of testing themselves against others or the environment.

13 Other older adults are more interested in exercise simply to maximize good health, pos-

ture, and energy. Social interaction, fun, and release from stress are more important to these adults. Coaches and program leaders will need to continue to tinker with the formula for sport that meets the needs of these older athletes. More frequent but shorter work-outs with less intensity seem to be the best schedule for older adults. Time to socialize during or after activity is a strong attraction and should be made available in a comfortable setting.

As the population continues to age, it is vital that opportunities for physical fitness are adapted to meet the changing needs of aging adults.

14 Sexual preference will continue to be a topic of controversy in the coming years. Historically, sport has not been kind to gays and lesbians, particularly in performance sport. A relatively few successful homosexual athletes have publicly announced their sexual preference, but most have quietly concealed it to avoid controversy.

15 Gay and lesbians join local athletic clubs to enjoy physical activity, meet new people, receive emotional support, and have fun without the pressure of dealing with the historically homophobic sports world. As public acceptance of gays and lesbians grows, more athletes will have the courage to announce their sexual preference and insist on equal opportunities. The sports world will become more accepting of athletes, coaches, and sport administrators who embrace the gay or lesbian lifestyle.

16 Finally, mental and physical disabilities have historically eliminated people from sport participation. With the advent of laws that prevent discrimination against people with disabilities, sport participation has blossomed as well. The Special Olympics and the Paralympics have offered competitive and participation sport to people with disabilities at the national and international level. Local communities and schools have gradually sought to add sport programs for the people with

disabilities and wherever possible have sought to include these athletes in existing programs. Some sports have been modified and others invented that are appropriate for those with handicaps. Education, financial support, and coaches' training are keys to sustaining the growth in opportunities for these athletes.

Will Sports Change?

17 If you have any doubt whether sport will change in the future, look at the last 50 years. Since the 1950s, sport has expanded dramatically to become a huge corporate moneymaker. Professional football, basketball baseball, ice hockey, tennis and golf have made millionaires out of athletes and sustained the corporate organizations that regulate and control these sports. People once thought an athlete who earned $10,000 for a single season of play was amazingly rich. When Joe DiMaggio agreed in 1949 to the first $100,000 contract to play center field for the New York Yankees, it was thought as the zenith of sport compensation—yet today's superstars are signing contracts worth up to $10 million per year for up to seven years! Even taking inflation into account, athletes' salary rose 10-folds over the last quarter century.

What changes can this young athlete expect to see in the next 10 years?

18 As previously mentioned, social changes have opened up opportunities for people of all races and ethnic groups, for women and for athletes with disabilities. In spite of these significant changes, more are yet to come.

Total words: 1470
Total reading time: __________minutes________seconds

* *The text is based on Social Issues in Sport by John Wood.*

Vocabulary and Expressions

skyrocket /ˈskaɪˌrɒkɪt/ *vi.* to rise extremely quickly or make extremely quick progress towards success

influx /ˈɪnflʌks/ *n.* the arrival of a large number of people or things at the same time

ingenuity /ˌɪndʒəˈnjuːɪtɪ/ *n.* someone's ability to think of clever new ways of doing something

bottom line the final line in the accounts of a company or organization, stating the total profit or loss that has been made

provenance /ˈprɒvənəns/ *n.* the place of origin of something

elusive /ɪˈluːsɪv/ *adj.* difficult to describe, find, achieve, or remember

testosterone /ˌtesˈtɒstərəʊn/ *n.* a male hormone that causes a stage of growth in older boys and development of their sexual organs

don /dɒn/ *vt.* to put clothing on one's body

tinker /ˈtɪŋkə / *vi.* to make small changes to something, especially in an attempt to repair or improve it

Comprehension Check

1. The first sentence in paragraph 1 tells that social trends are difficult to predict, while the first sentence in paragraph 2 says that certain social trends seem clear in American society. Do you think this is contradictory? Why or why not?
2. What does "as" mean in the underlined sentence in paragraph 2? Translate the sentence into Chinese.
3. According to the passage, what should be taken into consideration while designing sport programs for older adults?
4. Why is the author so sure that more changes will happen in sports?
5. How do you define the relationship between social changes and sports after reading the passage?

Critical Thinking Starters

1. Except the social changes mentioned in Text A, what other social changes are possible to happen in the global environment?
2. Sports are often seen as a central, unifying platform to rally an audience and raise awareness and/

or funds around a particular cause. The most common examples are the thousands of run/walks, marathons and endurance races that happen every year, raising funds and awareness around a myriad of diseases and critical social issues, such as equality. Some people believe that this is a good way for advocacy, awareness and fundraising, while others think this diverts sports away from its essence. What do you think about this?

More to Know

The International Day of Sport for Development and Peace (IDSDP) is an annual celebration that highlights and promotes the power of sport as a catalyst for social change in all corners of the world.

Since 2014, following a decision by the United Nations (UN) General Assembly, the IDSDP has been celebrated each year on 6 April. The IOC, in its capacity of Permanent Observer to the UN, has been supportive of this initiative as it values its potential to recognize sports organizations' role in and contribution to social change and human development.

The first celebration in 2014 saw an overwhelming response from the Olympic and sports movement, with the organization of hundreds of runs, sports tournaments, educational and peace-building activities, as well as exhibitions and discussion forums to address and highlight the power of sport as a catalyst for social change, development and peace.

The IDSDP offers a new opportunity to promote sport and physical activity as a cost-effective and meaningful tool that can address a wide range of needs related to: education, health, social inclusion, youth development, gender equality, peace building and sustainable development. It also provides a notable platform to advocate among governments for more investment in sport, related infrastructure and quality physical education for youth.

This event celebrates the work that is being carried out around the world by the IOC, National Olympic Committees, International and National Sports Federations, sports clubs, governmental and non-governmental organizations, neighborhood associations and all other entities and volunteers who believe that sport is an effective tool for social development.

Using sport to promote development and peace has been at the core of the IOC's mission since its creation in 1894. Pierre de Coubertin, the IOC's founder, was explicit in his desire to use Olympism as a means to promote harmony among individuals and nations. It is therefore apt that this International Day emphasizes the positive impact of sport and physical education at all levels from casual practice to competitive sport.

The annual IDSDP is also a fitting complement to the celebration of Olympic Day, which, introduced by the IOC in 1948, commemorates the founding of the modern Olympic Movement, each year on 23 June. Millions of people in countries around the world participate in a wide variety of Olympic Day activities, from sport to educational and cultural activities.

Expert's View

What's an advance in science or technology that you think will change the landscape of sports in the coming years?

I'm going to give two. One is individualized training. I'm interested in what's happened with sports science in the decade since the sequencing of the human genome. Although there's a lot left to learn, just as we've learned the differences in my gene that's involved in acetaminophen metabolism from yours—I might need three Tylenols while you need one to get the same effect, or maybe no amount works for me—we're finding genes that make some people more trainable to particular training programs than others. Not only genes, but actually direct physiology, whether it's properties of muscle fibers or things like that, that can help you figure out what the best training plan is for an individual. Just as there's no perfect medication regimen for any individual, because we're so biologically unique, there's no one single perfect training plan that works for everybody.

Some countries that are starting to put this into effect. Denmark and the Netherlands are doing things like muscle biopsies, and moving athletes around sports based on that. Or if the athletes are plateauing in training, you can tailor training to their specific physiology to get better effects. That's really neat, and can be done with fairly easy interventions. I think we're going to continue moving in that direction, toward individualized training to get the optimal training environment for every individual.

The other thing I wanted to mention: occlusion testing, where you block certain parts of perceptual information digitally or virtually. Either in the field with special types of glasses and things like that, or in videos by deleting parts of players' bodies or time segments of the action, to figure out what information athletes actually need to predict what's coming in the future faster than they could do consciously. You can use that to understand what they should be exposed to the most, what kind of practice scenarios are not wasting time, essentially. It turns out that pitching machines are completely wasting time, because they don't teach you the perceptual cues of a pitcher's body that let you anticipate a pitch. This is why softball pitchers can always strike out major-league baseball hitters. I think this occlusion testing is helping us focus our training time only to athletes' better perceptual skills. And it might even be connected to some of the virtual reality stuff that Chris is talking about. That would be a great way to use it on the field.

by David Epstein, Sports science journalist

Activity Time-Out

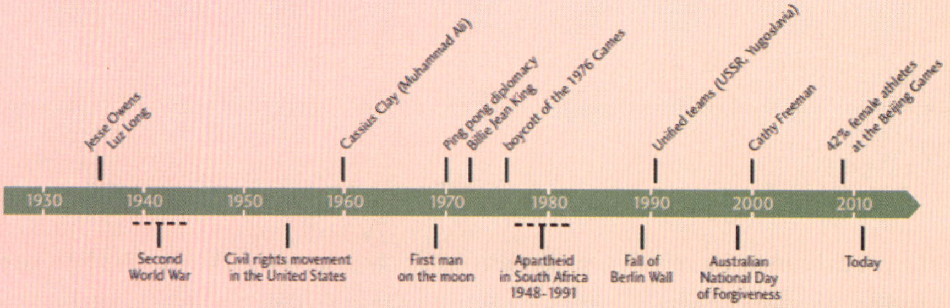

This timeline highlights the links between big historical events (social, political or human) and the contributions of athletes and sport for their set up for future generations. Select one of them and search for information about it. Share your findings in class.

Sports in Focus

Taekwondo is a traditional Korean martial art, which means "the way of kicking and punching". In taekwondo, hands and feet can be used to overcome an opponent, but the trademark of the sport is its combination of kick movements.

Taekwondo has been developing with the 5000-year long history of Korea, being called by several different names in the course. In Korea, Taekwondo began as a defense martial art called "Subak" or "Taekkyon," and developed as a way of training body and mind in the ancient kingdom of Koguryo, under the name of "Sunbae." In the Shilla period, it had become the backbone of Hwarangdo that aimed at producing leaders of the country.

Taekwondo today is similar to the martial arts in other oriental countries and shares some features with them, because in the course of its evolution it has gained many different styles that existed in the martial arts of the countries surrounding Korea, like Japan and China.

But Taekwondo is very different from many such oriental martial arts. First, physically it is very dynamic with active movements that include a mirage of foot skills. Second, the principle physical movements are in simpatico with that of the mind and life as a whole. Third, it possesses dynamic poses from another perspective.

Taekwondo can be characterized by unity: the unity of body, mind, and life, and the unity of the pose and confrontation, and cracking down. When you do Taekwondo, you should make your mind peaceful and synchronize your mind with your movements, and extend this harmony to your life and society. This is how in Taekwondo the principle of physical movements, the principle of mind training, and the principle of life become one and the same. On the other hand, the right poomsae（品式）lead to the right confrontation, which will eventually produce great destructive power.

Taekwondo pursues harmonious growth and improvements of life through its unique activities. This is why one could say Taekwondo is a way of life. To ultimately enable ourselves to lead more valuable lives, we would do well by finding the guiding principles deeply hidden in Taekwondo.

Relevant Words

belt	trunk protector	dobok
groin guard	head protector	forearm and shin guards

Text B

Sport and Globalisation

1 Modern sport is bound up in a global network of interdependency chains that are marked by global flows and uneven power relations. Consider the consumption of sports events. People across the globe regularly view satellite broadcasts of English Premier League and European Champions League matches. In these games the best players drawn from Europe, South America and Africa perform. The players use equipment—boots, balls, uniforms etc.—that are designed in the West, financed by multinational corporations such as Adidas and Nike and hand-stitched, in the case of soccer balls, in Asia. This equipment is then sold, at significant profit, to a mass market in the towns and cities of North America and Europe. Several transnational corporations are involved in the production and consumption phases of global soccer—some of whom both own the media companies and have, as in the case of Sky TV, shareholdings in the soccer clubs they screen as part of what sociologists term the "global media sport complex".

2 The global flows that pattern world sport have several dimensions. These include: the international movement of people such as tourists, migrants, exiles and guest workers; the technology dimension is created by the flow between countries of the machinery and equipment produced by corporations and government agencies; the economic dimension centers on the rapid flow of money and its equivalents around the world; the media dimension entails the flow of images and information between countries that is produced and distributed by newspapers, magazines, radio, film, television, video, satellite, cable and the world wide web; and finally, the ideological dimension is linked to the flow of values centrally associated with state or counterstate ideologies and movements. Note, for example, how the opening and closing ceremonies of the Athens Games were designed to project images and messages about Greece to both its own people and to a global audience. All five dimensions can be detected in late twentieth century sports development and appear likely to continue in the future. Then how can we make sense of these global sport processes?

3 Three points need to be grasped. First, studies of sport that are not studies of the societies in which sports are located are studies out of context. Here, emphasis is being placed on the need to examine the interconnected political, economic, cultural and social patterns that contour[1] and shape modern sport. Ties of trade, warfare, migration and culture are of long standing in human his-

[1]contour/'kɒntʊə/ vt. to form the general shape or outline of an object

tory. More recent globalisation processes have unleashed new sets of "interdependency chains", the networks that have (inter)connected people from distant parts of the globe. It is in this context of global power networks, that the practice and consumption of elite modern sport can be best understood. Secondly, in order to trace, describe and analyze the global sports process it is wise to adopt a long-term perspective. An historical and comparative approach can help us explain how the present pattern of global sport has emerged out of the past.

4 The third point of significance concerns the concept of globalisation itself. The concept refers to the growing network of interdependencies, political, economic, cultural and social, which bind human beings together—for better and for worse. Globalisation processes are not of recent origin and nor do they occur evenly across all areas of the globe. These processes are very long-term in nature but during the twentieth century the rate of change gathered momentum. Despite the "unevenness" of these processes, it is more difficult to understand local or national experiences without reference to these global flows. In fact, our living conditions, beliefs, knowledge and actions are intertwined with unfolding globalisation processes. These processes include the emergence of a global economy, a transnational cosmopolitan culture and a range of international social movements, which lead to a greater degree of interdependence and an increased awareness of a sense of the world as a whole.

5 Globalisation processes, then, involve multi-directional movements of people, practices, customs and ideas that involve a series of power balances. Although the globe can be understood as an interdependent whole, in different areas of social life established and outsider groups and nation states are constantly vying with each other for dominant positions. We may be at the earliest stages of the development of a "transnational culture" or "global culture", of which sport is a part. This process entails a shift from ethnic or national cultures to "supranational[2]" forms based upon either the culture of a "superpower" or of "cosmopolitan" communication and migrant networks.

6 Global sport, then, seems to be leading to the reduction in contrasts between societies but also to the emergence of new varieties of body cultures and identities. Several of the more recent features of globalisation can also be identified. These include: an increase in the number of international agencies; the growth of increasing global forms of communication; the development of global competitions and prizes; and the development of standard notions of "rights" and citizenship that are increasingly standardised internationally. The emergence and diffusion of sport in the 19th cen-

[2]supranational/ˌsuːprəˈnæʃənəl/ *adj.* involving more than one country; having power or authority which is greater than that of single countries

tury is clearly interwoven with this overall process. The development of national and international sports organisations, the growth of competition between national teams, the world-wide acceptance of rules governing specific, that is "Western", "sport" forms, and the establishment of global competitions such as the Olympic Games and the men's and women's soccer World Cup's, are all indicative of the occurrence of globalisation in the sports world.

7 If consideration is given to the issue of international sport success in the late twentieth century and in the early part of this new century it is clear that this involves a contest between systems located within a global context. Sport success depends on several elements: the availability and identification of human resources; methods of coaching and training; the efficiency of the sport organisation and the depth of knowledge of sports medicine and sport sciences. These national sport system mechanisms are a necessary but not sufficient explanation of international sport success. In addition to these elements sport development within a particular society also depends on the status of that nation in the sports international rank order. Less developed nations tend to under-utilise their talent and performers and/or lose them to more powerful nations in the global sports process. Global sport processes can thus lead to the under- or dependent development of a nation's talent.

8 The migration of performers, coaches, administrators and sport scientists within and between nations and within and between continents and hemispheres is also a pronounced feature of late twentieth century sport. Migration of this elite talent has become a decisive feature that structures the experience of sport in different societies. The movement of technology and the manufacture of clothing, footwear and equipment is a world-wide industry that wealthier nations are able to access to a far greater degree than their poorer counterparts. The global sports industry needs to be examined in terms of the implications for sustainable sport systems. In addition to these global flows, the images of sport stars and tournaments flow round the globe via the media sport complex. The interconnected web of media and corporate interests structures, though it does not completely determine, the sports experience for performers and consumers alike.

9 The global sports system accordingly involves the mechanisms of production, experience and consumption. Achievement sport involves the identification and development of talent; its production on a global stage, in a single or multi-sport event and its consumption by direct spectators or, through the media complex, a global mass audience. Traced over time there is a tendency towards the emergence of a global achievement sport monoculture—a culture where administrators, coaches and teachers promote and foster achievement sport values and ideologies and where com-

petitions and tournaments are structured along highly commodified and rationalised lines. Within the global sports system there is not only an international rank order of nations, but these nations can be grouped, more or less, along political, economic and cultural lines, into core, semi-peripheral and peripheral blocs. At the core of most team and individual based sports lie the countries of Western Europe, North America—excluding Mexico—and former "White" Commonwealth countries such as Australia. Semi-peripheral countries tend to involve former socialist countries and some emerging nations such as South Korea. Peripheral countries include most Islamic nations, the majority of African countries and those from South Asia. Whereas the West may be challenged on the field of play by non-core countries, the control over the content, ideology and economic resources associated with sport still tends to lie within the West. Yet, through state policy, non-core countries can use major sport festivals to solidify internal national identification and enhance international recognition and prestige.

10 Either in terms of hosting events or when the relevant decisions are taken, however, it is the West that dominates in international recognition, respectability, status and prestige. The more high tech and commodified the sport, the more dependent success is on the elements of the global sport process identified earlier. As a result, the West tends to win out. Indeed the last decade has seen the recruitment by Western nations not only of sport scientists and coaches from the former Soviet bloc, but also the drain of athletic talent from Africa and South America in sports such as soccer to the economically more powerful clubs of Europe. Non-core leagues remain in a dependent relationship with the dominant European core. In other sports such as track and field and baseball this drain of talent flows to the USA. The West also remains dominant in terms of the design, production and marketing of sports equipment; new innovations emerge within the West. Sport federations tend to be controlled by Western officials and global sport tournaments are usually located within the West.

12 In the past decade or so there have, however, been challenges to the achievement sport ideology and to Western domination. Though no longer in existence, the Soviet bloc mounted a sustained challenge to the West for some forty years, though it too became incorporated into the ideology of achievement sport. Non-Western success on the field of play, in specific sports such as badminton and middle and long distance athletics, is beginning to be matched by the involvement of non-Western personnel as coaches, officials, administrators and producers of sports goods, media outlets and the hosting of major tournaments. Though England was the "cradle of modern sport", the relative decline of Great Britain on the sports field—despite the improved, if overhyped success in the Sydney Olympic Games—is also matched by its fading influence in the corridors of power of

global sport politics. This may be indicative of how things might develop in this century for Europeans and perhaps Westerners more generally. One main source of potential dispute may well be the Olympic Games. As yet, however, the West are the winners in the global sport contest —hegemonic control remains with Westerners.

13 Global sport has not, however, led to complete homogenisation[3]: the consumption of non-indigenous cultural wares by different national groups was both active and heterogeneous[4]. Resistance to global sport processes has also been evident. Yet, there is a political economy at work in the production and consumption of global sport/ leisure products that can lead to the relative ascendancy[5] of a narrow selection of capitalist and Western sport cultures. Global sport processes can therefore be understood in terms of the attempts by more established white, male groups to control and regulate access to global flows and also in terms of how indigenous peoples both resist these processes and recycle their own cultural products. We are currently witnessing the homogenisation of specific body cultures—through achievement sports, the Olympic movement and sports science programmes—and simultaneously the increase in the diversity of "sports"/body cultures.

14 It is possible, however, to overstate the extent to which the West has triumphed in terms of global sports structures, organisations, ideologies and performances. Non-Western cultures, as noted, resist and reinterpret Western sports and maintain, foster and promote, on a global scale, their own indigenous recreational pursuits. Clearly, the speed, scale and volume of sports development is interwoven with the broader global flows of people, technology, finance, images and ideologies that are controlled by the West, and by Western men. In the longer term, however, it is possible to detect signs that the disjunctures, and non–isomorphic patterns, that characterise global processes are also leading to the diminution of Western power in a variety of contexts. Sport may be no exception.

Total words: 2152
Total reading time: __________minutes________seconds

* *The text is based on Sport and Globalisation by Joseph Maguire*

[3]homogenization / hɒˌmɒdʒənaɪ'zeɪʃən/ *n.*the act of making something uniform in composition
[4]heterogeneous / ˌhetərə'dʒi:nɪəs/ *adj.* consisting of elements that are not of the same kind or nature
[5]ascendancy /ə'sendnsɪ/ *n.* the state that exists when one person or group has power over another

Comprehension Check

1. What are the five dimensions of global sport flow? Explain each with examples.
2. What does the underlined sentence in paragraph 3 mean? Paraphrase it.
3. According to the passage, how is globalisation defined?
4. What does the author want to illustrate by the underlined part in paragraph 6?
5. What can globalization bring to sports? Is this process beneficial to the development of sports? Then why do some people resist the global sport process?

Pop Culture

During the Olympic Games of London 2012, Atos unveiled a dramatic vision for the future of the sport industry in 2020 with the launch of the Digital Edition of the ascent thought leadership program. This sets out how technology will radically change the sporting experience of athletes, viewers at home, fans in the stadium and events organizers by 2020.

Amongst the many controversial predictions made by the expert authors, was a forecast that by 2020, event organizers could stage events where athletes compete in the same race yet are located in different countries. Each athlete could run in his or her own city, and yet they could appear together as holograms in the same race.

Produced as a special edition magazine for the London 2012 Olympic and Paralympic Games, ***ascent at London 2012: a vision for sport and technology*** is a unique thought leadership study that provides a pan-industry view of the emerging technology trends that are driving innovation in sport.

The study is designed to help the International Olympic Committee (IOC), International Paralympic Committee (IPC) and every business involved in the sport's industry make key strategic decisions about their business and anticipate the challenges created by new technologies, now and in the future.

Vocabulary Building

Look up the following words and expressions in reference books and on the Internet.

Words and Expressions	Meaning
futurology	
internationalism	
reconciliation	
unilateralism	